# The Message of Deutero-Isaiah
## in its Sequential Unfolding

# The Message of Deutero-Isaiah in its Sequential Unfolding

BY

## JULIAN ⌊MORGENSTERN

*President Emeritus, Professor Emeritus of Bible*
*Hebrew Union College - Jewish Institute of Religion*

# Hebrew Union College Press

CINCINNATI · 1961

PRINTED IN THE UNITED STATES OF AMERICA

PRESS OF *Maurice Jacobs* INC.

224 N. 15TH ST., PHILADELPHIA 2, PENNA.

# Foreword

With this special edition of Dr. Julian Morgenstern's writings on Deutero-Isaiah, which appeared previously in the *Hebrew Union College Annual*, the Alumni Association of the Hebrew Union College - Jewish Institute of Religion expresses its tribute to a renowned fellow alumnus and colleague on the attainment of his eightieth birthday.

A graduate of the class of 1902 of the Hebrew Union College, Dr. Morgenstern served as professor of Bible in his alma mater from 1907 and as its president from 1921 until his retirement in 1947. For almost sixty years he has taught, led and guided the leadership of American Reform Judaism. His many studies on the Bible have shaped the thought of numerous scholars of all faiths and brought distinction to him and to our school.

We greet our beloved colleague on his eightieth birthday with the prayer that God extend his years and preserve his vigor of mind and body, that we may be privileged to continue to be warmed by his presence at the annual conventions of our Alumni Association.

Max Schenk,
*President, Alumni Association*
*March, 1961*

# ALLUMNI ASSOCIATION OF THE HEBREW UNION COLLEGE - JEWISH INSTITUTE OF RELIGION

## 1960–1961
## EXECUTIVE BOARD

MAX SCHENK, *President*
NORMAN M. GOLDBURG, *1st Vice-President*
DAVID MAX EICHHORN, *2nd Vice-President*
HERMAN ELIOT SNYDER, *Secretary-Treasurer*

| | |
|---|---|
| MEYER M. ABRAMOWITZ | ARYEH LEV |
| SIDNEY BERKOWITZ | MORRIS LIEBERMAN |
| MAURICE J. BLOOM | HARRY B. PASTOR |
| ARTHUR BRODEY | SANFORD E. ROSEN |
| ABRAM VOSSEN GOODMAN | LAWRENCE W. SCHWARTZ |
| MILTON GREENWALD | SAMUEL SILVER |
| RICHARD C. HERTZ | WILLIAM B. SILVERMAN |
| ABRAHAM I. JACOBSON | EDGAR E. SISKIN |
| NATHAN KABER | EARL S. STONE |
| BERTRAM KLAUSNER | ALLAN TARSHISH |
| JOSEPH KLEIN | SAMUEL TEITELBAUM |

JAMES A. WAX

*Ex-Officio*

BERNARD J. BAMBERGER
STANLEY R. BRAV
NELSON GLUECK
JULIAN MORGENSTERN

# Table of Contents

# The Message of Deutero-Isaiah
# in its Sequential Unfolding

# PART ONE

## I

## Introduction

COMMENCING in 1939 and continuing uninterruptedly until 1957, my seminar in Old Testament at the Hebrew Union College carried on an analytical study of Isa. 34–35; 40–66. We entered upon this task with no preconceptions whatever, other than a single conclusion, at which I had myself arrived some years previously and which by that time had been tested and developed in a manner which to me and my associates in the seminar seemed thorough and decisive. This conclusion was that early in 485 B. C., the year of the accession of Xerxes to the Persian throne, a severe catastrophe befell the Jewish community in Judaea. The country was overrun and ravaged by a coalition of neighboring states, Edom, Moab, Ammon and the Philistines, with the permission and the token support of the Persian royal administration. A large section of the Jewish people was massacred and another, comparable section was taken captive and sold, in the slave-markets of Tyre, Sidon and Gaza, into slavery to the Greeks, and thus came to be dispersed throughout the Mediterranean world. Jerusalem was captured and laid in ruins and its walls were destroyed. The second Temple, dedicated only thirty years previously, was burned to the ground. The Jewish community of Judaea was left a pitiful remnant of its former self. The evidence for and the details of this momentous and tragic event, perhaps the most tragic in all Jewish history until the advent of Hitler, I have collated carefully and presented in a study entitled "Jerusalem — 485 B. C.".[1]

Within this seminar we have always endeavored to pursue carefully and responsibly our own independent course of investigation and conclusion, disregarding initially, and until our study had progressed to the proper point, the hypotheses and the conclusions presented by earlier scholars, even those whose eminence and au-

[1] *Hebrew Union College Annual* XXVII (1956), 101–179; XXVIII (1957), 15–47, and XXXI (1960), 1–29.

thority in Biblical research we profoundly respected. Our principle was, so far as possible, to advance from the known to the unknown or from the more certain to the less certain. Accordingly we inaugurated our study of Isa. 34–35; 40–66 with a careful analysis, textual reconstruction, and interpretation of Isa. 63.15–64.11, since this unquestionably unified prophetic address seemed unmistakably to have as its historic setting the afore-mentioned national catastrophe.[2] We quickly found this assumption adequately confirmed. From this point we advanced through the years step by step, from chapter to chapter. We purposely reserved certain sections of the portion of the Book of Isaiah under investigation to be studied analytically, each section in turn by itself, in the following order, Isa. 56–66; 34–35; 49–55; 40–48; and all this excluding the various passages dealing with the Suffering Servant theme, which we set aside to become the final and climactic step in this research. After some eighteen years our task was practically completed.

Again and again the results of our investigation were totally unanticipated, surprising, and even startling in character and import. We established, to the satisfaction and conviction, so I firmly believe, of at least the majority of the members of the seminar through the years, that not only Isa. 56–66, but also 34–35 and likewise 49–55 have as their historic background events or movements in Judaism and in Jewish history later than the Zerubabel rebellion, early in 519 B. C., and also than the dedication of the second Temple in 516 B. C. A surprisingly large number of these prophetic utterances deal in one way or another with the catastrophe of 485 B. C. and the after-effects thereof over the ensuing years. Accordingly all of Isa. 34–35[3] and 49–66, including, as I hope to demonstrate upon some other occasion, the Suffering Servant sections, both in these chapters and in 42.1–4, 6 f., we have had to ascribe to Trito-Isaiah, with the specific understanding that by Trito-Isaiah is meant, not a single prophet, perhaps a disciple of Deutero-Isaiah, as has not infrequently been suggested, but rather a long succession of prophetic personalities over a protracted period, extending from 520 B. C. to well into the fourth century B. C.[4]

---

[2] This address we have interpreted, in detailed, analytic manner, in "Jerusalem — 458 B. C.," *HUCA* XXVII (1956), 147–150.

[3] The intimate relationship of the addresses in these two chapters to Isa. 40–66 has been adequately demonstrated by Torrey, *The Second Isaiah*.

[4] Cf. Morgenstern, "Two Prophecies from 520–516 B. C.," *HUCA* XXII (1949), 365–431; "Isaiah 63.7–14," *HUCA* XXIII (1950–1951), 185–203; "Two Prophecies

Accordingly, so the investigation of the seminar has established, the whole of Deutero-Isaiah is to be found in Isa. 40–48.[5] And even within these chapters the following passages, in addition to the brief Suffering Servant fragment in 42.1–4, 6 f., are not from Deutero-Isaiah, but are rather displaced fragments of Trito-Isaiah; 40.1–5, 9–11;[6] 41.17–20 (?), 27; 42.10–13,[7] 14,[8] 21; 43.14 (?); 45.8, 14,[9] 24a$\beta$b–25 (?); 47.2–4, 6; 48.16b, 22 (= 57.21). With the exclusion of these vv., some twenty-seven all told, equivalent approximately to one eighth of the total range of these nine chapters, what remains of Isa. 40–48 constitutes the whole of Deutero-Isaiah, every utterance of this exalted, prophetic figure which has been preserved. In many positive and significant respects his message, contained in its entirety within these chapters, represents the culminating point of the prophetic movement in Judaism.

## II

 THE ANTECEDENTS OF THE MESSAGE OF DEUTERO-ISAIAH

These nine chapters are characterized by a marked and easily recognizable literary style and a singular unity of historic setting, thought and purpose, which stamp them as the product of one, single prophetic personality and distinguish them decisively from Isa. 34–35; 49–66. The prophet's various addresses within these chapters are directed to one specific audience, the Jewish community in Babylonia. This consisted of the descendants, now in the second and third generations, of that portion of the Jewish nation which had been carried into exile

---

from the Fourth Century B. C. and the Evolution of Yom Kippur," *HUCA* XXIV (1952–1953), 1–74; "Isaiah 42.10–13," in *To Do and To Teach: Essays in Honor of Charles Lynn Pyatt* (1953), 27–38.

[5] For a list of earlier scholars who have reached this same conclusion cf. Pfeiffer, *Introduction to the Old Testament*, 453 f.

[6] Originally a unit with Isa. 52 and by a late editor transposed from there to their present position, manifestly to serve as the introduction, as indeed they do most effectively, to the entire section, Isa. 40–66; cf. below, note 22.

[7] Morgenstern, "Isaiah 42.10–13," cited in note 4.

[8] Which must be prefixed to chapter 62 and effectively links that prophetic utterance with 63.15–64.11 as the answer to the poignant question in 64.11, with which the earlier utterance closes.

[9] Which should probably be transposed to chapter 60 and be interpolated there between vv. 11 and 13, and so replace the present v. 12, apparently a late, editorial gloss.

from Jerusalem and Judaea to Babylonia by Nebuchadnezzar some fifty years, more or less, previous to the prophet's advent among them. Not at all improbably in the prophet's audiences there were also some survivors of the original deportees.

It was to this same group of exiles, or rather to their fathers, that Jeremiah had sent his message, some fifty or more years earlier, bidding these Jews settle down in the land of their present sojourn, adjust themselves sympathetically to their new environment, beget children and childrens' children, seek and promote the welfare of the various local communities into which they would have become incorporated, and there pray on behalf thereof to Yahweh, their ancient, national deity.[10] This was a message of far-reaching significance, in first degree and immediately for Judaism, and in second degree and ultimately for world-religion; for it was the very first affirmation by any prophet or spokesman of Yahweh that it was possible for a Jew to worship Yahweh outside of Palestine. It meant in the first place the repudiation by Jeremiah of the fundamental and up to this moment still unchallenged principle of primitive Semitic religion, that the primary connection of any deity was with the land, and only secondarily with the people dwelling therein.[11] Still at about the middle of the eighth century B. C. Amos, despite a, on his part, dawning conception of universalism, had subscribed unreservedly to this principle,[12] and had accordingly affirmed, by implication at least, the utter impossibility of an Israelite worshiping Yahweh anywhere beyond the confines of Israel, Yahweh's own land. Now for the first time the new principle was distinctly formulated, by Jeremiah, that Yahweh was primarily and essentially the god, not of the land, but instead of the people, Israel, and accordingly in Babylonia, or, by implication, wherever Israel might, for any reason, come to be or to dwell, in any land however remote, even unto the very ends of the earth, there Yahweh could still be found and supplicated by any Israelite group, or even by any single Israelite, who there eagerly sought Him and desired to worship Him. And there, in this foreign land, however distant from His own land it might be, Yahweh could still protect His people and prosper them, provided of course that they for their part remained faithful to Him.

[10] Jer. 29.1–7.

[11] Robertson Smith, *The Religion of the Semites*, 3rd ed., Stanley A. Cook, Editor, 92 ff.

[12] Morgenstern, "The Universalism of Amos," in *Essays Presented to Leo Baeck on the Occasion of His Eightieth Birthday* (1954), 122 f.

One matter of deep, historic import Jeremiah's letter to these Jewish exiles in Babylonia discloses, viz. that almost immediately after arrival in Babylonia they had begun to settle down, to adjust themselves readily to their new, cultural environment, and even to prosper therein. They could marry and beget children freely and could build houses for their families and dwell therein in security and comfort. All this conformed completely to the long-established policy of Assyrian kings and of the Neo-Babylonian monarchs after them, in transporting sections of the various peoples conquered by them from their native lands to districts in the vast Assyrian and Neo-Babylonian Empires sufficiently remote from their former homes to ensure the improbability of these deportees ever being able or even seeking to return thither. There these exiles were settled, with the expectation that they would remain forever resident, and there, with full and purposed freedom to exploit the economic resources of their new land to the utmost, for this redounded of course to the economic advantage of the Empire and tended likewise to ensure its stability as a large political entity, they would come before long to feel completely at home. There their children and children's children were born, and there quite naturally, in this land of their birth, these latter came in due time to feel completely at home. Plainly just this was the developing economic situation of the Jewish exiles in Babylonia which Jeremiah's letter envisaged. And equally plainly, precisely this, though naturally in heightened degree, was the economic situation of the Jewish exiles in Babylonia to whom Deutero-Isaiah addressed his message.

• Certainly these Jewish deportees in Babylonia were exiles; but in no sense were they slaves. They were in exile, גלות, yes, permanently resident in a foreign country far from their ancestral and in memory still cherished homeland, but in no wise were they in oppressive captivity, שבי. It is significant indeed that in Isa. 40–48 only the former term occurs with reference to Israel, and that too only once,[13] while the latter term occurs also only once,[14] but not with reference to Israel at all, but rather to Babylon, which is represented as about to be carried off to שבי, to captivity and enslavement in a foreign land, a national fate purposely represented as infinitely worse than mere exile, Israel's status in Babylonia. On the other hand, שבי, enslavement in captivity in foreign lands, is the condition of Israel

---

[13] Isa. 45.13.
[14] Isa. 46.2.

in Isa. 52.2 (bis); 61.1.[15] But the verb, נלה, or any of its derivatives occur in all of Isa. 49–66 only once, and that in a passage (49.21) where it and the word which follows it seem to be a gloss, since both are lacking in G, and also since the presence of these two words there disturbs the meter decidedly. This evidence, slight though it is, suggests that Isa. 40–48, i. e. Deutero-Isaiah, envisages Jews carried away from their native land by Nebuchadnezzar into exile, נלות, in Babylonia, whereas Isa. 49–66 envisages Jews scattered in all directions, even unto remote parts of the Mediterranean world, and there existing in a state of שבי, oppressive captivity and enslavement to foreign masters. And this suggests still further that practically all of Isa. 49–66, i. e. Trito-Isaiah, must be later than the tragic catastrophe which befell the Jewish community in Palestine in 485 B. C., one of the effects of which was the carrying off into שבי in various lands of the western, Greek world of a very considerable section of the Judaean Jewish community.

This very significant conclusion with regard to the basic relationship of Isa. 49–66, and especially of 49–55, to this catastrophe of 485 B. C., with the resultant corollary that this entire section must be later than that date, and therefore can not be in any sense the utterances of Deutero-Isaiah, is confirmed by a considerable mass of evidence, the import of which is unmistakable.

Isa. 60.4, 8–22[16] is an address which can be readily dated. It begins by picturing graphically the impending return to Zion, under Yahweh's protection, of her sons and daughters. They will return in ships,[17] enough ships to constitute a fair-sized fleet. Manifestly then they come from lands across the Mediterranean, i. e. from the Greek world. But Zion is still in ruinous condition; its walls are destroyed and the land round about is wasted. But very soon all this will be changed. Zion's walls will be rebuilt, and this too by foreigners, impliedly those very foreigners, Israel's conquerors, who had wreaked all this devastation. It will be rebuilt and repopulated and quickly become once again a city of wealth and beauty, a center of world-commerce, worthy indeed to be the place in which Yahweh delights. Nay more, Zion's former conquerors and oppressors will now render homage to her; their kings will be brought in fetters[18] unto her, and

---

[15] And regularly in Ezra (2.1; 3.8; 8.35) and Neh. (1.2 f.; 7.6; 8.17) and in other writings of this relatively late period.

[16] For vv. 1–3, 5–7 cf. "Two Prophecies from 520–516 B. C.," cited in note 4.

[17] For כיל read, with Kittel, Biblia Hebraica³, בְּלִי.

[18] Certainly v. 11bβ, in its MT form, is incomplete in thought, while metrically

the entire world will become her possession forever. In other words, the long-expected Jewish world-empire will, through Yahweh's favor, at last come to realization. There can be no question whatever that this address is the utterance of an ardent adherent of the Nationalist party within the little Palestinian Jewish community. Moreover, he looks back upon a great catastrophe which had befallen his beloved city and people, and that too so recently that its crushing effects still persist. Certainly this catastrophe can not be the destruction of Jerusalem and the exile of its people by the Babylonians in 586 B. C. The fact that at least a considerable section of the people must return to Zion in ships, must come accordingly from across the Mediterranean, where, so the clear implication is, they had been held as enslaved captives, establishes conclusively that the national catastrophe here mirrored so vividly was that of 485 B. C. That this address was uttered fairly soon after this event, hardly more than a generation later, when the effects of the catastrophe were still felt in all their severity, is an almost unchallengeable conclusion.

But precisely the same national situation, the same in every essential detail, thoughts, faith and yearnings, is portrayed, and that too quite as realistically and ardently, in Isa. 49.8–26. There too Zion is in ruins and the country is devastated. Zion is pictured as Yahweh's wife, rejected and divorced by Him and bereft of all her children, left completely alone, forsaken and disconsolate. But Yahweh is about to respond favorably to her supplications. He will take her again unto Himself. Her children will soon return to her, coming from distant lands, from the North, from the sealands of the Mediterranean, and from remote districts of Egypt, returning in circumstances of ease and luxury, with kings and queens as their personal servants, conditions manifestly the complete reversal of those under which they were then living in these foreign lands, at least as this ardent Nationalist spokesman imagines them to be. Moreover, they will return in such numbers that the former confines of the city will be too small by far to contain its restored population. Zion's walls will be rebuilt, and that too by those same, cruel enemies who had

it lacks a beat. Manifestly a word has been lost at the end of the line (cf. Morgenstern, "The Loss of Words at the Ends of Lines in Manuscripts of Biblical Poetry," *HUCA* XXV [1954], 63). Following a hint furnished by Targum Yerushalmi, which renders נהוגים by זיקין, we may quite confidently supply בְּזִקִּים as the missing word. II Kings 25.7 (=Jer. 39.7; 52.11; II Chron. 33.11; 36.6); II Sam. 3.34 suggest that kings taken captive were usually transported in fetters to the place of their captivity. Practically the same thought as is set forth here finds expression in Ps. 149.8.

destroyed them,[19] after which these former oppressors will depart, will get themselves so far off that, impliedly, they will never again be able to trouble restored Israel. Certainly the subjection of foreign kings and queens to slavery implies Jewish world-dominion and empire. This address too, which has so much in common with that in 60.4, 8–22, can, like that address, be the utterance only of a still loyal and trusting Nationalist, who looks back upon an extreme national disaster, and again, not at all that of 586 B. C., but rather that of 485 B. C., and who, in point of time, stands much closer to the later catastrophe than did Deutero-Isaiah to that of 586 B. C. Quite plainly this address has absolutely nothing in common either in historic setting, in thought, or in audience addressed with Isa. 40–48. In fact the destiny here represented as divinely appointed for restored Israel, viz. to triumph over its former conquerors and all its enemies, reduce them to subjection and thus, by implication, become the head of a Jewish world-empire, is in every respect the complete antithesis of the role of the servant of Yahweh and the agent of His universal salvation, which, as we shall learn, Deutero-Isaiah heralded as Yahweh's eternal purpose and ordained destiny for His people.

One further consideration enables us to fix the date of utterance of both of these hopeful and stirring addresses within a period of approximately forty years. In both addresses the walls of Jerusalem are still in ruins, but their rebuilding in the near future is confidently predicted by the eager, trusting Nationalist authors of the two addresses. Certainly then both addresses must be earlier than the rebuilding of the walls of Jerusalem by Nehemiah in 444 B. C. Accordingly the two addresses may be safely dated within the period 485–444 B. C., and probably nearer the end of this period than its beginning, an unusually close dating for Biblical writings.

The following table records the repeated expression of the same thoughts and motives which find such vivid and forthright presentation in Isa. 60.4, 8–22 and 49.8–26, and that too with employment of the same figures of speech, elsewhere in Isa. 49–55:

Zion Yahweh's repudiated wife: Isa. 50.1; 54.1–10
Zion bereft of her children: Isa. 51.18, 20; 54.1
The Judaean community sold into slavery in distant lands: Isa. 50.1; 52.2 f.

---

[19] In v. 17a, following a suggestion of *G*, for מהרו בניך read מְהֵרָה יְבָנוּךְ. This wording offers an effective parallelism to v. 17b both in thought-content and in stylistic and metrical form.

Zion in ruins and the land wasted: Isa. 51.3, 17–20; 52.9; 54.3
The return of Zion's children: Isa. 54.2 f.
Zion's destined triumph over its former conquerors and oppressors:
  51.23
Destined Jewish world-empire: Isa. 54.3

Very significantly, not one of these themes nor the graphic, figurative forms in which they are cast, with but one, single, possible
exception, finds expression in or the slightest contact with the thought
or with the manner of presentation thereof of Isa. 40–48. And even
that one, single, possible exception, the return of Zion's exiles, is
portrayed so differently in 40–48 than in 49–55 that there can be no
doubt whatever that the two sections envisage two altogether different
returns; in 40–48 a return from גלות, exile, in Babylonia; in 49–55,
with one, single exception,[20] just as also in 60.4, 8–22, a return from
שבי, captivity and slavery in various foreign lands of the vast, Mediterranean area. Accordingly, even in respect to this one theme, of the
return of dispersed Israel to its native land, Isa. 40–48 and 49–55
deal with altogether different historic situations, the former with the
exile to Babylonia following the Babylonian conquest of Judaea in
586 B. C., and the latter with the sale of a vast number of Jewish
captives into slavery in the Mediterranean world as one of the effects
of the catastrophe of 485 B. C.

Beyond all question then each of the passages cited in the above
table and the various addresses of which they are part, i. e. the
greater portions of Isa. 50, 51, 52 and 54, have exactly the same
historic setting as Isa. 49.8–26 and 60.4, 8–22. They too look back
to the catastrophe of 485 B. C., and so must be later than that event.
Therefore under no condition can they be the utterances of Deutero-
Isaiah.

Of these various prophetic addresses in Isa. 49–55 one in particular can perhaps be dated, and that too with considerable assurance,
somewhat more precisely than merely by the broad statement, "a
generation or so later than 485 B. C." In Isa. 52.1 and 11 a markedly
ritualistic note is sounded. In v. 1bc the emphatic statement is made
that into Jerusalem, the holy city, the uncircumcised and the unclean
shall never again enter, impliedly, and that too very clearly, to despoil
and defile it, the latter procedure manifestly in a completely ritualistic
sense. Earlier commentators, who, practically without exception,
automatically attributed this address to Deutero-Isaiah, interpreted
this passage as meaning that never again would the Babylonians,

---

[20] Cf. below, pp. 9–18.

Judah's conquerors in 586 B. C., a people who did not practice circumcision, be permitted by Yahweh to enter the city. Impliedly then this would be an expression of Judah's eventual triumph, through Yahweh's help, over its former conquerors, an idea, it may be noted in passing, altogether foreign to the thought of Isa. 40–48, and likewise meaningless therein after the advent upon the stage of history of Cyrus, the Persian, the Yahweh-destined conqueror of Babylonia, according to Deutero-Isaiah. But this interpretation, manifestly one of sheer desperation, misses completely the ritualistic implication of v. 1c and also that of v. 11. This latter v. charges a certain group of Jews to turn aside and go forth "from there," i. e. unquestionably from Babylon, in order to come in due time and under Yahweh's guidance and protection to Jerusalem. Upon this journey they will be the bearers of "the vessels of Yahweh," unquestionably the vessels to be used in the cult of the Temple, now in ruins but impliedly soon to be rebuilt. Very properly these bearers of the sacred vessels are charged to touch nothing unclean and to "hold themselves apart"[21] from all others, manifestly so that their sacred burden might not be defiled and so rendered unfit for eventual use in the Temple cult.

Now this picture, thus unfolded in this one v., agrees precisely with that set forth in Ezra 8.24–30. There we read that Ezra "set apart," הבדיל, twelve priests of superior rank, to whom he entrusted not only the gold and silver in his keeping, but also the sacred vessels for the cult of the new, the third, Temple, which Artaxerxes, the Persian king had commissioned him to restore, the treasure which that king had turned over to him, the gold and silver for the reconstruction of the new sanctuary and the sacred vessels for ritual use therein. The emphasis upon ritual purity in this prophetic address agrees completely with the ritualistic program inaugurated by Ezra after his arrival in Jerusalem, which found its eventual culmination in the Priestly Code in the final quarter of the fifth century B. C. Moreover, the picture set forth throughout this address[22] of the return of these

---

[21] For הברו of *MT* read, with *G*, וְהִבָּדְלוּ.

[22] Inasmuch as we must refer to various passages of this very significant address in the development of our thesis, it will be well to present here the complete address, as we have reconstructed it in the seminar. As has already been intimated, we have linked with this address Isa. 40.1–5, 9–10. As is readily perceived, these vv., on the one hand, have no thought-connection whatsoever with the address contained in the major portion of that chapter, vv. 6–8, 12–31, and, on the other hand, their thought-connection with Isa. 52.1–12 is very close. Certainly Isa. 40.1–5, 9–10 do not constitute a complete address in themselves, but are manifestly displaced fragments of a

exiles from Babylonia to Jerusalem, passing safely through the many hardships and dangers which they would surely encounter en route,

---

larger, prophetic address. And Isa. 52.1–12, in turn, as it stands, seems badly disjointed, with sudden and troublesome breaks in thought between vv. 6 and 7 and again between vv. 10 and 11, breaks which are completely obviated when Isa. 40.1–5, 9–10 are properly integrated with Isa. 52.1–12. (Isa. 52.13–15 belongs of course to the Suffering Servant document.) Moreover, it is easily comprehensible just why Isa. 40.1–5, and with these vv. also vv. 9–10 were transferred from their original position to the significant place where they now stand, at the very beginning of a new and distinct section of the Book of Isaiah; for in this position they sound very effectively the keynote of this entire section, the affirmation of Israel's eternal relationship to Yahweh as His people and its return to native land and restoration to a position of security, under Yahweh's protection, and of dignity and respect among the nations of the world. But, as can be readily comprehended, the transposition of these eight vv. from their original position to their present location naturally caused not a little confusion and dislocation in the remaining portion of the original address. For this reason in the reconstruction of the original address some textual realignment is unavoidable.

The following is the original text of this significant address, as we have reconstructed it in the seminar.

| Meter | Text | Verse |
|---|---|---|
| 3/2 | נחמו נחמו עמי / יאמר אלהיכם | 40.1 |
| 3/2 | דברו על-לב ירושלם / וקראו אליה | 2 |
| 3/3 | כי מלאה צבאה / כי נרצה עונה | |
| 3/3 | כי-לקחה מיד יהוה / כפלים בכל חטאתיה | |
| 3/3 | עורי עורי <התעוררי> / לבשי עדיך ציון | 52.1 |
| 3/3 | לבשי בגדי תפארתך / ירושלם עיר הקדש | |
| 3/3 | כי-לא-יוסיף לבא בך / עוד ערל וטמא | |
| 3/2 | התנערי מעפר קומי / שבי ירושלם | 2 |
| 3/2 | התפתחי ממוסרי צוארך / שביה בת-ציון | |
| 3/3/3 | כי-כה אמר יהוה / חנם נמכרתם <עמי> / ולא בכסף תגאלו | 3 |
| 3/3/3 | כי-כה אמר < > יהוה / מצרים ירד עמי / בראשונה לגור שם | 4 |
| 3/3 | ושרו באפס עשקו / <ואני מעבדתו גאלתיו> | |
| 3/3 | ועתה מה-לי-פה נאם-יהוה / כי-לקח עמי חנם | 5 |
| 3/3 | שלליו יחללוני תמיד / וכל-היום שמי מנאץ | |
| 3/3 | לכן-ידע עמי שמי < > / כי-אני-הוא המדבר הנני | 6 |
| 3/3 | סורו < > צאו משם / טמא אל תגעו | 11 |
| 3/3 | צאו מתוכה הבדלו / נשאי כלי יהוה | |
| 3/3 | כי-לא בחפזון תצאו / ובמנוסה לא תלכון | 12 |
| 3/3 | כי-ההלך לפניכם יהוה / ומאספכם אלהי ישראל | |
| | קול קורא | 40.3 |
| 4/4 | במדבר פנו דרך יהוה / ישרו בערבה מסלה לאלהינו | |
| 3/3 | כל גיא ינשא / וכל-הר וגבעה ישפלו | 4 |
| 3/3 | והיו המעקשים למישור / והרכסים לבקעה <יהיו> | |
| 4/4 | <הנה> מה נאוו על-ההרים / רגלי מבשר משמיע שלום | 52.7 |
| 4/4 | מבשר טוב משמיע ישועה / אמר לציון מלך אלהיך | |
| 3/3 | קול צפיך נשאו / קול יחדו ירננו | 8 |
| 3/3 | כי-עין בעין יראו / בשוב יהוה ציון | |

and now joyfully and with their faith in Yahweh and in His power to protect and prosper His people confirmed in the sight of all mankind,

| | | |
|---|---|---|
| 3/2 | פצחו רננו יחדו / חרבות ירושלם | 9 |
| 3/2 | כי־נחם יהוה עמו / גאל ישראל | |
| 3/2 | חשף יהוה > < / זרועו > < / לעיני כל־הגוים | 10 |
| 3/2 | וראו כל־אפסי ארץ / את־ישועת אלהינו | |
| 3/2 | על־הר גבה עלי־לך / מבשרת ציון | 40.9 |
| 3/2 | הרימי בכח קולך / מבשרת ירושלם | |
| 3/3 | הרימי אל תיראי / אמרי לערי יהודה | |
| 3/3 | הנה־אלהיכם > < / בָחָזָק יבוא / וזרעו משלה לו | 10a |
| 3/3/3 | ונגלה כבוד יהוה / וראו כל־בשר יחדו / כי־פי יהוה דבר | 5 |

40.1    Reassure, encourage My people, saith your God;

2      Enhearten Jerusalem and proclaim unto her,
Verily, her suffering is fulfilled, yea, her guilt is appeased;
    For she has taken from Yahweh's hand twofold for all her sins.

52.1    Awake, awake, rouse thyself, don thy jewelry, O Zion;
Put on thy gala attire, O Jerusalem, (thou) Holy City;
    For into thee shall enter never again one uncircumcised or unclean!

2      Bestir thyself, from the dust rise up, O captive Jerusalem;
Free thyself from the bonds of thy neck, O captive daughter of Zion!

3      For thus hath Yahweh spoken: For nothing were ye, My people, sold; so not for money shall ye be redeemed!

4      For thus hath Yahweh said: To Egypt went My people down of old in order to sojourn there;
But its ruler for naught oppressed it, but from its servitude I redeemed it.

5      So now what have I (to do) here, saith Yahweh; for My people have been taken for nothing;
Its despoilers blaspheme Me constantly, and the whole day long My name is profaned!

6      Therefore My people shall know My (true) name, that I, the Eternal One, am indeed the One Who Decrees!

11     Depart, go forth from there; aught unclean touch not!
Go forth from within her; hold yourselves apart, ye bearers of Yahweh's vessels!

12     For not in panic shall ye go forth, nor in headlong flight shall ye journey on;
For he who goeth at your head is Yahweh, and he who bringeth up your rear is Israel's God!

40.3    A voice calleth:
In the desert prepare ye Yahweh's road; in the Arabah level off a highway for our God.

4      Every depression shall raise itself, and every mountain and hill shall sink low;
And the uneven stretches shall become a plain, and the gullies shall become (each) a valley.

52.7    Behold, how beautiful upon the mountains are the feet of the bearer of good tidings, who announceth weal, and that too in such substantial and visible manner that all nations could not but have observed, and so must perforce attest Yahweh's

---

Who heraldeth good, who proclaimeth salvation, who sayeth to Zion: Thy God ruleth (again)!

8 Thy watchers raise their voice, together they shout aloud with joy;
For with clear vision shall they behold the return of Yahweh to Zion.

9 Exult, together shout aloud, ye ruins of Jerusalem!
For Yahweh hath enheartened His people, He hath redeemed Israel.
Yahweh hath bared His arm before the eyes of all the nations,
So that all the ends of the earth may behold the salvation of our God.

40.9 Upon a lofty mountain get thee up, O Zion, herald of good tidings!
Raise thy voice with might, O Jerusalem, herald of good tidings!
Raise (it), fear not; say unto the towns of Judah,

10a Behold, your God cometh with might, and His arm exercises dominion for Him;

5 And the radiance of Yahweh shall be revealed; and all flesh shall together behold (it); for the mouth of Yahweh hath decreed (this)!

40.1. The apt manner in which the vv. which we have transposed from Isa. 40 fit in here in the positions to which we have assigned them, their complete unity of thought, style and meter with Isa. 52.1–12, and the degree to which this textual reconstruction enhances the poetic beauty and the vigor and appeal of this address are apparent almost from the very first.

40.1–2 state in stirring manner the theme of this address, a message of reassurance to Jerusalem that its salvation and restoration are near, are indeed narrowly impending, all at the hands of its God, who Himself is about to return to it. Note the recurrence of נחם in 52.9, and note also that this very meaningful word, having specific reference to the catastrophe of 485 B. C. (cf. *op. cit., HUCA* XXVIII [1957], 16–18), which occurs in Trito-Isaianic passages fifteen times and in Lam. five times, is used by Deutero-Isaiah not even one single time. This is further and quite cogent evidence that Isa. 40.1–5, 9–10a must be later than 485 B. C., and so can come only from Trito-Isaiah.

Naturally the speaker in vv. 1–2 is the Deity, and the persons addressed, who are bidden to bring a message of reassurance to Jerusalem, are His prophetic spokesmen of that day, of whom the author of this address is one. Their words to Jerusalem, in obedience to this divine commission to them, commence of course with 52.1.

40.2. The statement of v. 2bc, that Jerusalem has received at Yahweh's hand punishment in twofold measure for all its sins, would seem to imply suffering in such extreme degree that the reference can be only to the bitter catastrophe of 485 B. C. Or perhaps, as was suggested in the seminar upon two different occasions, the reference here may be to the twice-repeated destruction of Jerusalem, that by the Babylonians in 586 B. C. and this of 485 B. C. However, whichever of these two possible interpretations of this passage be correct, it is certain that the v. itself, and with it the entire address of which it is an integral part, must be later than 485 B. C. — כי at the beginning of each stichos of v. 2b is the כי of certainty or affirmation; therefore. as the meter here manifestly requires, it receives in each instance a full divinity and power and His deep solicitude for His people, agrees fully with that implicit in Ezra 8.21–23, 31 f. For there Ezra tells of

---

beat. — For צבא with the connotation, "bitter, exacting, painful labor," cf. Job 7.1; 10.17; 14.14; Dan. 10.1; Sir. 7.15. Here quite plainly the word connotes the suffering imposed by Yahweh upon Israel as punishment, manifestly disciplinary in character. The thought here expressed approximates closely Jeremiah's doctrine of מוסר (cf. J. A. Sanders, *Suffering as Divine Discipline in the O. T. and Post-Biblical Judaism,* [1955]).

52.1 Certainly this v. in its *MT* form is metrically unbalanced. Quite obviously a word has been lost in 1aα. It is a reasonable assumption that this word was התעוררי (cf. 51.17), and that it was lost by haplography with עורי עורי and perhaps also with התנערי in v. 2a. — For עזך read, with Kittel, עדיך. This simple emendation provides a very effective parallelism with the thought of the following distich. — Certainly, conforming to the idiom of Biblical Hebrew, יבוא must be emended to לבוא.

52.2. For שבי, read, with practically all commentators, שביה, precisely as in the parallel position in the next distich. — For מוסרי read, with most commentators, ממוסרי. The first מ was lost no doubt by haplography; for פתח מ' cf. Jer. 40.4.

52.3. In the second stichos of the first tristich a word has certainly been lost, a word necessary to complete the three-beat meter. This word can be only עמי. The supplying of this word in this particular position makes the parallelism with the corresponding stichos of the tristich immediately following most effective. This repetition of עמי in this double-tristich parallels exactly that of שביה in the double-distich of v. 2; in fact we may readily discern a parallelism between the double use of שביה in v. 2 and the double use of the contrasting term, עמי, in v. 3, a contrasting parallelism which enforces vividly and cogently the message of reassurance to Israel which this address conveys. The statement here and again in v. 5, that Israel was sold into slavery for practically no price at all indicates, and this very compellingly, that the reference is again to the catastrophe of 485 B. C.

52.4a. אדני overloads the meter by one beat, and, since it is unessential to the thought, should certainly be omitted.

52.4b. The mention of Assyria is surprising indeed, and doubly so in an address directed to a Judaean audience, descendants of the people of the Southern Kingdom, which was destroyed, not by Assyria, but by Babylonia. Moreover, the thought of v. 4a by itself is incomplete, for the context demands a reference to some misfortune which befell Israel in Egypt comparable in some way to that which the Jewish community in Palestine had only recently experienced, and specifically an experience of slavery in Egypt which paralleled that which followed upon the catastrophe of 485 B. C. and from which, so this address intimates, Yahweh is about to deliver His people. Accordingly, a relatively minor emendation, for ואשור read ושרו. The reference is of course to the king of Egypt. Certainly the second metrical unit of v. 4, obviously a distich, is incomplete both in the thought which the context here requires and in metrical form. Quite obviously a complete stichos has been lost, one which told of Yahweh's deliverance of His people from Egyptian bondage. Accordingly the clause here supplied by conjecture must approximate closely the content, and probably even the wording, of the missing stichos. The supplying of this lost stichos restores v. 4a to its original form as a 3/3/3 tristich which parallels in every way, and that too most effectively, the 3/3/3 tristich immediately preceding in v. 3.

52.5. For the necessary textual reconstruction of v. 5b and the import thereof cf. Blank, "Isaiah 52.5 and the Profanation of the Name," *HUCA* XXV (1954), 1–8.

his unwillingness to ask the very friendly and cooperative Persian
king for military protection for himself and his band upon this long

---

In addition to emending with Blank, יהילילו נאם־יהוה to יחללוני, I would also emend
משלו to שלליו (cf. Jer. 50.10; Ezek. 39.10; Zech. 2.12) and would likewise transpose the
ו of ותמיד to the following word, וכל־היום, and thus with it introduce the second half
of the distich. — פה, "here," i. e. in the present, historic situation, in which Israel
finds itself enslaved once again, and that too again in a foreign land, in much the same
manner as it had formerly been enslaved in Egypt. The thought implicit here is that
even as Yahweh of old delivered His people from slavery in Egypt, so must He now
once again deliver them from slavery in the land of their present bondage. This
appreciation of the full import of ועתה מה־לי־פה here confirms the wording which we
have conjectured for the missing stichos of the distich immediately preceding.

52.6.   In v. 6 the words לכן ביום ההוא are altogether meaningless, superfluous
and disturbing of both context and meter. With their omission the very meaningful
thought of the distich and also perfect metrical order are recovered. — For הוא, "the
One Who Is; the Ever-Existent One," as a name of Yahweh apparently coined and
certainly frequently used by Deutero-Isaiah and also by his successors cf. Morgenstern, "Deutero-Isaiah's Terminology for Universal God," *Journal of Biblical
Literature* LXII (1943), 269–280, and especially p. 273.

52.11.   משם, "from there," i. e. from Babylonia; note the import of the suffix
of מתוכה in the corresponding stichos of the next distich. — Quite plainly the one סורו
overloads the thought, is readily dispensable, disturbs the meter, and so should be
omitted.

52.12b.   For הלך read ההלך; the manifest parallelism with ומאספכם in the corresponding position in the second stichos of this distich requires that this word here
also be determined, and so have the article. The one ה was lost undoubtedly by
haplography.

40.3   The two words, קול קורא, manifestly stand outside the meter, and thus,
and also by their altogether impersonal character, suggest quite vividly the manner
in which in a drama the name of the speaker is indicated in the margin. — The two
imperatives, one in each distich of the v., are certainly not directed to Israel or to
any other people. They can be directed only to Yahweh's immediate, super-earthly
servants, the angels or whoever they might be. These are the ones bidden to prepare
the highway through the desert for the impending journey of Yahweh and His people.
Furthermore, the statement that this highway would lead through the Arabah is
illuminating indeed, for it tells that this contemplated route which the exiles, returning from Babylonia, were to travel was the southern route, leading from Southern
Babylonia across the desert, probably to the site of present-day Jauf, then on through
the Wadi Sirḥan into the Arabah, and then across the Jordan and on to Jerusalem.
Unquestionably this highroad through the desert was suggested by the route from
Babylonia to Teima, the favorite residence of the last Neo-Babylonian monarch,
Nabunaid, undoubtedly much travelled during the reign of that monarch.

40.4.   The v. seems to imply that, in fulfillment of the command in v. 3, at the
bidding of the heavenly agents the land over which the highroad for Yahweh will
pass will level itself and likewise straighten itself so that travel upon it will become
easy and the travellers upon it will come directly and surely to their goal. — Instead
of העקב, here a difficult word indeed, into which the artificial connotation, "rough
places," would have to be forced, read, with 42.16, המעקשים, "the crooked or winding
stretches"; actually this passage is definitely reminiscent of 42.16. Correspondingly

and hazardous journey, although he does record that the king was
ready to grant his every request. In fact the king had apparently of

---

והיה must be emended to והיו. — At the end of the second distich of 40.4 a word,
essential to the meter seems to have been lost (cf. "The Loss of Words at the Ends of
Lines" etc., cited in note 18). By supplying יהיו not only is this loss repaired but also
an effective chiasm with the first stichos of the distich is achieved.

52.7. This v. consists of two distichs, of which the second is a 4/4, while the
second stichos of the first distich likewise consists of four beats. This suggests very
compellingly that the first stichos of the first distich should also contain four beats
instead of the present three, since the metrical form, 3/4, seems not to exist in Biblical
Hebrew poetry. By supplying הנה at the beginning of this first stichos the 4/4 meter
is achieved and at the same time the picture is made decidedly more vivid. —
Quite frequently in Biblical Hebrew a verb in its normal form will express the
iterative idea of its primary meaning; thus בנה, not only "to build" but also "to
rebuild" (Josh. 6.26; Isa. 45.13; 58.12; 60.10; 61.4; Amos 9.14; Zech. 6.12). So here,
מלך "to resume the kingship; to reign again" rather than merely "to reign." Certainly
this interpretation adds much to the import and effect of this passage.

52.8. For this interpretation of עין בעין cf. Num. 14.14.

52.7-8. These two vv. advance the thought one significant step. They picture
vividly the approach of the returning exiles to Jerusalem, their destination, after
having safely and happily completed the first stage of their long, difficult and danger-
ous journey, the march through the desert and the Arabah. The vv. imply that the
messenger, whom the returning band of exiles have sent on in advance to announce
their coming, has approached sufficiently close to Jerusalem for the city-watchers to
perceive him and, appreciating the full import of the momentous message which the
mere sight of the messenger seems to convey, to raise their voices in exultation.
Vv. 9-10 then reveal the full import of this incident, thus heralded and just on the
point of transpiring, while 40.9, 10a, 5 bring the address to an extremely stirring
climax by bidding Jerusalem proclaim, and in such manner as can be heard, not only
by all the towns of Judah, but also by the entire world, the glad tidings of all that
this entire chain of events means.

52.10. 52.10aα in its *MT* form can be read only as of four beats. But since the
prevailing meter in this section of the address seems to be 3/2, it is well to emend
זרועו את־זרוע קדשו to את־זרוע קדשו.

40.10a. אדני יהוה again, just as in 52.4, presents one beat too many for the
meter. יהוה alone would suffice and may well be the original reading. However, since
the context seems to require a word here which would tie up the thought here expressed with "the towns of Judah" of the preceding distich, אלהיכם seems much more
expressive and decidedly preferable to יהוה. — Instead of בְּחָזָק vocalize בְּחֹזָק (cf.
Amos 6.13).

40.5. For this interpretation of כבוד יהוה cf. Morgenstern, "Biblical Theopha-
nies," *Zeitschrift für Assyriologie* XXV (1911), 139–193; XXVIII (1913), 15–60;
"The Gates of Righteousness," *HUCA* VI (1929), 1–37. The full implication of this
v. is that upon the New Year's Day, the day of the fall equinox, Yahweh will enter
His restored Temple in Jerusalem in the traditional manner, with the first rays of
the rising, equinoctial sun (cf. Isa. 60.1 and "Two Prophecies from 520-516 B. C."
[cited in note 4], 387–393) shining in through the eastern gate, kept tightly closed
through all the remainder of the year but opened wide shortly before sunrise of this,

his own accord offered military protection for the journey, but this Ezra had emphatically rejected, with the assurance to the king that the hand of Yahweh was over all those who appealed to Him, to guard them from all mishap.

What is at issue here is perfectly clear. Ezra, the Zadokite, is putting to a very realistic test the message proclaimed more than a full century earlier by his fellow-Zadokite, Ezekiel, a message undoubtedly zealously cherished through all these years by that prophet's fellow-Zadokites in Babylonia, that at the proper time Yahweh would bring exiled Israel back to its native land, would there implant within it a new heart, purged of all impulse to evil, which, in turn, leads to unfaithfulness to Him, and would take it again unto Himself as His people, and all this primarily in order to graphically and convincingly demonstrate His divinity and power in the sight of all peoples, and thus rehabilitate His reputation as a powerful god among the gods of all the nations, and so come once again to be respected and feared by all men.[23] Plainly Ezra reasons that, should he and his band make this long and hazardous journey trustingly and courageously and at

---

the most important day of the year, for just this very significant ceremony, and closed again at nightfall of the same day, to remain closed throughout the ensuing year. This ceremony was known as הִגָּלוֹת כְּבוֹד יהוה, "the self-revelation of the radiance of Yahweh"; (cf. Ex. 16.10; Lev. 9.6, 23; Num. 14.10; 16.19 et pass.). Ezek. 40.1; 43.1–4; 44.1–4 depict this same New Year's Day rite in some detail, and this too in connection with the dedication of the new, remodelled sanctuary. And since there is ample and convincing evidence that Ezek. 40–48 is of Ezranic authorship, the work of Ezra or of some of his followers (cf. Hölscher, Hesekiel, der Dichter und das Buch, BZAW 39 [1924], 189–212; the evidence is, however, far more abundant and cogent than that which Hölscher, the first proponent of this hypothesis, has presented), and since also, so we maintain, this prophetic address envisages the coming of Ezra and his band to Jerusalem in 458 B. C., with the specific commission from Artaxerxes I to restore or reconstruct the ruined Temple, it follows that this address and Ezek. 40–48 contemplate the same historic event. Here, just as there, the climax of the ritual dedication of the restored sanctuary is the entrance of Yahweh into it in the ancient, traditional manner, at sunrise of the New Year's Day in the form of the first rays of the rising, equinoctial sun, the כְּבוֹד יהוה, coming in through the open, eastern gate. Isa. 40.5 adds the very significant thought, that all mankind will behold this event and, by implication, will thus know that Yahweh has resumed His kingship over His land and people (cf. 52.7) and has demonstrated convincingly His divine power, and has thus rehabilitated His reputation as a god, and so has fulfilled, as we shall see very soon, the expectation and pronouncement of both Ezekiel and Ezra. This picture is indeed a fitting, effective and climactic conclusion to this stirring address, and accordingly is cast very properly as a 3/3/3 tristich.

[23] I have called this the doctrine of "for His name's sake"; cf. my several articles, "Moses with the Shining Face," HUCA II (1925), 18–20; "Psalm 48," HUCA XVI (1941), 26–38; "Psalm 23," JBL LXV (1946), 20 ff.

last arrive safely and triumphantly at their destination, it would confirm in concrete and convincing manner Ezekiel's prediction and promise, and this not only to the nations at large but also even to Israel itself, and would prove conclusively to all that Yahweh, Israel's god, is indeed a true and mighty deity, one in whom Israel may safely trust and one with whom the nations must truly reckon. Precisely this is the implication of Ezra 8.31 f. But precisely this is the implication also of the prophetic address in Isa. 51.1–12 in its original, full form. In the light of these compelling considerations there can scarcely be any doubt that not only must this address be later than 485 B. C., but also that it must be interpreted in connection with the coming of Ezra and his band to Jerusalem, and therefore can not in any way be from the tongue or pen of Deutero-Isaiah.

Moreover, in the light of the obvious relationship of this address to the catastrophe of 485 B. C., the still persisting effects of which it portrays so vividly, it is impossible to avoid the conclusion that the coming of Ezra and his band to Jerusalem, and that too with a commission from Artaxerxes, the Persian king, to restore the Temple, burned to the ground in 485 B. C., must have taken place not too long after that catastrophe, that, in other words, the Artaxerxes in question must have been Artaxerxes I rather than Artaxerxes II, as is today maintained with more or less assurance by many Biblical scholars, and that all this occurred in 458 B. C., the seventh year of Artaxerxes I, just twenty-seven years after the great catastrophe, rather than in 398 B. C., the seventh year of Artaxerxes II, sixty years later and almost a century after the catastrophe.

Other considerations of more than passing significance confirm our major conclusion that all the prophetic utterances of Deutero-Isaiah are to be found only in Isa. 40–48, while the whole of Isa. 49–55, except potentially for the present the Suffering Servant passages in all of Isa. 40–66,[24] must, along with Isa. 56–66, be classified as Trito-Isaiah.

In the first place, it should be noted that, with the exception of the Suffering Servant passages, the term, עבד יהוה, "Servant of Yahweh," or the representation of Israel as the servant or agent of Yahweh, a basic theme, as we shall see, of the message of Deutero-Isaiah, occurs or finds expression, even in the faintest form, not even once in all of Isa. 49–66. This fact by itself is almost decisive in

---

[24] I hope to show, upon some other occasion, that all the Suffering Servant passages in Isa. 40–66 together constitute a distinct, literary unit, of dramatic character, which is definitely later than 485 B. C., and so must likewise be classified as Trito-Isaiah.

confirming our conclusion that in Isa. 49–55 no Deutero-Isaianic material whatever is to be found.

Furthermore, Yahweh has, according to Deutero-Isaiah, chosen Israel as His servant in order that it may be the agent or mediator of His salvation for all mankind. This thought of universal salvation, mediated through Israel, is, as we shall see, likewise basic to the entire message of Deutero-Isaiah. Very significantly, the one and only word by which Deutero-Isaiah designates this salvation is תשועה.[25] But in Isa. 49–66 this word occurs not one, single time. On the other hand, ישועה, which is used not even once in Isa. 40–48, occurs in 49–66 eleven times, six times in 49–55 and five times in 56–66. Moreover, with the exception of Isa. 49.6, 8, a fragment of the Suffering Servant document, Yahweh's salvation, in all of Isa. 49–66, is destined for Israel alone, with the nations of the world having absolutely no part in it. In fact in all these chapters this salvation of Israel by Yahweh is always of national, political character, salvation from dominion over and oppression of it by other nations. This concept of Yahweh's salvation is manifestly the very antithesis of that of Deutero-Isaiah.

It is also a matter of considerable import that in all of Isa. 40–48 which must be assigned to Deutero-Isaiah, and that is of course by far the greater part, Jerusalem is referred to only six times,[26] and that too only in poetic and rather remote and conventional manner. This is easily comprehensible. As we shall learn, Deutero-Isaiah's addresses were all delivered in Babylonia and were directed immediately to only the Jewish community exiled in that land. In his thought and message Jerusalem played no more than a secondary role. On the other hand, in Isa. 49–66 Jerusalem is referred to under that name thirteen times and under the name, Zion, fifteen times. Manifestly in the thought of the various Trito-Isaianic writers Jerusalem played a constant and omnipresent role, due to the simple fact that, in significant contrast to Deutero-Isaiah, all of them without exception, and this includes the author of the Suffering Servant document, were addressing their message to an audience whose home was Jerusalem and its vicinity, in other words to the Jewish community of Palestine.

This cumulation of decisive evidence should suffice to establish beyond all possibility of challenge that the totality of Deutero-Isaiah's

---

[25] Isa. 46.13 (bis), 45.17. 45.8, in which ישע occurs, is a gloss. In Isa. 49–66 ישע occurs three times (51.5; 61.10; 62.11). It is therefore obviously a Trito-Isaianic term.

[26] 41.27; 44.26b, 28b; 45.13; 46.13; 48.2. 40.2, 9 are, as we have shown, Trito-Isaiah.

addresses which have been preserved are to be found only in Isa. 40–48, while all of 49–55, like 56–66, and this including all the Suffering Servant passages, even those in 40–48, must be ascribed to Trito-Isaianic writers, who, for the most part, lived and spoke after, and in large measure in direct relation to, the great, national catastrophe of 485 B. C.[27]

After this long, but altogether necessary, digression, we may resume our primary task, the consideration of the message of Deutero-Isaiah, as this unfolds itself in Isa. 40–48.

In the course of evolution of his prophetic message, when he was no longer a youthful, eager, fiery denouncer of Judah for its oft-repeated faithlessness to and transgression against Yahweh, Jeremiah evolved his doctrine of the new covenant.[28] He affirmed repeatedly that the presumptively bitter experience of the exile, with all the personal suffering which, so he assumed, this must necessarily entail, would be for מוסר, discipline, divinely administered, corrective discipline of the rebellious and sinful people. And in due time, when this discipline would have achieved its purposed effect, and Israel in exile, now fully comprehending the nature and degree of its former faithlessness and now thoroughly regenerate, would have returned to Yahweh, its god, in complete sincerity, then Yahweh, whose power and will on behalf of His people were, so Jeremiah's earlier message to the exiles had clearly implied, effective even in foreign lands, would reassemble dispersed Israel, bring it back from exile to native land, reestablish it there in security, take it again unto Himself as His people,

---

[27] However, as I have shown elsewhere ("Two Prophecies from 520–516 B. C." [cited in note 4]), Isa. 55.1–5 must be assigned to 520 B. C. and Isa. 60.1–3, 5–7 to 516 B. C.

[28] Jer. 31.30–33. A number of distinguished Biblical scholars, and notably Duhm, have denied, or at least have seriously questioned, the Jeremianic authorship of these vv. and of the message of the new covenant which they convey. But, as will become increasingly clear, Ezekiel's doctrine of "for His name's sake," formulated and proclaimed not later than 572 B. C., presupposes and in large measure grows out of this doctrine of the new covenant. Furthermore, it is to be presumed that this doctrine had been formulated sufficiently long before Ezekiel's proclamation of his doctrine for the unreality of Jeremiah's assumption of Israel's spiritual regeneration through the anticipatedly bitter experiences of the exile to become clearly realized. Accordingly, if not from Jeremiah himself, the doctrine of the new covenant would certainly have to be ascribed to some anonymous prophet, and that, too, one of comparable stature, contemporaneous with Jeremiah. And since we know of no such prophet, there seems no good reason for not accrediting this lofty doctrine to Jeremiah in complete accord with Biblical tradition. And indeed Jeremiah's parable of the figs (Jer. 24) certainly implies just such a corollary as this doctrine of the new covenant.

and enter with it into a new covenant, a covenant which of course
He would never again have cause to repudiate. For, unlike the old
covenant, which He had had to repudiate, the old covenant, made
at Sinai, the terms of which were inscribed upon two stones, hidden
away in the ark in the innermost recesses of the Temple, and which
faithless Israel had forgotten or defiantly disregarded, the prescriptions
of this new covenant would be written ineradicably upon the heart of
every true son of regenerate Israel, and thus would become an integral
part of his very being, and so could never be disregarded or forgotten,
but would shape his every thought, impulse and action in such manner
that never again could he possibly cease to know Yahweh and His
way or turn aside therefrom into the devious paths of rebellion and
sin. Accordingly this new, inviolable covenant would be an eternal
covenant, which would bind Israel to Yahweh, its god, as His people
in perfect and ever-enduring union. Such was Jeremiah's doctrine of
the new covenant.

But, as must have become clearer with each passing day and
year, and as Jeremiah himself must in due time have come to realize
all too clearly, after the first hardships of deportation, entailing
anguished separation from loved ones, resettlement in a distant,
strange land and more or less difficult adjustment to the altogether
new environment, were ended, the exile ceased completely, at least
for the majority of the deported Jews, to be an experience of מוסר,
of disciplinary and corrective suffering and eventual regeneration,
and became instead a state of normal, and by no means unhappy,
daily existence. Quite speedily the exiles adjusted themselves sympathetically to their new environment and began to feel completely
at home there and in general to prosper. Particularly must this have
been true of the generations which were born and lived their entire
lives in Babylonia. This was now their true home. Jerusalem was
only a memory, hallowed perhaps, but a memory none the less, which
in only secondary measure determined their loyalties and way of life.
They were now Babylonians in birth, culture and spirit.

And not at all unnaturally, Jeremiah's admonition to them to
pray to Yahweh in their new land and home seems to have evoked
little sympathetic response. A few of the exiles for one reason or
another, the deported Zadokite priests of the former Temple for
example, may have heeded the prophet's bidding; but they were the
almost unnoticeable minority. For the vast majority Jeremiah's
admonition voiced a religious principle not only too novel to be
adequately comprehended, but also one which lacked appeal. Why
should they continue to pray to Yahweh, and that too in a foreign

land, they must have debated with themselves as well as with one another. What had He done for them, and what could He do for them now in this strange land, in which, despite Jeremiah's message to them, they persisted in believing, He had no place nor authority whatever? They had been made to realize, to their own cost, that, so at least their present situation suggested, He could not even protect His people in His own land, where, if anywhere, His power and authority should have prevailed. What then could He do for them in a foreign land, far distant from His own country, a land in which other gods, gods who had proved concretely that they were far mightier than He, held sway? Furthermore, despite the novel idea voiced in Jeremiah's message to them, was it not a fundamental principle of religion, as they, the masses, still understood it, that god and land were so intimately and inseparably linked to each other that when one visited a foreign country, and particularly when one abode there for a time, or, and especially, settled or was settled there permanently, as seemed to be their status, he had to acknowledge and pay homage to the god or gods of that land, if he would there enjoy divine protection and favor?

True, Jeremiah had bidden them believe that their present condition of exile was only temporary, that it was not at all powerful and victorious foreign gods who had imposed this condition upon them, but rather Yahweh Himself, their own, native god. And He had allowed this presumably unhappy situation to encompass them, not at all because of His own impotence in competition with these foreign deities and His consequent inability to effectively protect His people, even in His own land, but actually because of His own implicit strength, because in all this He was in truth carrying out His own wise and loving purpose. He had allowed this supposititious calamity to befall them as מוסר, as disciplinary punishment for their previous, long-protracted faithlessness to Him and to their covenant-obligation to Him, so that they might ponder upon and learn the evil of their ways, and with this the depth and persistence of His love for His people, and thus become regenerate and return to Him in truth. And when this happy condition would prevail at last, after a long period of trial and discipline, seventy years perhaps, then Yahweh would reveal Himself in His true being, would assert His power, even in this foreign country, and would bring exiled Israel back to His and its native land, and there would take it again to Himself as His people, and would renew His covenant with it.

But for the majority of the exiles, particularly as their sojourn in Babylonia drew on and a new generation, born in the land, gradually replaced the actual deportees, the appeal of Jeremiah's admonition, with its vague and remote promise of return to the land of their fathers, steadily diminished. It spoke to them in terms which they could no longer translate into living reality. The fact could not be gainsaid, so it seemed to many, that thus far Yahweh had been shown to be far less powerful than other gods, and particularly than the world-conquering, triumphant Babylonian deities, and completely unable to protect His people even in His own land. After this convincing demonstration of relative power, why should they put further trust in Him, particularly in this remote, foreign land, where certainly, despite Jeremiah's startling affirmation that even here Yahweh could act on their behalf, the native gods alone were dominant? Why then should they not, conforming to the traditional and still generally valid principle of early Semitic religion, tender their allegiance to the all-powerful gods of this land and worship them loyally, in conformity with the established beliefs and cult-practice of Babylonian religion?

And as for the promise of eventual return to native land, what appeal might that have for them? Had they not, the steadily growing majority, been born in this land? And were they not prospering here, at least many of them, and this manifestly with the favor and blessing of the gods of the land? Was not this then, and not Israel, their true native land? And, a very compelling consideration indeed, were not the culture of this land and its people, their immediate neighbors, and in consequence their own manner of living, immeasurably superior to that which their fathers had known and fashioned in their former national home-land? Why then should they even contemplate or desire to return thither? Certainly here in Babylonia they were better off by far, both economically and culturally, than they could ever hope to be back in the land of their fathers, the land of Yahweh. What could that distant land offer them, and what could a weak, impotent Yahweh, its god, bestow upon them, which they did not already possess in greater extent and in more attractive form here in this, their true native land?

So the vast majority of the Jewish exiles in Babylonia must have reasoned, and this too altogether naturally. Accordingly Jeremiah's message must have fallen in the main upon deaf ears and unresponsive hearts. More and more, as one generation followed another, these Jewish exiles must have integrated themselves with the land of their birth and their abode, with its native population, and with its culture. True, in loyalty to their past, their ancestors and their national tradition, they may have cherished in some degree the memory of their former land, their ancient god there and their origins. But in way of life, in spirit, in national aspirations and in social and religious affiliations they tended, with each passing generation, to identify themselves more and more with their environment, to become a part of the Babylonian nation and devotees, more or less ardent, of Babylonian religion and of the Babylonian gods.

And so, before many years had passed, following Jeremiah's message to them, it must have become apparent to all that the prophet had been completely mistaken in his assumption that the exile would be an experience of מוסר, of disciplinary suffering, inflicted by Yahweh upon His people with distinct purpose, that, at least from the standpoint of relationship to Yahweh, it would have no regenerative effect whatever upon Israel nor induce it to return to its god in such sincere and whole-hearted manner as to justify Him in bringing it back from exile in Babylonia to its native land and there taking it again as His people and entering with it into a new and ever-enduring covenant. But despite the steadily expanding awareness of the unregenerating effect of the exile upon the Jewish community, either that in Babylonia or seemingly also that which remained resident in Palestine, and the consequent lack of cause for Yahweh to fulfill His conditional promise of restoration to native land and of renewal of His covenant with Israel there, as communicated through Jeremiah, the promise itself took firm and persistent hold upon the thought, the imagination, the hope and the faith of the Jewish community in Judaea and of at least some of the Jewish exiles in Babylonia. Despite its obvious illogicality the belief became ineradicably fixed in their minds and hearts that ultimately, whenever the right moment would come, Yahweh would bring back the exiled section of His people from Babylonia to Palestine, there would reunite it happily with that section thereof which had remained constantly resident in the land, and there He would take this restored Israel to Himself once again and renew His covenant with it, a covenant now which, regardless of how Israel might live and act henceforth, would endure forever, would never be broken, would be truly an eternal covenant. This doctrine of the new, ever-enduring covenant became from this moment on basic in Jewish thought and belief and shaped in very considerable measure Judaism's subsequent development and likewise the ultimate evolution of Christianity from it.

The first to formulate this doctrine of the new covenant in this new form, a form which, needless to say, was certainly not anticipated by Jeremiah, and to formulate it in terms of a realistic program, was Ezekiel, apparently during the closing years of his prophetic ministry, accordingly at about 572 B. C., and therefore some twenty years, more or less, after Jeremiah had first promulgated the doctrine in its initial form. This period was certainly enough for the truth to become abundantly realized, that, measured by Jeremianic standards and expectations, Israel would never become sufficiently regenerate to merit the renewal of the covenant as Jeremiah had envisaged it. In Jeremiah's message, that it was possible for Israel to worship Yahweh even in distant Babylonia and to supplicate His substantial blessing upon it there, and likewise in his proclamation that at the proper time Yahweh would bring Israel back from exile in Babylonia to native land, with its implication that even in Babylonia, far from His own land, Yahweh could and would demonstrate His power and prove it superior to that of the local, Babylonian deities, even the mightiest among them, and would successfully effect His purpose of delivering His people from the place of their earlier deportation and long, enforced sojourn, there was implicit a certain measure of positive universalism. It was the suggestion that, contrary to the impression which, presumably, Babylon's conquest of Judaea had conveyed to all the nations, Yahweh was indeed a persistently powerful deity, powerful not only in His own land, but in other, even distant, lands as well, a true world-deity therefore, one who could work His will in any land and in any part of the world, a deity therefore with whom the nations must thenceforth reckon and whom they must therefore respect and even fear.

This particular implication of Jeremiah's doctrine of the new covenant constituted the starting-point of what seems to have been Ezekiel's final message as a prophet of Yahweh. To him Yahweh was indeed a world-god, and a powerful god too, one who could assuredly hold his own with all other world-gods, the gods of all the powerful nations of the world, a god who was therefore entitled to rank high among them. But because of Israel's sin and its faithlessness to Him Yahweh had been obliged to punish it drastically, by permitting it to be conquered by Nebuchadnezzar and, in considerable numbers, be carried off into exile in distant Babylonia. Yahweh's purpose in all this was plain and sure. And beyond all question Israel had merited this extreme punishment at His hands. But apparently Yahweh had failed to foresee one important consequence of this procedure on His part, viz. what the natural reaction of all the nations other than Israel, and even of Israel too to a certain extent, to this treatment by Him of His errant people would be. Certainly the true nature and extent of Israel's faithlessness to its god and the consequent justification of Yahweh's disciplinary treatment of it these other nations could not comprehend. But under any condition one of the primary duties of any able and responsible god, so they would necessarily reason, was to protect his people at all times, to ward off all danger and threatening calamity and, above all else, save it from conquest, destruction and loss of identity as a nation and a people. If he could not do this, if he failed in this primary responsibility to his people, what manner of god could he be? What must the nations and peoples of the world think of him? They could not but regard him as a deity completely impotent, totally unable to do aught of consequence for his people, a deity therefore who merited, not the respect and high esteem of the nations, but only their disregard and contempt.

Just this was now Yahweh's position in the eyes of all the nations of the world. Although His treatment of His faithless people was, from His and its standpoint, justifiable in every way, it had cost Him far too much. In this age of steadily evolving universalism in international relations and of the god-concepts attendant thereupon, Yahweh had inadvertently forfeited His reputation among the nations. So long as His people remained in exile in a foreign land, the nations could think of Him only with disdain, as a completely impotent deity, with whom they need not reckon in any way whatever. Because of Israel's faithlessness and sin and the inescapable obligation resting upon Him to punish it in extreme measure, as it undoubtedly deserved, Yahweh's reputation as a god, as a true world-god, had suffered severely, perhaps even irreparably. And Yahweh was jealous for His reputation, intensely jealous. He was truly a world-god, as much so and as powerful as any; and this the nations and their gods must be made to realize. And to achieve this end only one way was open. What had caused Him to sink so low in their esteem must now be undone, must be completely reversed. In this implicit competition with the gods of other nations His reputation, what the nations and all the world would think of Him, in what esteem they would hold Him, was a consideration which had come to transcend by far the merited discipline of His people. Therefore He had no alternative. He had to undo what He had wrought. Despite its having dearly merited the punishment He had visited upon it, He must now deliver His people from exile in a foreign country and bring it back to its ancestral land, His land, and there rehabilitate it and take it to Himself once again as His people.

Moreover, in so doing there was one distinct advantage accruing to Yahweh. To protect His people in its native land, the land in which He was sovereign, and to ever prosper it there was, as has been said, the primary obligation of every national deity. True, many had failed in this task, and their respective nations had looked in vain for salvation from threatening national catastrophe, each to its own god. Other gods, however, had proved their power and had established for themselves positions of respect and even of fear in the eyes of the nations of the world by successfully fulfilling this obligation, each to its own nation and people, and perhaps also by making its own nation triumphant through military conquest over other nations and thus building up in greater or less degree a substantial empire.

But what god was there in all the previous history of mankind who, once his people had been decisively conquered and had been deported in very considerable number to some remote country, had shown himself able to reassemble these deportees or their posterity and deliver them from this enforced sojourn in this foreign land and bring them back safely to their homeland and securely establish them there as his people once again? Such an achievement would imply victory by him, not only over the nation native to the land of his people's exile, but also over the gods of the land, the very gods who had given their people victory over his nation, and who presumably would purpose to keep this conquered people forever subdued and in exile. Moreover, he would gain this triumph over these gods in their own land, where presumably they alone were dominant. Surely such an achievement was much more difficult, and therefore a far truer test of the character and power of any god, than was merely protection of his people in his and its own land, and that too when its strength and resources were still unimpaired, against an invading enemy, no matter how powerful this latter might be. Just this, this almost super-divine task, Yahweh would now perform on behalf of His exiled people and would carry it through successfully in every detail. And by so doing He would effectively demonstrate His true, incomparable, divine power and thus establish, beyond all possibility of challenge, His position as a god among the most powerful gods of all the nations of the entire world and His status as a true world-god, with whom the nations, all the nations, must henceforth reckon and whom they must fear and revere. Thus Yahweh would rehabilitate His name, His reputation, among the nations.

But certainly Israel had not, by its own conduct, merited such salvation and restoration. Rather it had deserved all that had befallen it; for in the final instance it was Israel which, because of its iniquity and faithlessness and the consequent compulsion resting upon Yahweh to discipline it, was responsible for bringing His name into disrepute among the nations. And certainly too, contrary to Jeremiah's anticipation, the effect of the exile had not been at all to make Israel regenerate and cause it to repent, to eagerly desire to return to and be reunited with its god. If anything, Israel in exile had drifted farther and farther from Yahweh and become more and more steeped in its faithless, sinful ways. It was this unrepentant Israel whom Yahweh was now undertaking to redeem. But with a sinful, rebellious, unrepentant, unregenerate people Yahweh, the supremely righteous god, he who from the very first contact with his people and the establishment of the covenant-relationship between himself and them had been recognized by them as the god of truth, integrity, justice and faithfulness, could not possibly maintain positive and sympathetic relations, the relations which must always exist between loyal god and loyal people. Therefore, since manifestly, contrary to Jeremiah's expectations, Israel in exile would not of its own accord return to Yahweh, and since, despite all its faithlessness, Yahweh had indispensable need of Israel for the fulfillment of His new and larger purpose, and since with an unrepentant, recalcitrant people Yahweh could not maintain permanently positive, happy relations, Yahweh would of His own accord, for the sake of His reputation as a world-god, change Israel's sinful and rebellious nature to one of righteousness and faithfulness. As an act of sheer grace, and without the slightest meriting thereof on Israel's part, He would remove from Israel's breast that hard, stubborn, unimpressionable heart of stone, which through all the long past had prompted it to rebellion and sin against Him, and would substitute for it a new heart, a heart of flesh, a heart soft and warm, sympathetic and amenable to His counsel, admonition and discipline, an understanding and faithful heart. And with this new heart now beating steadily and responsively within its breast, Israel could not but henceforth keep faith with Him, forever walk with Him in truth and righteousness, and deservedly be and remain His people unto eternity.

Actually Ezekiel does not in this connection say specifically that Yahweh will formulate a new covenant and bring Israel into new covenant relations with Himself.[29] But there can hardly be any question that this relationship between Yahweh and the now, in the most literal sense, regenerate Israel, by divine action made totally incapable of future faithlessness and sin, is a covenant relationship. And precisely like the new covenant of Jeremiah, this new god-people relationship, thus formulated and proclaimed by Ezekiel, was destined to endure forever. Beyond all challenge Ezekiel's picture

---

[29] But cf. Ezek. 16.60–63; however, this passage is almost certainly a late interpolation and non-Ezekelian.

of the restoration of Israel by Yahweh from captivity in Babylon to
native land, of the new, positive and ever-enduring relationship as
god and people between Yahweh and Israel, and even the role of
Israel's heart therein,[30] were the direct and, not improbably, the
conscious outgrowth of Jeremiah's doctrine of the new covenant.
In fact it is reasonably certain that without Jeremiah's doctrine of
the new covenant as his starting-point Ezekiel would never have
arrived at this final and, in some respects, this climactic stage of his
complete prophetic message.

Such was Ezekiel's doctrine of "for His name's sake" in its origin
and its import.[31]

## III

### THE MESSAGE OF DEUTERO-ISAIAH

Some thirty years or so after Ezekiel had proclaimed his doctrine of
"for His name's sake," Deutero-Isaiah entered upon his prophetic
ministry. All told, what seem to be seven addresses by him are preserved in Isa. 40–48. Each of these addresses or literary compositions
is contained in a single chapter, with the one exception that chapters
42–44 seem to constitute a single, unified address, which, however,
in its present form manifests not a little textual disarrangement of its
original, logical thought-sequence. Of these seven compositions four,
those in chapters 45–48, can be dated quite accurately in relation to
each other, while the three remaining addresses, in chapters 40–44,
may be dated, if not with the same preciseness, none the less with
reasonable accuracy in relation to the addresses in 45–48 and also
in relation to each other. Thus it is possible to trace the gradual
unfolding of Deutero-Isaiah's message.

Two unchallengeably reliable clues point the way in this dating
process. The first of these is the successive stages of Cyrus' military
program, as this is revealed in several of these addresses. In chapter
40 no mention of nor reference to Cyrus occurs. In chapter 41 Yahweh
is represented as debating or contending in courtroom argument with
the peoples of the world and, so the further implication is, with their

---

[30] No doubt the role of Israel's new heart in Ezekiel's picture was suggested, in
part at least, by the role of the heart of every son of Israel, upon which Yahweh's
תורה is to be inscribed, in Jeremiah's vision of the new covenant (Jer. 31.32; cf. also
24.7). We may see in this further evidence of the dependence of Ezekiel's doctrine
upon that of Jeremiah.

[31] Ezek. 20.1–44; 36.16–36.

gods, in order to establish by definitive proof who is the one, true God, the God of all the world. As we shall see, this is an oft-recurring theme of this great prophet, and he, first of all the prophets of Israel, and apparently the very first of all the outstanding exponents of religion in the history of mankind, has at last arrived at the concept of one world-God, the Creator of the entire universe, the one, single, existent God; and for him that one world-God is of course Yahweh, the god of Israel. He challenges these nations and likewise, by implication, their gods to prove the divinity of the latter by determining who of all the gods it is who has summoned Cyrus to do his bidding and has given or is giving him victory over all peoples, who has subdued or is subduing nations before him and humbling kings beneath his feet. Here (vv. 2 f.) and again in v. 25, where Yahweh affirms positively and definitively that it is He, and no other god, who has done all this, the tenses of the verbs are confused and uncertain, so that it is impossible to establish with certainty whether here Cyrus' campaigns are in the past, the present or the future. Certain internal evidence, vague and indecisive though it is, suggests, however, that the campaigns and triumphs of Cyrus, as here referred to, are of the past, though of course not of a too distant past. And if so, then the address in chapter 41 must have been spoken by the prophet somewhat later than Cyrus' conquest of Babylon late in 539 B. C.

In the long address in chapters 42–44 Cyrus is referred to only incidentally, in 44.28a, where he is called Yahweh's shepherd, i. e., as the term, "shepherd" in early Accadian inscriptions[32] and in the Biblical literature of the exilic and early post-exilic periods[33] frequently connotes, His king, His world-king, elevated by Yahweh to world-kingship as the agent of His world-purpose. 44.28b and also 26b refer to Cyrus indirectly by implying that the primary task, or at least a portion thereof, which he, by Yahweh's decree, is to perform, is to rebuild Jerusalem, so that it may be inhabited once again, and to restore the Temple. However, careful analysis establishes with reasonable certainty both that 44.26b–28 have little or no relationship to the thought of the verses which immediately precede or of the address as a whole, and are therefore out of place where they stand, and also that they are in themselves hardly a literary unit, since v. 28b not only duplicates in part what has already been stated adequately in v. 26b, but is also couched in a literary form which differs slightly but significantly from that of vv. 26b–28a. The latter

---

[32] Mowinckel, *He That Cometh* (translated by G. W. Anderson), 47.
[33] Cf. Isa. 44.28; Jer. 23.1, 4; Ezek. 34.2, 7.

group of verses should be transposed[34] to chapter 41, to intervene
there between v. 4a and 4b, where it fits perfectly metrically and
likewise amplifies the thought of 4a and 4b effectively by stating what
was Yahweh's initial decree, viz. the drying up at creation of the
waters of the original world-sea and the appearance of dry land, and
what was His most recent decree, viz. that Cyrus should be His world-
king and the agent of His will, and that accordingly Jerusalem should
be restored and repopulated by him, impliedly for the fulfillment of
some ultimate, larger, divine purpose. On the other hand, 44.28b
should be transposed to come between 45.19 and 20a, where it, in
turn, both fits perfectly metrically and also supplies an integral and
essential thought. Manifestly then in the address itself, recorded in
chapters 42–44, Cyrus is referred to not at all.

In chapter 45 Cyrus is called Yahweh's "anointed one," in other
words His king. Yahweh has appointed him to this exalted position
so that he might subdue nations and depose their native kings. In
their stead Yahweh girds Cyrus as world-king, and this too despite
the fact that Cyrus does not yet know Him, and so does not realize
as yet that it is He, Yahweh, and no other god, who has made him
world-conqueror. Yahweh has prospered Cyrus throughout his entire
career, to the end that Cyrus may at last come to realize that it is
He, the god of Israel, who has done all this for him. And all this, its
ultimate purpose, Yahweh has done for the sake of His servant, Israel,
and also in order that it may come to be recognized from one end of
the earth to the other that He, Yahweh, alone is God, the one, true
world-God, and that besides Him there is no god. From the very
beginning Yahweh has stimulated Cyrus to action and has prospered
him in all his undertakings for the ultimate purpose that he might
rebuild Yahweh's city, Jerusalem, and restore His exiled people to
its native land. Such is the picture of Cyrus and, though as yet not
comprehended by him, of his relations to Yahweh, to Israel, and to
the world, as these have from the very beginning been purposed and
planned by Yahweh.

Manifestly in this picture Babylon has already passed into Cyrus'
possession, and Cyrus has become, as head of the newly established
vast Persian Empire, the supreme world-ruler. But, so the prophet
insistently affirms, not Marduk, the chief deity in the local Babylonian
pantheon, has chosen him and prospered him in all this, has made him
victorious everywhere and elevated him to the lofty position of

---

[34] Though probably in the order corresponding to the logical development of the
thought here expressed, viz. 27–28a, 26b.

world-king, as he, perhaps in considerable measure for political considerations, in order to ingratiate himself with the native Babylonians and win their loyalty and support, asserts again and again in his inscriptions, but only Yahweh, Israel's god, and He alone. It is a reasonable inference that Deutero-Isaiah was familiar with this declaration of Cyrus, undoubtedly immediately after the fall of Babylon widely publicized by oral proclamation as well as by written record, and was prompted by it to affirm, in vv. 1–7, that it was actually Yahweh, and He alone, and no other god, i. e. impliedly not Marduk at all, nor yet Cyrus' native Persian deities, Ormuzd and Ahriman, who had done all this for Cyrus. And when Cyrus would come to realize this, and thus know Yahweh truly, as eventually he must, he would then be moved to acknowledge Yahweh as the one and only true God, and to bring to fulfillment Yahweh's ultimate purpose, or at least an integral and important part thereof, the restoration of His people to its ancestral land and the rebuilding of His holy city, and of course of the Temple therein, the place of His worship. Unquestionably this address must be dated after the fall of Babylon to Cyrus in October, 539 B. C., though apparently not too long thereafter, perhaps early in 538 B. C.; for seemingly Cyrus' edict, permitting the return to native lands of the various peoples who had been exiled therefrom by the Babylonians, while probably anticipated, had at the time of this address not yet been formally proclaimed.

Moreover, it is now readily apparent that 44.28a, 26b, which we have transposed to chapter 41, between v. 4a and 4b, reaffirm the thought of 45.13b, manifestly there announced by the prophet for the very first time. And if 44.28a, 26b be indeed integral in chapter 41, as we propose, this would indicate that the prophet's address in chapter 41 must have been formulated and delivered subsequently to that in chapter 45. Corroboration of this hypothesis will be forthcoming in due time.

In chapter 46 the only reference to Cyrus is the vague statement in vv. 10b–11, that for the fulfillment of His purpose Yahweh has called one from the East, a vulture, impliedly so called because of the suddenness and speed with which he would swoop down upon his prey, the man of his plan, i. e. the agent through whom His well-considered plan will at last, with His own mediation, come to fulfillment. Manifestly here Babylon has not yet fallen before Cyrus. In fact it is possible to fix with reasonable assurance the exact date of this address. The picture, painted quite graphically in vv. 1 f., or even, with additional implications, in vv. 1–4, of the images of the Babylonian deities, and particularly those of Bel-Marduk and his divine son, Nabu, being borne in solemn procession, a wearying and exhausting burden to their bearers, is almost certainly that of the ritual of the Akitu Festival, the Babylonian New Year Festival, celebrated during the first thirteen days of Nisan, i. e. in the early spring. On the eighth day of this festival the images of the gods were borne in solemn procession from Ešagila, the Marduk temple in Babylon, down the sacred highway to a quay upon the bank of the Euphrates River. There they were loaded upon boats and carried up the river to their destination, the *bît akîti*, the shrine, far from the city, which stood, or was thought to stand, upon "the Mountain," the cosmic mountain upon the eastern horizon, which covered the place of exit from the netherworld. There the gods, represented by their idols, abode until the eleventh day of the festival, when they returned, with the resurrected deity, Bel-Marduk, at their head, reversing the course of their journey thither. The final stage of this return was the solemn march of the gods, with their idols borne by their devotees or priestly attendants, from the river-quay back to Ešagila, where the idols were restored, each to its normal position within the great sanctuary.[35] It is to this festal procession of the idols of the Babylonian gods that the opening verses of this prophetic address apparently refer. In all likelihood therefore this address was spoken by the prophet during the celebration of the Akitu Festival, and specifically during or immediately following the sacred procession of the gods, either that away from the Marduk sanctuary or that of the return thither. And inasmuch as Babylon had not yet fallen to Cyrus, but, as v. 13 assures, this fall is imminent, we may with reasonable assurance date this address at the last Akitu Festival before Cyrus' conquest of Babylon, i. e. in the early spring of 539 B. C.

Chapter 47 is actually not a prophetic address in any sense whatsoever. When its original form will have been restored, later in this study, it will become clear immediately that it is a bitter denunciation of Babylon in the form of a powerful dirge, cast throughout in 3/2 meter, the metrical form characteristic of Biblical elegiac poetry. The poem is animated by a deep-rooted, even vindictive, hatred of Babylon. It announces, but more in the form of an eager wish than as an assured, Yahweh-ordained judgment, the impending, utter collapse of Babylon as a nation, the mistress of the world. Actually the name, Yahweh, occurs in the original poem not even a single time. The author is manifestly a poet, one of exalted power; but he is certainly not a prophet, or at least he is not yet a prophet. Actually there is no

[35] Cf. Thureau-Dangin, *Rituels Accadiens*, 147 f.

reason whatsoever for not regarding Deutero-Isaiah as the author of this stirring poem. In fact several bits of evidence, the accumulative import of which is quite compelling, point directly to Deutero-Isaiah as the author. But the total absence in the poem of the prophetic motive and tone, coupled with the fact that it makes no mention at all of Cyrus nor suggests that the eagerly wished for and confidently expected overthrow of Babylon may well be at his hands, points strongly to the conclusion that this poem was one of Deutero-Isaiah's earliest literary efforts, composed probably before Cyrus had achieved military success sufficient to suggest to the poet that he might well be the eventual conqueror of Babylon. And this, in turn, suggests further that it may well have been the rapid and successful progress of Cyrus' campaigns, and with this the growing conviction that he was indeed the eagerly awaited conqueror of mighty Babylon, and, furthermore, that he was destined for this service by Yahweh, and this too for a purpose larger and more beneficent by far than the mere overthrow of Babylon, a purpose which concerned directly Yahweh's own people, Israel, and particularly Israel in exile, which transformed the youthful, brilliant poet into the exalted, far-visioned prophet. Under any condition it is reasonably certain that the poem which constitutes the original nucleus of Isa. 47 is older, perhaps by a year or two, than any of the actual, prophetic addresses of Deutero-Isaiah.

In 48.6aα, 14b–15, 6b–8[36] the prophet declares that Yahweh has called Cyrus as His agent in order that he may work His will against Babylon. Moreover, the prophet announces further, this is the capstone, as it were of Yahweh's eternal world-plan, the final stage in the fulfillment thereof, only recently determined upon by Yahweh, never previously disclosed, and now revealed unto Israel for the first time. This last statement is significant It establishes with certainty that this is the prophet's very first mention of Cyrus and of the role which Yahweh, the Creator of the universe, has assigned to him in the execution of His eternal world-plan. But if this be so, then it follows unmistakably that this address in Isa. 48 must have been formulated and delivered earlier than any of the other addresses in which Cyrus is mentioned or even indirectly referred to, i. e. then earlier than the addresses in chapters 41, 45 and 46. This conclusion is confirmed, in some measure at least, by the fact that this address makes no reference to Cyrus' campaigns other than that Yahweh has

---

[36] The rearrangement of the text in this order produces a unified and significant thought-development altogether essential to the prophet's argument in this address. For the reconstruction of the complete address cf. Part II, below, pp. 68 ff.

called him as His agent and will make him successful in the discharge
of his responsible task, the ultimate goal of which is the conquest of
Babylon. Apparently this goal is still somewhat remote. Cyrus'
military program is manifestly under way, but seemingly has as yet
not advanced to the point where his siege and conquest of Babylon
might be expected in the immediate future. But if this address in
chapter 48 be earlier than the addresses in chapters 41, 45 and 46, it is
at least a reasonable, working hypothesis that it is earlier likewise
than the two remaining addresses of the prophet, those in 40.6–8, 12–31
and 42–44, that, in other words, it was the prophet's earliest, his
initial prophetic utterance. This assumption will be amply confirmed.

In this same initial address, in vv. 9–11, the immediate continuation of vv. 6b–8 in the address as rearranged, the prophet goes on to
say that the reason why Yahweh had not revealed to Israel sooner
this most recent stage in the evolution of His eternal world-plan, in
which Cyrus was to be His active agent, was that Israel could not be
trusted, that from the very moment of its conception, even before its
emergence as a people, Israel had shown itself untrustworthy, deceitful
and rebellious. Actually, so the clear implication is, Israel had merited
in ample measure that Yahweh should have repudiated it and have
allowed it to be completely annihilated. One consideration, however,
forbade Him doing this. For His name's sake, for the sake of His
reputation, He has restrained His wrath, has been patient with His
faithless people, and has not permitted it to be cut off, to be destroyed,
and so cease to exist as a people. Instead He has purified it, though
not as silver is purified, but rather in the furnace of suffering. For
His own sake has He acted thus, for under no condition can He permit
His name to be profaned or that which should redound to His credit
to be ascribed to some other deity.

A moment's thought must establish conclusively that here Deutero-
Isaiah is doing no more than to reaffirm Ezekiel's doctrine of "for
His name's sake," and this too in the most literal manner and with
use of much of Ezekiel's own terminology. Plainly he had immediate,
personal knowledge of Ezekiel's doctrine, with all its implications,
as it had been enunciated by that prophet some thirty years earlier,
and in this seemingly initial address he did little more than reaffirm
the older prophet's doctrine, and merely appended to it, in Yahweh's
name, the further announcement (vv. 12a, 17a, 20 f.) that the moment
for Israel's destined return from exile in Babylonia to its native land
is drawing near, that Cyrus is His appointed agent to bring this about,
and that (vv. 17b–19) if Israel will only comprehend all this and
appreciate Yahweh's gracious purpose for it and shape its way of life

in conformity with Yahweh's instructions, then it may expect a glorious and never-ending future as Yahweh's own people.

Furthermore, Israel's return from Babylonia to its homeland will be by way of the desert. There Yahweh, its Redeemer, will provide miraculously for all its needs and will bring it safely through all dangers, even as He did at the time of the exodus from Egypt. And when it will have attained its goal, it shall proclaim far and wide, so that it may become known to the very ends of the earth and that all nations and peoples may hear and know, that Yahweh has indeed redeemed His people, has through His own might brought it forth from distant exile, and, surmounting all obstacles and dangers, has restored it to its native land and renewed with it His old, god-people relationship. Thus the nations will be made to recognize and have regard for Him as, at the very least, a true world-god. And thus Yahweh's reputation among the nations will have been effectively vindicated. Such is the major theme of Deutero-Isaiah's address in chapter 48. It may be remarked in passing that nowhere in this address is Israel called specifically "the servant of Yahweh," nor is there here the slightest suggestion of any such role destined for it.

With this realization of Deutero-Isaiah's direct dependence, at least in this address, upon the final message of Ezekiel, his immediate prophetic predecessor, we may affirm with abundant justification that he inaugurated his own prophetic career as the self-consecrated spokesman of Yahweh as a spiritual disciple of that earlier prophet, though whether consciously so or not insufficient evidence does not permit us to determine. As we shall consider further citations of the Ezekelian doctrine in Deutero-Isaiah's later addresses and the gradual unfolding of his message from this starting-point to the formulation and proclamation of his own distinctive doctrine of Israel as the servant or agent of Yahweh, we shall find additional confirmation of the hypothesis that Deutero-Isaiah inaugurated his prophetic ministry as a spiritual disciple of Ezekiel, and that the address in chapter 48 was indeed his initial utterance as a prophet of Yahweh.

To one other doctrine, of prime importance in his total message, the prophet gives expression in chapter 48, and this too in a manner which establishes even more decisively that this address is his initial prophetic utterance. He denounces (vv. 1–5) the Jewish exiles in Babylonia, even those who consciously and with a certain conventional and superficial loyalty affirm their Judaean origin and their persistent devotion to Yahweh, their ancestral god, but all this not in truth and sincerity; for they are always quick to ascribe whatever may transpire and may affect them, not to Yahweh, but rather to the Babylonian gods, represented by their idols, to whom they have learned to pay homage here in this land of their enforced sojourn and in this altogether new cultural environment. This manifest disloyalty to Yahweh and this allegiance to the Babylonian deities on the part of Israel in exile by the time of Deutero-Isaiah undoubtedly transcended by far that which Ezekiel had witnessed some thirty years earlier. Yet for His name's sake, so the prophet declares in this address, Yahweh may not let Israel be cut off completely; neither may He permit the credit and honor which are His due to be claimed by or ascribed to some other god. Therefore not only must He redeem Israel from exile and restore it to its ancestral land, but He must also demonstrate convincingly to Israel that He, its god, is indeed a true and powerful deity, well able to fulfill His purpose with and His promise to it. Certainly before the nations and peoples at large can be expected to acknowledge His divinity, His own people must be brought to full appreciation of His true, divine character and power, and therefore with conviction and pride to accept and publicly proclaim Him as its god.

Accordingly, a literary or hortatory technique which he employs again and again, the prophet represents Yahweh as challenging all other gods, and of course specifically the Babylonian deities, whom His people in exile have come to regard as supreme and as the ultimate, divine authors of everything which transpires in the universe, to debate with Him. The specific issue is who of all these gods, including Himself, can accurately foretell future events. Underlying this challenge is the principle that only that god who creates or initiates something, who fashions and uses it in order to carry out his own preconceived purpose and plan, and who therefore is alone aware of and responsible for it, can foresee and announce in advance precisely when it will happen, how it will work, and just what its effects will be. And even more specifically, only that divine being who has created the entire universe, who was at the beginning and will be throughout all time, can recount or can foretell anything and everything with certainty, everything which has transpired in the past, which may happen in the immediate today or tomorrow, or which may come to pass in the remote future. Now let these other gods, these so-called gods, who are really only inanimate idols and naught else, let them stand up in debate with Him, in the hearing of all the nations of the world, but particularly in the hearing of His own disbelieving, faithless people, and prove their true divinity. And with that effective, biting sarcasm, of which, so he demonstrates repeatedly, he is a supreme master, the prophet, speaking in the name of Yahweh, after challenging these other deities to foretell and announce the events which are happening now or are about to happen in the immediate future, and apparently after a long moment of silent waiting, with not a word nor a sound being heard from them, asks them pointedly (v. 6aα), "You, do you not foretell?"

Then, still representing Yahweh as speaking (vv. 16a, 3, 12b–13a) he challenges these foreign gods to draw near and hear Him foretell future events. This He can do just because He is the Creator of the universe and of all that is therein. Therefore He knows in advance, and so can foretell and announce, everything that will transpire; for it is His creation, His universe, and He has decreed its course and that of all creatures within it, and that too with distinct purpose and plan. He was at the beginning, when He brought this world into being, and He will be until the very end. He is the Creator and the Eternal One. And as proof thereof He will now foretell what is about to happen, new things, just now decreed; for it is He who has summoned Cyrus and will make him victorious wherever he may campaign, until at last, in fulfillment of His purpose, Babylon itself will fall before him. And when these events, just decreed and now foretold and announced for the first time, come to pass, then all mankind, but especially Israel, His people, will know with true and abiding conviction what manner of god He, Yahweh, really is.

Very significantly, although he affirms that Yahweh is an eternal, ever-existent deity and the true Creator of the universe, Deutero-Isaiah does not in this address as yet go so far as to declare that Yahweh is the one God, the true and only world-God, and that these supposed gods, represented by their idols, are no gods at all, have no reality whatsoever, and so are utterly powerless, incapable of doing aught. Manifestly he is drawing near to, but plainly has not yet quite reached, this ultimate truth, this basic and recurrent theme of his evolving message, although, as we shall see, that followed soon thereafter. Unquestionably the prophet's distinctive doctrine is here just beginning to take definite shape and must advance still quite some distance before it achieves full and climactic formulation and proclamation. And in this consideration we may see further evidence that in Isa. 48, the final chapter in that section of the Book of Isaiah which we have ascribed to Deutero-Isaiah, we have this prophet's initial utterance as the divinely commissioned spokesman of Yahweh unto His people.

As has been stated already, chapter 47 is not in any sense a prophetic address, but is rather an elegiac poem, of very high literary merit, an apostrophe to Babylon, announcing its certain and narrowly impending conquest, humiliation and doom as a nation. Because of various considerations we have ascribed this poem to Deutero-Isaiah, and specifically to the early, pre-prophetic period of his career. As has been pointed out, this poem, precisely like the subsequent prophetic addresses, is characterized by an intense hatred of Babylon and a profound contempt for its gods and its religious institutions. Typical of this, and one cogent reason for ascribing this poem to Deutero-Isaiah, is the effective satire, characteristic of the prophet, as we shall see, with which, in vv. 12–14 he derides the Babylonian religion, as symbolized by its *bârû*-priests,[37] its official and authoritative forecasters and announcers of the future, in the name of their gods, for their complete failure to foresee the impending doom of Babylon and to save at least themselves therefrom. Implicit, though still in incipient form, is of course the thought, later definitely formulated in chapter 48 and subsequent addresses, that the Babylonian gods, whose functionaries these priests are, are themselves totally unable to foresee truly and, through their priests, announce beforehand coming events, so that their people might prepare themselves for the impending crisis, and that therefore they are in truth no gods at all.

The address in chapter 46 reveals a slight advance in the evolution of the prophet's thought and message. As has already been intimated, the occasion of this address was, so we have inferred, the celebration of the annual Akitu Festival, the Babylonian New Year Festival, during the first thirteen days of Nisan in 539 B. C. The prophet here addresses Jewish exiles in Babylonia who are apparently, as worshipers of the Babylonian gods, participating in some manner in the cultic celebration of the festival. In this address the prophet presents for the first time two specific themes. The first of these is the positive affirmation of what, we have seen, was only, though very plainly, implicit in the address in chapter 48, viz. that these Babylonian deities are no gods at all, but are only idols and nothing more, each fashioned by a human being, an artisan, hired for this task by some other human being, who provides the precious metal and pays him for his labor. This heavy lump of metal, for that is all it actually is, must be loaded upon the shoulders of its devotees and borne along in the festival procession until its bearers are completely exhausted. And when, at the close of the festival ritual, it is deposited in its customary place in the sanctuary, can it as much as move itself from this spot? And even more, can it respond to the anguished appeals

---

[37] Cf. Zimmern, *Die Keilinschriften und das Alte Testament*, 3rd ed., p. 589, note 5, and the references cited there.

for help directed to it? And still more, can it save its worshipers from danger and distress? The implicit answer to these questions, the correctness of which all must acknowledge, is that the idol can perform not one of these functions. But just these are the services which men must expect from their gods, if these are true gods. How then can deluded Israel compare with these utterly lifeless and powerless idols its own god, Yahweh, than whom there is absolutely no other god? How can it liken to these inanimate and totally impotent pieces of metal its god, who has created the entire universe with purpose and plan, and who alone, as the sole Creator and Planner, can therefore foretell coming events, since everything which transpires must conform to His plan? It is He therefore, and none other, who has called Cyrus from the East to be His agent in the fulfillment of His present world-purpose. And this world-purpose, whose consummation is drawing ever nearer, is the salvation of His people in exile, its restoration to Zion and its glorification there.

In this address the prophet has manifestly advanced quite some distance beyond his initial position of reaffirmation of Ezekiel's doctrine of "for His name's sake." His own distinctive doctrine is now beginning to take concrete shape. For the first time he affirms positively and absolutely that Yahweh, Israel's god, is the one and only God, that besides Him there is no other god at all, and least of all any god who might be compared with Him, with the implication that, as a result of such comparison, His own reputation as a god might suffer. Likewise in this address the prophet inaugurates his oft iterated denunciation of other gods, and particularly of the Babylonian gods, as naught but idols, inanimate and impotent objects of wood or metal, creators of nothing at all, but themselves the creation of human hands, who can do naught whatsoever for either themselves or their deluded worshipers, but are in truth only an exhausting burden to them. In no way may they be compared to Yahweh, the one world-God, Israel's god, who not only need not be carried by, but Himself carries and upholds, His worshipers at all times, and is even now preparing to deliver them from their present, humiliating position as exiles in a foreign land and restore them to glorious existence in their ancestral home. These two themes, denunciation of all other gods as inanimate, impotent idols and affirmation that Yahweh is the sole world-God, here developed only simply and briefly, as accords with an initial expression of them, will find repeated, ever expanding, and more positive and effective affirmation in the prophet's subsequent addresses.

As has already been intimated, the address in chapter 45 is later

than the three addresses in chapters 48, 47 and 46, and was delivered
by the prophet shortly after Cyrus' conquest of Babylon and the
definitive establishment of Persia as the one existent world-empire,
probably then early in 538 B. C. In this address Deutero-Isaiah
reaches the culmination of his evolution as a prophet and of his
distinctive prophetic message.

He begins this momentous address, speaking of course in the
name of Yahweh, by hailing Cyrus as Yahweh's anointed. This is a
significant thought indeed. Hitherto this title, משיח, "anointed one,"
or more specifically, משיח יהוה, "Yahweh's anointed one," had been
applied only to Saul and thereafter to David and his descendants, the
dynastic kings of Judah. Now, at just this juncture, shortly after the
establishment by Cyrus of Persia as a true world-empire, transcending
in size and also in folk-composition and integration of peoples the
Neo-Babylonian Empire which it replaced, for the prophet to apply
this unique and meaningful title to Cyrus was a procedure fraught
with deep import. Not only did it imply very positively that Cyrus
had accomplished all this and had achieved the position of supreme
world-ruler, not at all through Marduk's help, as he had publicly
proclaimed (vv. 1–5), nor yet, as he may have really believed in
the intimacy of his own mind, so the prophet suggests, through the
aid of his own native, Iranian gods, the dual deities, Ormuzd and
Ahriman, respectively the divine sources of light and darkness, of
good and evil (v. 7), but through the support of Yahweh, and of
Yahweh alone, but it also implied more, much more.

For there had been in the past, and there could ever be, only
one "anointed of Yahweh" at a time. Therefore, were Cyrus now
actually "Yahweh's anointed," the ruler of this greatest world-empire
mankind had until this moment ever known, the world-king in all
truth, and, as the title implied further, the world-king who was, in
conformity with Yahweh's manifest purpose, to be succeeded in this
office by his own posterity, who was, in other words, destined by
Yahweh to be the founder of an eternal, ever-enduring dynasty,
ruling over an eternal, ever-enduring world-empire, it could mean
only that the prophet did not envisage any descendant of David
ever again claiming or holding this title as of right and by Yahweh's
will and in conformity with His purpose, and with this even more,
that the prophet, speaking, as has been said, as Yahweh's mouthpiece,
disclaimed for Israel forever thenceforth all independent, political
status, all existence as a self-governing nation under its own Davidic
king. Rather, he contemplated the world, the entire world, as a single
political unit under one world-ruler, Cyrus and his dynasty, and

Israel therefore as an integral part, a province as it were, or, perhaps better, a folk-unit, thereof. Certainly in his vision of Israel's future place and function in this new, unified world, as destined by Yahweh in conformity with His all-embracing and ever-continuing world-purpose, there was nothing whatever of regained political independence and renewed national existence under its own native king, one of the Davidic line. Manifestly in Deutero-Isaiah's vision of Israel, restored by Yahweh to existence in its ancestral land, political statehood had no place whatsoever. There Israel was to be, not a political unit, not a nation, not a kingdom, but rather a people, Yahweh's people.

In this connection the prophet reaffirms, and in a manner more positive and absolute than in 46.9, that Yahweh is the one and only God, the one world-God, He and none other. Besides Him there is no other god, not even Marduk and the other members of the Babylonian pantheon, nor yet Ormuzd and Ahriman, Cyrus' native Persian deities. He is the sole Creator and Administrator of the universe, and this not idly but with preconceived and specific purpose.

Moreover, since He is the sole Creator of the universe, and since, too, from the very first moment of existence He had acted and fashioned the world with specific, beneficent purpose, it follows that everything which has already transpired or may yet transpire in history, as it affects not merely Israel, but also all nations, all mankind, must have been purposed by Him and be in conformity with His universal plan. For this reason it is that He, and He alone, can foresee coming events, can foretell and announce to men, His creatures, what is to be, what is about to transpire. And for this reason it is, because His will and purpose alone determine what is to be, that ability to correctly foresee and announce coming events is a true and proper test of divinity, for it proves, beyond all possibility of challenge, that He, and He alone, is God, the one, true world-God, and that the other, so-called gods, the gods of the various nations, are not gods at all, have no reality, do not exist, are truly nothings.

Furthermore, the preconceived, specific, benevolent purpose, for which He has created this world is that it might be inhabited, be inhabited of course by men (v. 18). Moreover, since He, the one world-God, has chosen Israel to be, not a political entity, a nation, at all, but rather to be His people, and has destined it to play this role permanently, throughout all time, this too must be for some divinely conceived purpose of universal character. Therefore Israel is His, Yahweh's, servant, the agent or instrument through whom His ultimate world-purpose will attain fulfillment. This is the very first application by the prophet of this title, "servant of Yahweh," to

Israel, the very first occurrence of this term in his addresses thus far. And in this address he employs this title only once (v. 4), and apparently somewhat incidentally, quite as if it were a term altogether new to him, coined at just that moment, and therefore the full, potential import of which he did not yet realize.

In this address there is not a single specific reference to the doctrine of "for His name's sake," which the prophet had inherited from Ezekiel. He has now, so it would seem, sensed the inadequacy of that doctrine, its inadequacy in relation to his new and expanding realization that Yahweh is not merely another world-god, one among many other deities of like character, Israel's national god, who has benevolent relations with it alone, and who is concerned with His reputation, what the other nations and their gods may think of Him and how they may evaluate Him, particularly in relation to themselves and in comparison with their own gods. If Yahweh is indeed the one and only God, the sole Creator of this earth and of all mankind upon it, and if then the other gods, the gods of the nations, all of them, are naught but impotent unrealities, then certainly Yahweh need no longer concern Himself with what the nations might think of Him and how they might rate Him as a world-god in comparison with their own gods. His only real concern need be how the nations might be brought to appreciate this truth and so might discard their present gods completely, relegate them to oblivion, and offer unto Him, and to Him alone, the homage which is His due from them. With this formulation by the prophet of this new and distinctive doctrine, that Yahweh is the one and only God, the sole God of the entire universe, and that there is no other god at all, the old doctrine of "for His name's sake" loses all meaning and force. Deutero-Isaiah has at last advanced clearly and positively beyond the ultimate point in prophetic revelation reached by Ezekiel, his immediate predecessor as a prophet and his spiritual mentor, and now stands upon his own feet as a prophet of independent vision, thought and message.

Furthermore, if, as the prophet has just affirmed, Yahweh had created the world for a definite and clearly conceived purpose, and if then from all mankind, from all the peoples whom He had fashioned, He had chosen Israel as His particular people, then this too He must have done for some specific purpose, some specific purpose in relation to all mankind. And since it is His immediate purpose to restore Israel to its native land, and primarily in order to effect this He has called Cyrus and elevated him to his present, imperial position as world-ruler, then certainly His ultimate purpose in all this is not merely to thereby convincingly demonstrate to all the nations and peoples of the world His irresistible power, and thus prove that, contrary to their present belief, resulting from Israel's conquest and exile some fifty or more years earlier, He is indeed a true god, who merits their respect and even their fear, as the Ezekelian doctrine had affirmed. Rather it is something which transcends this by far, some infinitely larger purpose, of true world-character, which must be related to Yahweh's ultimate purpose in creating the world, likewise, as we have seen, announced for the very first time in this same momentous address, viz. that it should be inhabited by men, by men dwelling together in unity and accord, by men who would in due time recognize Him as God, their Creator, the one, sole God of the entire universe, and who would accordingly worship Him alone and seek to live the life which He had instituted for them. In the eventual fulfillment of this ultimate purpose Israel is destined to play a specific role. For this role He has chosen it and hailed it as His servant. And in order that it may discharge this role in proper and responsible manner He is about to bring it forth from exile and back to its ancestral land, where manifestly it can function most truly and effectively as His servant and thus bring to fulfillment His ultimate purpose with it. Now what might this divinely ordained service be, as the prophet sees it?

By this time it should have become apparent that Deutero-Isaiah's doctrine of Israel as the servant of Yahweh, of Yahweh, the one, universal God, is the natural and direct outgrowth of Ezekiel's doctrine of "for His name's sake" and of Israel's role therein. The combination of what may properly be regarded as the three doctrines basic to the prophet's distinctive thought and message, that Yahweh is God, the sole world-God, the Creator of the world, that He has created the world with clearly conceived purpose, to be inhabited, and certainly to be inhabited happily, by men, and that He has chosen Israel to stand in a peculiarly intimate, god-people relationship with Himself, made the prophet's development and proclamation of the role of Yahweh's servant or agent for Israel in the fulfillment of Yahweh's world-purpose both logical and inevitable. As has been stated, in this address in Isa. 45, he applies the title, "servant of Yahweh," to Israel for the very first time, and manifestly without immediately comprehending all the potential implications of the term, the manifold forms and directions in which this service to Yahweh, the one world-God, by Israel might express itself. It is reasonable to expect that in subsequent addresses the prophet would develop these potentialities and would announce the various, specific services in the name or on behalf of Yahweh, in the realization of His eternal world-purpose, for the performance of which Israel was chosen by Yahweh. It will be in-

teresting and likewise significant to determine, though upon some
other occasion, the various ways in which subsequent generations,
the heirs of Deutero-Isaiah's fruitful·and stimulating message, interpreted Israel's divinely appointed role as Yahweh's servant-people.
For the present our concern is the direction, manner and range of
the prophet's own development of this basic theme of his steadily
unfolding message.

Before the constantly advancing and ever-victorious armies of
Cyrus, made victorious by Yahweh, and by Him alone, so the prophet
affirms emphatically, and this too as one important stage in Yahweh's
total plan, and obviously an early stage at that, the nations, each in
turn, so the prophet clearly implies, had appealed to their various
gods, at first no doubt confidently, but finally in utter desperation,
each calling upon its own particular god or gods to protect it and save
it from conquest, slaughter, despoliation and national doom. But not
one of these gods, not a single one, had proved equal to the task. Not
one had been able to answer his people's anguished supplication and
deliver it from conquest and subjection by Cyrus. Each god, in a
long succession, had shown himself weak, impotent, incapable of
bringing salvation to his people. It was quite as if not one of these
gods really existed, as if they were in truth no gods at all. The universal
appeal, resounding throughout the world, ringing agonizingly from
the hearts of all nations and peoples, was for salvation, for a god who
could save them from warfare and destruction, for a true savior-god.
Where could such a god be found? But unless he were found, and
found relatively soon, what would become of mankind and of this
world?

From the standpoint of Deutero-Isaiah and his message, from the
present moment of Cyrus's conquest of Babylon and the inauguration
by him of the Persian world-empire this question meant this; if these
costly wars, which had paved the way to Cyrus' present exalted
position, and this too as the initial stage of Yahweh's world-plan,
should be protracted interminably, and the massacre of countless
human beings never be ended, what then would become of Yahweh's
total world-plan in its ultimate purpose, that He had fashioned this
world to be inhabited by men? As things had transpired in the life of
nations up to the present moment, mankind would eventually ex-
terminate itself, and instead of being inhabited, as Yahweh had
purposed, the world would in the end become empty and dead, and
Yahweh's ultimate purpose would be frustrated completely. Truly not
merely nations, first this nation and then that, but all mankind
together, all mankind as one, needed a divine savior, a god who could

indeed save, save each individual nation and save all mankind as a unit, a god who could at the same time make all warfare to cease and enable nations to live together henceforth quietly, amicably, happily, and free from fear. What god such as this was there, and where might he be found?

To this insistent question, of such universal character, Deutero-Isaiah offers the answer, to him the only possible, logical and certain answer. That desperately needed and eagerly sought god, that universal savior-god, was Yahweh, Israel's god, and none other, none other because actually there was none other, no other god at all. He was in all truth a, or rather the, Savior-God, the מושיע, "the Deliverer, the Savior." And although the nations could not recognize this as yet, He had already inaugurated the initial stage of this salvation program by uniting the entire world, all mankind, into one positive political unit, one world-empire, under the beneficent rule of His Messiah, His chosen "Anointed One," Cyrus, the one whom He had called from the East to be His agent for the attainment of this goal. Now, with all mankind thus united as a single political unit, one world-empire, and this efficiently and benevolently administered by His appointed agent, His world-king, all warfare must of necessity cease forever; for within this closely unified and justly governed political unit there would be neither occasion for nor possibility of warfare and strife between nations ever henceforth.

This initial portion of Yahweh's world-plan had been successfully carried through by Cyrus, Yahweh's agent, although, as the prophet stressed (vv. 4 f.), Cyrus himself had as yet not comprehended this, his true, Yahweh-appointed role. And if Cyrus himself did not comprehend as yet, then how much the more could the nations of the world, the victims of his conquests, also not realize as yet that there was indeed one, but only one, divine source of salvation, one, and only one, true Savior-God, and that this Savior for all mankind was Yahweh, Israel's god? And even if perhaps they might in some way, in this age of dawning universalism, have some faint intimation that there might perhaps be some such god, one single, universal God of all mankind, how could they be brought to comprehend that this one Savior-God was neither Marduk, nor yet Ormuzd, nor any other god, but only Yahweh, the god of Israel, the god of this little, still exiled people, the one true world-God? How could they be made to realize that He was the one, sole Savior-God in and for all the world, that He was indeed the Savior-God for whom all the nations were waiting so eagerly and despairingly, and that from Him, and only from Him, could and would salvation come to them?

Just here lay the service which Israel, Yahweh's people, chosen by Him as His servant, was to perform. If Yahweh would save it, would deliver it from exile and bring it safely through all dangers back to its ancestral land, and would there rehabilitate it as His people, dwelling in security and forever loyally serving Him there, it would demonstrate concretely and convincingly to the nations and to all mankind that He is indeed a god able to save, the only god who, through all these many long years of warfare and destruction, had actually saved His people and restored it from exile to freedom in its own land. And what He could thus do, and actually will have done, for His own little people He would do likewise for them, for each of them, if only they would believe in Him and approach Him in the proper spirit. Therefore the time has indeed come for Israel's salvation and restoration to native land, and that too in order to prove to the nations conclusively that Yahweh is not merely a powerful national deity, quite as powerful, and therefore quite as deserving of respect and fear, as the gods of other nations, as the earlier doctrine of "for His name's sake" had affirmed, but that He is also a god who can save, a god who, in view of the total failure of all the other gods of the nations to save, each merely his own nation and people, can be for them, as well as for His own people, the one and only true Savior-God, the one, sole God of all the world. For this end, the true climax of His total world-purpose, Yahweh must now save Israel, His people, must redeem it from exile and restore it, despite all attendant difficulties and dangers, to its native land. And there restored, Israel must henceforth keep faith with Him and live in the sight of all mankind as His people. Thus Israel, by its deliverance from exile and restoration to native land and to peoplehood there, and with this happy state enduring forever, will give living and eternal testimony unto all mankind of Yahweh, its god, as the one, true Savior-God, the one and only world-God, for all peoples to see and be convinced and accept. This is to be Israel's task as the servant of Yahweh, and this is the service which Yahweh has, from the very first, chosen it to perform in His name and for His glorification and for the salvation of all mankind.

As has already been indicated, Deutero-Isaiah's doctrine of Israel as the servant of Yahweh evolved directly and logically from Ezekiel's doctrine of "for His name's sake," with the simple reaffirmation of which Deutero-Isaiah inaugurated his prophetic ministry. And this tracing of the evolutionary process step by step indicates once again and even more decisively that the chronological sequence of Deutero-Isaiah's prophetic utterances thus far, until some moment early in 538 B. C., following soon after Cyrus' capture of Babylon, was, as has been posited already, chapters 47, 48, 46 and 45. This suggests that, for some reason unknown and unimaginable, the words of the anonymous prophet of the exile were appended in inverse chronological sequence to the collected addresses of the true Isaiah, the prophet of the latter portion of the eighth century B. C.

In the latest of these four addresses, that in chapter 45, Deutero-Isaiah reaffirms, and that too more positively and expansively than he had affirmed it previously and for the first time in the address in chapter 46, that Yahweh, Israel's god in first degree, is actually more than this, more than merely *a* world-god, along with the gods of other nations, that He is *the* one and only God, the single world-God. To this he has now added the significant doctrine of absolute universalism, uttered hitherto by no prophet or religious pioneer, either of Israel or of any other people of antiquity, a doctrine altogether new, formulated now for the first time in the history of religion, that the entire universe is indeed one unit, created by one God alone, and created by Him with distinct purpose, the unification of all mankind, His creatures, their fusion into one, single political unit, under the administration of one, single world-ruler, chosen by Him for this role, therefore His Messiah, His "Anointed One," His appointed king, imbued by this rite of anointment, either actually or symbolically, with His divine spirit. This world-king shall rule in such manner that, even though not specifically stated by the prophet, but clearly implicit in his message, all warfare shall cease,[38] nations shall dwell together henceforth in perfect and ever-enduring peace, and shall thus, through Yahweh, the one and only Savior-God, find that salvation for which they had sought, so hopefully at first, and then so despairingly and so completely in vain, each from its own god or gods, and shall thus come to realize with absolute conviction, not only the impotence and futility, but also and even more the complete unreality and non-existence of what they had erringly imagined to be gods, their gods,

---

[38] It remained for another, undoubtedly later, and perhaps even quite a bit later, prophetic personality, one who might very properly be regarded as a spiritual disciple of Deutero-Isaiah, to formulate this vision of the cessation of all warfare between nations and the consequent, ever-enduring, perfect peace throughout the entire world, and the adjustment of the nations of their own free will to the way of life for all mankind instituted by Yahweh as the one World-God, in a concrete and stirring word-picture, a picture so appealing and which in many respects constitutes the very climax of Israelite prophetic thought and utterance that, not at all surprisingly, it is recorded twice in the Bible and is ascribed to two different prophets, Micah (Micah 4.1-4) and Isaiah (Isa. 2.1-4). Manifestly this latter ascription has a slight measure of historical justification, since the vision is essentially the doctrine implicit in Deutero-Isaiah's message concretized in a vivid eschatological picture.

and likewise that Yahweh, the one and only God, is their true Savior, and that only through Him can they find the salvation which they seek. And finding this, they will of course turn to Him, acknowledge Him as God, as the one world-God, will pay homage to him and swear by His name and His alone. Thus, and only thus, will this world, created by Yahweh, become truly habitable by men, His creatures, even as from the very first He had purposed it to be.

To achieve this supreme goal, Yahweh must now deliver His people, Israel, from its present exile, bring it safely through all attendant dangers and reestablish it in its ancestral land, there to live henceforth in security and in perfect faithfulness to Him, its own particular god from the very beginning, and by this continuous, happy existence in its ancient home-land demonstrate convincingly to all the nations that Yahweh is indeed the true Savior-God, able and eager to save all nations and peoples in the same manner as He had saved His own people, and thus win them to recognize, acknowledge and pay homage to Him as the one world-God. This is Israel's appointed role as Yahweh's servant, as now initially conceived by this exalted prophet, just this and naught else.

Actually Deutero-Isaiah nowhere, even in his later addresses, defines in specific terms just wherein Israel's service to Yahweh would lie. As contemplated by him, however, this service, so it seems, was to be passive rather than active in character. Restored by Yahweh to native land, what Israel, Yahweh's servant, was to do there was in the sight of all the nations to live a normal life as a people, politically as a loyal constituent of the Persian world-empire, which Yahweh, its own god, had called into being, and religiously as a people or community, the devoted worshipers of Yahweh, gladly and eagerly conforming to the way of life which He had ordained for it. Through its safe return, under Yahweh's protection, to its ancestral land and its living there faithfully as His people ever thereafter, Israel would bear testimony of Yahweh and of His true nature, power and benevolent purpose in the sight of all the nations. By steadfastly adhering to this simple program Israel would perform dutifully and adequately the service which Yahweh demanded of it.

This involved then, so at least it seems, no procedure of active proselytism on the part of Israel, no purposeful and sacrificial endeavor to convert nations and peoples to positive worship of Yahweh and to impose upon them a Yahweh-ordained, realistic way of life. Rather the nations were to learn of Yahweh and of His power and His purpose to save them also, even as He had saved His own people, and of His way of life, enjoined not for Israel alone but also for all mankind, only from what they might observe for themselves of Israel's present secure and happy state, and from this, and from this alone, to spontaneously gather conviction and faith.

All this sublime thought, this exhilarating vision and alluring program for the achievement of world-salvation and world-unity, even as Yahweh, the sole Creator of the entire universe, had purposed from the very beginning, is contained in Isa. 45, either expressed concretely and positively or else more or less immediately implicit therein. Some of these implications, though, as we shall see, by no means all, the prophet developed further in subsequent addresses. But actually the prophet's entire message, either directly set forth or else in varying degree implicit, is contained in this single address in Isa. 45. We have accordingly, and, we believe, quite justifiably, represented this address, even though it is not by any means his final utterance, as the culminating point in the prophet's entire ministry.

But to resume: Israel's role then as Yahweh's servant was to be essentially passive. It was merely to be the very first people to be saved by Yahweh and then ever thereafter to live in perfect faithfulness with Him and in resultant perfect security and blessedness, and thus attest by concrete and convincing example to Yahweh's character and power as a savior-god, as the one Savior-God, not merely for itself alone but also for all nations and all peoples, the one and only world-God. This, and this alone, was the service which Yahweh expected, or even demanded, of Israel as His servant, so Deutero-Isaiah affirmed. It was to be a service of attestation. Israel was to bear witness to Yahweh. It remained for the prophet, as he came to comprehend ever more fully and clearly the true nature and import of the role of servant of Yahweh, which he, speaking as Yahweh's mouthpiece, had assigned to Israel, to apply to it the specific title of witness, witness unto Yahweh.

And this he does in what is obviously his very next address, that in chapters 42–44. There he portrays Yahweh as once again challenging the gods of all the nations, represented of course by their idols, to contest with Him in order to prove who among them, if any at all, is a true god. However, the primary test this time is not, as it had been in all Deutero-Isaiah's earlier addresses, ability to correctly foresee and announce coming events. This test is referred to here only incidentally (43.9) and is apparently now relegated to a secondary role. Instead the decisive consideration will now be far more immediate and challenging in character, the testimony of witnesses as to the ability of this god or that to bring salvation to his people, his worshipers. Each god has his witnesses. The witnesses of the foreign gods are the workmen, artisans of both wood and stone, who had fashioned their various idols. In a long passage (43.9; 40.19–20; 44.9–20; 42.17), which is indeed one of the classic pieces of derisive satire of all world-literature, these witnesses are made to testify, obviously somewhat reluctantly, that these images which they have fashioned are really lifeless objects and nothing more. They can neither see nor hear nor comprehend nor know aught, and therefore they certainly can not foretell in the slightest measure what the future may have in store. Still less can they hear and respond to the agonized appeals of their worshipers to save them, to save them from impending destruction. In fact they can not save even themselves. Of all this their witnesses must testify, unwillingly perhaps but also inescapably. In no sense may these so-called gods be regarded as potential sources of that salvation which the nation of each and likewise all mankind together seek so eagerly and so desperately.

In opposition to them Yahweh's witness is Israel, His servant. And whereas thus far the prophet has applied this meaningful title, servant, to Israel only once, in 45.4, in this address he designates Israel by this title five times. Manifestly by this time this title has become fixed, and perhaps even slightly conventional, in the prophet's mind. Accordingly he couples with it a new title, which he employs now for the first time, a title which, as we have already indicated, had to follow soon after the address in chapter 45, with its significant thought-development and new and far-reaching implications, the title indispensable in the setting of this later address, witness. This new title the prophet applies to Israel three times in this address (43.10, 12; 44.8), and the first time in parallelism with the earlier title, servant, quite as if to imply a very intimate relationship between them, that the service for which Yahweh had chosen Israel was from the very first to testify of Him, that He is indeed the one and only God, the Eternal One, than whom there is no other Savior.

But thus far Israel has been an altogether ineffective witness of Yahweh, ineffective because it itself has been both blind and deaf to the real truth, and so did not itself really know Him nor comprehend His purpose and His irresistible power, and therefore had no real faith in Him. But a true witness must have complete faith in that of which he testifies. Therefore, since Yahweh has indispensable need of Israel for the fulfillment of His ultimate world-purpose, needs it in fact so much that He has paid a very high price for it (43.3b–4), He Himself will blot out all Israel's iniquities and faithless acts for His own sake (43.25; 44.22; cf. also 42.8), so that He might again take it, now a purified people, purged of all sin, to Himself as His people. This is of course a reaffirmation, the prophet's final reaffirmation, of the doctrine of "for His name's sake." But here, unlike in the earlier addresses, it is no longer basic to the prophet's message, but is more or less incidental. In fact in this address the renewal by Yahweh of His god-people relationship with Israel is no longer "for His name's sake," for the rehabilitation of His reputation as a god among the nations, but is instead for the fulfillment of His purpose of world-salvation, a far more exalted goal indeed. Accordingly the prophet no longer employs the old, Ezekelian phrase, למען שמו, "for His name's sake," but instead the simpler, more direct, and certainly far more inclusive and meaningful term, למעני, "for Mine own sake," i. e. "for the sake of My universal purpose." Manifestly Deutero-Isaiah has now advanced far beyond the Ezekelian doctrine with which he had inaugurated his prophetic ministry.

And now that Israel has been purged by Yahweh of its sin, impliedly never to prove faithless to or reject Him again, He will do a new thing in its behalf, one which He now announces for the first time, and thus, as further evidence of His divine nature and power, foretells, and the fulfillment of which will demonstrate with ultimate conviction, and this too not only to Israel, His servant, but also to all the nations, that He is indeed a god able to save. He will now redeem Israel from exile and bring it safely through the desert intervening between its present place of exile and its native land, despite the manifold hardships and dangers attendant upon such a journey, and will establish it securely once again in its ancestral home. And there He will pour out His spirit and bestow His blessing upon all the generations of the future, so that they will ever thereafter loyally manifest their allegiance to Him. Thus, saved and redeemed by its god, by Him who was from the very first its own particular god, its Holy One, restored to ancestral land, and there secure, happy and prospering, Israel will be Yahweh's witness and will ever thereafter bear testimony, will itself be the universally visible testimony, in the sight and for the eventual conversion of all the nations, to the truth, that Yahweh alone is the true world-God, the one and only Savior-God for all mankind.

Such is the theme of this, the prophet's longest and most involved address. In the main it is essentially a reaffirmation and close integration of all the basic principles and doctrines to which he had given expression in his earlier addresses. To these he adds the principle, implicit already in the earlier address, in chapter 45, but here clearly formulated and formally presented for the first time, that, as Yahweh's servant, Israel is the witness who bears testimony of Him and of His ability and will to save all peoples and all mankind. Just this is the specific service which, so the prophet now affirms, Yahweh has chosen Israel to perform. By this testimony Israel will demonstrate irrefutably to the nations that their gods, their idols, are not gods, are nothing at all, are utterly powerless to do aught, and that therefore, would they find salvation for themselves, such true salvation as Israel will have already experienced, for its eternal security, happiness and blessing, let them too turn to Yahweh, Israel's god, acknowledge Him as the one true world-God, the one and only Savior-God, and put their trust in Him and render homage unto Him.

And to one further new principle the prophet gives expression in this address, seemingly incidentally, and yet with deep import. In 43.15 and 44.6 he calls Yahweh by the specific title, "King of Israel" and "your King." Again, in 41.21, he speaks of Yahweh as "Jacob's King." Otherwise, in all seven addresses, Deutero-Isaiah does not employ the word, *melek*, "king," even once. By thus calling Yahweh Israel's King the prophet certainly implies once again that he does not envisage the Israel of the future as a political entity, a nation; for in such case he would certainly have contemplated a human king, a scion of David, as reigning over it; and in such case the title, "Israel's King," would not have been applicable to or worthy of Yahweh. Therefore no interpretation of this meaningful title for Yahweh is possible other than that just proposed, that the prophet envisages restored Israel only as a religious, and in no wise at all as a political, entity.[39] This Deutero-Isaianic concept of Yahweh as Israel's King, with its implied repudiation of political nationhood forever henceforth, called into being one school of thought and one distinct party and program within the Jewish community of Judaea in the early post-exilic period and definitely shaped the evolution of Judaism within that period and thereafter.

The address in chapter 41 repeats much of the prophet's earlier thought and argument, but links with this a few considerations which are essentially new. The address begins with, the prophet's now plainly

---

[39] Elsewhere in all the prophetic writings of the O. T. only in Zeph. 3.15, and possibly also in Isa. 33.22, both passages unmistakably of post-exilic composition and therefore later than, and probably more or less dependent upon, Deutero-Isaiah, is Yahweh spoken of specifically as Israel's King. Wherever elsewhere in the prophetic writings He is spoken of as King, it is distinctly as King of the heavenly hosts (Isa. 6.5) or as King of the entire world, the universal King (Jer. 10.10; 46.18; 48.15; 51.57; Zech. 14.9, 16, 17; Mal. 1.14). All these passages which hail Yahweh as universal King are unquestionably of post-exilic authorship, and so are later than and manifestly dependent upon Deutero-Isaiah.

conventional technique, a challenge by Yahweh to the gods of the other nations, and, by implication, in first degree to the Babylonian deities, and Bel-Marduk, the head of the Babylonian pantheon, in particular, and perhaps also to the Persian gods, Ormuzd and Ahriman, as well, to prove their divinity, as contrasted with that of Yahweh, by debate, or perhaps by a trial in court. The question at issue, the positive answer to which will determine infallibly in whom, and in whom alone, divinity abides, is the old one, who among all these gods it was that summoned Cyrus, assigned to him his particular task, and prospered him in such manner that he has by now conquered many nations, crushed their rulers and brought these peoples under his dominion. And even more than this, who was it who foretold this program of Cyrus, announced in advance its course and outcome, and who therefore was its true and sole author? This contest establishes anew and more definitively, and therefore with its decision stated more pointedly (vv. 24, 29), than ever before, that these so-called gods and their idols are absolutely nothing at all, and their work and its effects are totally non-existent.

Thus it is proved once again that Yahweh, Israel's god, is the one and only God, the Eternal One, the true world-God. And He is Jacob's King and Israel is His people, whom, despite the seeming import of their present state of exile, He has not rejected, but instead has from of old, even from the time of Abraham, from Israel's very birth as a people, chosen to be His servant (vv. 8–9). No longer need it fear or be dismayed for any cause whatsoever, for He, and none other, is its divine Champion, who imparts strength to it and upholds it with His own power (v. 10). And those who enrage themselves against it and contend with it and war against it shall, through Yahweh's intervention, be put to shame and be destroyed so utterly that no trace of them whatever will remain.[40]

Immediately the question arises, who were these enemies who enraged themselves so bitterly against Israel in exile.[41] Certainly they

---

[40] Vv. 11–13. Whether vv. 14–16 are a unit with what precedes or were appended thereto by some editor living at a later time and in an altogether different historic setting is not certain. In these vv. the picture of the destruction of Israel's enemies, and that too with Israel itself as the active agent thereof, is quite vivid and goes considerably beyond the program of deliverance of Israel by Yahweh contemplated in vv. 11–13, and also outlines a program for Israel not at all consistent with its role as Yahweh's servant and the herald of His salvation for all peoples. Because of these considerations it seems wise to regard these three vv. as a Trito-Isaianic appendix to the original address.

[41] The same expression occurs again and in precisely the same connection in 45.24b. Certainly 45.24aβb–25 has no immediate thought-connection whatever with

could not have been the Babylonians, in whose midst and apparently
in the friendliest, neighborly relations with whom Israel in exile had
by the prophet's time been living for a full half-century. Still less
could these enemies have been the Persians; for there is every reason
to believe that prior to Cyrus' conquest of Babylon the contacts of
Israel in exile with Persia had been at the very most few and remote
indeed. Nor could these enemies have been any other foe of national
character, for nowhere in these verses nor anywhere else in the seven
recorded addresses of Deutero-Isaiah is there the slightest intimation
of any nation or people now hostile to Israel, nor does anything that
we know of this particular period in world-history suggest this. Certainly its situation at this time in both Babylonia and Judaea was
not such as to give rise to national hostility to it from any direction.

Accordingly only one conclusion is possible, viz. that these enemies
of Israel must be internal, from within its own ranks. The uniqueness
of the expression, "those who inflame themselves," i. e. those who
work themselves into a rage, against them, might seem to confirm
this hypothesis, to suggest that this was not a normal enemy of
national character, cherishing an ancient and deeply-rooted hostility
to Israel, but rather that these were personal enemies, individuals,
whose antagonism was of rather recent origin and largely personal
in character.[42] The appreciation of this fact seems to open up an
entirely new chapter in the personal history of the prophet.

It is reasonably certain that this address is later than those in
chapters 45–48 and very probably also than that in chapters 42–44,
so at least the setting of its general thought, and especially of its
particular theme, within the evolutionary course of the prophet's
total message suggests. In none of these addresses has there been the
slightest intimation of hostility, national or otherwise, to Israel or
reason for it to fear or despair. This is an altogether new note in the
prophet's total message. But if this address be indeed later than the
several addresses in chapters 42–48, then it follows that it must have
been uttered after 538 B. C., though how much thereafter it is impos-

the address recorded in the remainder of the chapter. Accordingly it may well be a
displaced fragment of some other address of Deutero-Isaiah, an address the entire
remainder of which has apparently been lost, but one which had something in common with this address in 41.1–13 and undoubtedly reflected the same advanced stage
of the prophet's evolving thought and message.

[42] Note that חרה, in the *nif.* "to inflame oneself; to become enraged," occurs in
this conjugation only three times in all Biblical literature (Isa. 41.11; 45.24; Cant.
1.6), and that in each instance it is in the plural, quite as if this manifestation of
anger and hostility was on the part of single individuals rather than of a single,
unified group or nation.

sible to determine, since here all indications of specific, historic setting
and resultant dating are entirely lacking. Certainly prior to this
message Deutero-Isaiah had been functioning as prophet and delivering his successive addresses for at the very least some four or five
years, or perhaps even somewhat longer. His addresses were all, even
including the apostrophe to Babylon in chapter 47, directed specifically
to the Jewish exiles in Babylonia. From the very beginning of his
prophetic ministry he had denounced them unrestrainedly and bitterly
for their manifest faithlessness to Yahweh and had sought to revive
their faith in Him and devotion to Him, and thus prepare them for
their divinely promised return to the land of their fathers and for
restored peoplehood with Yahweh there. But we can hardly escape
the conviction that for the most part his words had fallen upon deaf
ears, and that only a scanty minority had hearkened sympathetically
to his message and accepted it with eager conviction. We may even
imagine that his oft-repeated, acrimonious denunciation of these exiles
provoked among them steadily increasing resentment and growing
antagonism, directed not merely against him personally but also
against those few who openly subscribed to his unfolding message and
shaped their thoughts and planned their lives and destiny in conformity therewith.

We may even imagine further that in course of time a breach
sprang up between the two groups, the sympathizers with the prophet
and their opponents, and grew steadily wider and deeper, until
eventually they became, so we may properly term them, two distinct
parties within the Jewish community in Babylonia, one the vast
majority of the exiles and the other the small, even tiny, minority,
each openly antagonistic to the other and, quite probably, with the
major party, in its inflamed hostility to the minority and to the
prophet, their spokesman, not infrequently resorting to extreme and
even violent action. We can understand also that eventually the
prophet might well come to designate this minority, sympathetic
with him and receptive of his doctrine and its program, as Israel,
the true Israel, the Israel whom Yahweh had chosen from the beginning
to be His people, His servant and His witness. And it would be to
this true Israel, this tiny group of exiles, that this message of reassurance in chapter 41, culminating in the divine promise of triumph
over their enemies, those who enrage themselves against them and
contend with them, the disbelieving and faithless mass of the Jewish
exiles, was directed.[43]

---

[43] Note that in Cant. 1.6 it is the maiden's own kinsmen who enrage themselves

This same message, addressed, it is reasonable to assume, to this very same audience, is repeated, and even more vigorously and graphically, in 40.6–8, 12–18, 21–31.[44] The thought of this address runs thus: Yahweh is the God who encompasses the universe. To Him neither individuals nor nations may be compared, nor may any likeness, and least of all that of a human being, be ascribed to Him; for man is only mortal and quickly vanishes, whereas the decree of Yahweh, formulated by Himself alone, without counsel from any source, endures forever. He, and He alone, has created the universe, and that too in absolute perfection, so that not even the most minute constituent of it is missing. Moreover, He has called this universe into being, part by part, in orderly succession, merely by pronouncing its name (v. 26).[45] Therefore let not Israel, Yahweh's

(נחרה, the same verb as here), against her, just as here, so we suggest, it is fellow-Israelites who enrage themselves against their kinsmen.

[44] As has already been indicated, vv. 1–5, 7–9 are from Trito-Isaiah, an integral part of a very significant address, the remainder of which is to be found in Isa. 52; cf. above, note 22. Likewise vv. 19–20 disturb the context where they stand and also seem to have no relationship whatever with the thought of this chapter. Very probably they are a displaced fragment of the long address in chapters 42–44, with the thought of which they have the closest affinity. In all likelihood they stood originally in this address, as we have reconstructed it in the seminar, immediately following 43.9 and preceding 44.9; cf. Pt. II, below, pp. 68 ff. There they serve as a perfect introduction to the thought of 44.9 ff., explaining, as they do, just why the artisans who make the idols are the proper witnesses, so far as these idols and the gods whom supposedly they embody are concerned, for they must testify, and that too as the ultimate authorities, just how these idols are fashioned and, furthermore, that after they are made they are utterly impotent and can not even move themselves from the places where they are set.

[45] Cf. Gen. 1 and note the use both there and here of ברא in this technical connotation, "to create through pronouncement of the divine word," i. e. then "to create by divine decree." This word, with this specific connotation, occurs thirteen times in Isa. 40–48, far more frequently than in any other single Biblical writing. Plainly it reflects the prophet's exalted concept of Yahweh and of the manner of divine creation by Him. In fact there is good reason for believing that it was Deutero-Isaiah who gave to this verb this specific, technical and theologically meaningful connotation, and probably even himself coined this verb and added it to the vocabulary of the Hebrew language; for there is ample ground for assigning every Biblical passage outside of Isa. 40–48 in which this verb or its single derivative, בריאה, occurs, to a period later than Deutero-Isaiah. (Even Jer. 31.22b is regarded by Movers, Hitzig, Cornill, Duhm and Giesebrecht as non-Jeremianic, and is therefore almost certainly later than Deutero-Isaiah.) If so, he undoubtedly borrowed and Hebraized the Accadian verb, barû, "to see; to foresee; to prognosticate" (cf. above, note 37, and note also that in Babylonian religion the barû-priests were the official foreseers and prognosticators of coming events; cf. Zimmern, Beiträge zur Kenntniss der Babylonischen Religion, 81, 226). This procedure on his part would accord in every way with the principle which he stressed repeatedly, that the ultimate test of divinity

people,[46] despair nor imagine, because of its present, unhappy situation, that He has lost sight of it or forgotten it. His power and His understanding are limitless and untiring, and His support of those who grow weary, in His service of course, is unfailing. Therefore let those who hope in and wait for Him continue to have faith, for they shall surely surmount all obstacles and, impliedly, also all opposition.

It should be noted that, in striking dissimilarity to all the other recorded addresses of Deutero-Isaiah, there is in this address not a single word of denunciation or castigation. From beginning to end it is a message of comfort and reassurance, an unconditioned promise of deliverance, protection and support by Yahweh, the Incomparable One, for all those who unfailingly put their trust in Him and seek to conform to His will and purpose for them, as He has revealed this to them. Of the various significant themes characteristic of this prophet and affirmed by him again and again in his earlier addresses, only one finds expression here, that of Yahweh, Israel's god, as the sole Creator of the world and therefore the one, incomparable, universal God, with its corollary, that Israel is His people. But despite the absence of reference to the other positive doctrines, which together comprise the totality of the message of this supreme prophet, there is not the slightest ground for questioning the Deutero-Isaianic authorship of this address. And inasmuch as it is, like the address in chapter 41, a message of comfort and reassurance to His plainly troubled and despairing people, and even seems to transcend that address in the depth and vigor of its promise of unfailing, divine support, it may, with reasonable certainty, be regarded as having been uttered by the prophet at a moment somewhat later than its companion-piece in chapter 41. It would accordingly be the very latest of the seven addresses of this prophet which are contained in the Bible and perhaps the very last address to have been spoken by him.

---

is ability to foretell coming events, and this only because the ultimate first cause of all events in life and history, past, present and future, is the one God who has created the entire universe, and, moreover, has created it with purpose, and who therefore Himself brings all events to pass in conformity with and in fulfillment of this purpose. Accordingly to create and to foresee and foretell or announce coming events are two divine functions so closely and inseparably integrated that they are practically one. Therefore the Accadian verb, barû, "to foresee; to prognosticate," transformed into the Hebrew verb, ברא, could come quite readily and logically to mean "to create (as a function of deity)," and therefore specifically "to create by the mere utterance of the divine word or decree."

[46] For the supplying of the missing עמי at the end of v. 27a cf. Morgenstern, "The Loss of Words at the Ends of Lines in Manuscripts of Biblical Poetry," *HUCA* XXV (1954), 55.

## IV

## SUMMARY

But granting this, then it follows that the seven recorded addresses of Deutero-Isaiah are, in Isa. 40–48, with the exception of the elegiac poem in chapter 47, arranged in inverse chronological order, that they range successively in order of deliverance by the prophet from the earliest, in chapter 48, to the latest, in chapter 40. How or for what reason these addresses came to be grouped in this manner, and what the import thereof may be, we have no way of knowing, or even of surmising, for evidence bearing upon these questions is totally lacking. But be that as it may, reading the addresses in this order, we are enabled to comprehend clearly the gradual evolution of the prophet's distinctive message. There is no need to rehearse in detail what has already been said. It suffices to state that Deutero-Isaiah inaugurated his prophetic ministry at about 540 B. C., or perhaps even a year or two earlier, but certainly not until after Cyrus had appeared upon the stage of history and had even advanced his program successfully to the point where the discerning mind could readily perceive that world-conquest was his purpose, that sooner or later he would certainly achieve this goal, and that accordingly Babylon and the Neo-Babylonian Empire would surely fall before him.

Moreover, the prophet entered upon his consecrated task as a spiritual disciple of Ezekiel, reaffirming, and that too initially with little or no modification thereof or addition thereto, the latter's doctrine of "for His name's sake," that it was Yahweh's purpose to restore unregenerate Israel from exile in Babylonia to its native land, there Himself to purge it of its iniquity and its impulse to sin and faithlessness to Him and to take it again as His people; and this for the sake of His reputation, to concretely and convincingly demonstrate His real power, to the end that the nations might recognize Him as a true world-god and respect and honor Him accordingly. What motivated Deutero-Isaiah to prophetic ministry in the name of Yahweh, the god of Israel, was undoubtedly the progress of Cyrus' campaigns in Western Asia, the confident anticipation that Babylon would eventually fall before him, the deeply rooted, personal conviction that it was actually Yahweh, and no other god, who had stirred Cyrus to military activity and had made and would continue to make him victorious, and the faith that all this was for a specific purpose, that Yahweh's covenant with Israel was eternal, ever-enduring and that through Cyrus exiled Israel would be restored to the land of its fathers, even as Jeremiah had prophesied some fifty years earlier, and that thus Yahweh's reputation as a true and powerful world-god would be vindicated, as Ezekiel, in his turn, had predicted some twenty years later.

However, not until early in 539 B. C., did the prophet, in chapter 46, arrive at, and give initial, positive affirmation of, the doctrine, which, however, was undoubtedly implicit in his very first address and awaiting eventual formulation, that Yahweh is the one and only God, that there is no other god, and that accordingly the gods of the nations, represented by, and even identified with, their idols, are not gods at all, are in fact no more than the inanimate pieces of wood or metal from which these idols are made, and are utterly incapable of doing aught, of hearing or speaking or even of moving themselves from the places where they may have been deposited by human hands, much less of saving their bewildered and despairing people from impending conquest and destruction, or even of saving themselves.

It is almost self-evident that with the formulation of this doctrine of the absolute oneness of Yahweh as the single, true world-God, Deutero-Isaiah had outgrown completely Ezekiel's doctrine of "for His name's sake" and had advanced to a doctrine distinctly original and novel, the first stage in the gradual evolution of his total, unique message. For Ezekiel's doctrine assumed as its initial premise the existence of other gods, national in character but international or supranational in power, with whom Yahweh must naturally be compared, and, because of the present condition of His conquered and exiled people, to His decided discredit, humiliation and dishonor. But so soon as Deutero-Isaiah arrived at his doctrine of Yahweh as the sole Creator of the universe, and therefore as the one and only true world-God, he had of necessity to reject, or at least to discard, the Ezekelian doctrine,[47] with its initial premise of the existence of many gods, and advance step by step from this initial stage of his own distinctive thought and doctrine to certain other principles and dogmas implicit in it, which he formulated and proclaimed in his later addresses.

Actually, however, it was not until after Cyrus' conquest of Babylon, late in 539 B. C., that the prophet achieved what might properly be regarded as the climactic fullness of his distinctive doctrine and message. At last he comprehended and proclaimed in positive and challenging manner that Yahweh, Israel's god, is the one and only

---

[47] Except for an occasional and purely incidental reference, as in 43.25; 44.22.

God, the Eternal One, the sole Creator of the universe, and that too with benevolent purpose, that it may be inhabited by men. But for this world to be inhabited, and inhabited securely and happily, warfare must come to an end, men must cease to destroy each other, and the world must be unified, organized as one political unit, one single world-empire under one supreme world-king, chosen for this role by Yahweh, the Creator, His true "Anointed One," Cyrus and, impliedly, his posterity after him. Thus, and only thus, through Yahweh and the fulfillment in this manner of His ultimate world-purpose, will mankind find the salvation, the true salvation, which until this moment it had sought so eagerly, so desperately and so futilely. And at last, finding this salvation, it will, naturally and properly and in fulfillment of one phase of Yahweh's total world-purpose, reject completely the false gods, whose complete inability to save had been convincingly demonstrated, and will turn to the one, sole God of the universe, who has wrought this salvation for them, and will swear by and worship Him, and Him alone.

But how shall they find Him and how recognize Him, when they do find Him? For this very purpose Yahweh, the one world-God, has chosen Israel, has chosen it from the very beginning of its existence as a people, even from the time of Abraham, its remotest ancestor. He has chosen it as His people and His servant; and He, in turn, is, in first degree, its god. And the service which it is to perform is to bear witness of Yahweh unto the nations, to be the agent or instrument through whom all the nations and all mankind will come at last to comprehend the true nature, power and purpose of Yahweh, the one Savior-God, the one, sole God of the world and of all mankind which inhabits it. Here Deutero-Isaiah reverts to and reaffirms Ezekiel's doctrine of "for His name's sake," but with a slight but significant difference in application. Through Israel's restoration to its native land, authorized by Cyrus as the result of Yahweh's prompting and bidding, and through Yahweh's bringing it in safety through all the hardships and dangers of the desert, through which the way from Babylon to Judah led, until at last it attained its goal, through this manifestation of Yahweh's will and power to save, and to save, not only His own people, but all peoples, all mankind, the nations will learn who Yahweh really is, not merely *a* world-god, but *the* world-God, the one, universal God, their true and only Savior. And then to Him they will all turn eagerly and acknowledge Him as the sole God of all the world and the only potential source of salvation, as therefore their God, and to Him, and to Him alone, they will render homage and by His name alone, as the one, sole, existent God, they will swear.

For this purpose Yahweh has chosen Israel as His particular people, as His servant.

There is cogent reason for believing that when Deutero-Isaiah, in the address recorded in chapter 45, coined the title, "servant of Yahweh," for Israel, he did not, in fact could not, comprehend immediately all the many and widely ramifying implications concerning the possible nature and manner of the service latent in it. As he interpreted it, at least at first, Israel's service to Yahweh was to be that of witness of Him, to bear testimony, by its own salvation through Him in the sight of all the nations, of the power and purpose of Yahweh to save, not only His own people, but all peoples, all mankind, as well. Its service was to be passive, rather than active, in character, in that it would itself be the somewhat involuntary object of Yahweh's salvation, and thus the living example, and therefore the visible and convincing testimony, in the sight of all the world, of Yahweh's power and will to save nations and peoples and all mankind. Accordingly in his next address, the long address in chapters 42–44, the prophet, speaking of course, in Yahweh's name, applies to Israel the new title, "witnesses of Yahweh," and thus defines and amplifies the earlier title, "servant of Yahweh."

But very plainly, despite the many obvious potentialities of service implicit in the title, "servant of Yahweh," particularly when it is linked with the doctrine of Yahweh as the one, universal God, the prophet did not advance much beyond this point in his formulation and enunciation of the specific role of Israel as the "servant of Yahweh." Least of all did he conceive of and announce any particular, conscious and active service or services to be performed by Israel in its discharge of this role, although, quite obviously, many services active and positive in character and to be performed by Israel with full awareness of their import, were definitely implicit in the role. The progressive unfolding of his message seems to have been suddenly interrupted at just this initial point, the proclamation of Israel as the servant and witness of Yahweh, and to have advanced hardly at all beyond this. Why should this have been? Why should the prophet have halted at this relatively early point, and this too, apparently quite abruptly, in his development of this doctrine, so rich in potentialities, and now plainly basic to his total message as it had evolved thus far, and as it gave distinct promise of evolving further?

This question can be answered only by conjecture, but one which seems to accord with facts and to be altogether reasonable. We have seen that Deutero-Isaiah inaugurated his prophetic ministry with, in his early addresses, scathing denunciation of the Jewish exiles in

Babylonia who, while still nominally and, viewed from the prophet's standpoint, more or less hypocritically, professing allegiance to Yahweh, their ancestral, national god, at the same time openly acknowledged and paid homage to the gods of the land, the various deities of the Babylonian pantheon. He sought by cogent argument to convince these exiles of the unreality and impotence of these gods and of the idols, their visible and tangible symbols, and to win them back to faith in and loyalty to Yahweh, and thus prepare them for the by him confidently expected, Yahweh-mediated return to native land. But, as we have seen, with the exception of a seemingly small and, for the immediate moment at least, insignificant minority, his words fell upon deaf ears and may even have engendered considerable, open antagonism. And even though Cyrus' conquest of Babylon and establishment of the Persian Empire might well have seemed to corroborate the prophet's predictions and to confirm his authority as a true spokesman of Yahweh, to whom and to whose message of Yahweh's complete purpose with His people these exiles might very properly have now given heed, actually the effect of all this seems to have been the complete antithesis of what might have been expected. To these exiles it may well have seemed that their former conquerors, the native Babylonians, in whose midst they were dwelling, were now reduced to the same level as themselves, for they too were now a conquered people. Moreover, Cyrus' rule was mild and benign and his dominion rested lightly upon all the constituent peoples of his vast empire, regardless of where they might be dwelling.

Presumably therefore after the Persian conquest of Babylon the status of the Jewish exiles in Babylonia, in its political, economic and social aspects, improved somewhat and their integration with the native population of the land progressed steadily. Small wonder then that when Cyrus extended permission, not merely to the Jews, but also to other peoples in his empire who had been carried thither as exiles by earlier Assyrian and Babylonian monarchs, to return to their ancestral lands, very few of these Jewish exiles availed themselves of this privilege. After all, so they must have reasoned, why should they depart from Babylonia, now the birthland of themselves and their children, the land wherein they had prospered and were prospering, in order to return to the distant land of Israel? True, that was the land of their fathers. But what could it offer in comparison with the countless advantages which their present home-land conferred upon them? Small wonder that Deutero-Isaiah's argument and appeal to these exiles met with, on the part of the large majority, only indifference and even resentment, resentment which probably mounted steadily, as the prophet persisted in his denunciations, until, following the proclamation of Cyrus' edict of return and its rejection by the vast majority of Jewish exiles, it flowered into open and perhaps even active antagonism to the prophet and his handful of followers.

As we have seen, the spirit and theme of the two latest recorded addresses of the prophet, those in chapters 41 and 40, differ radically from those of his earlier addresses. They have changed from argument and pleading with the totality of Jewish exiles and attempt to convince them that their return as a body to their ancestral land was truly purposed by Yahweh and sure to be realized at the proper moment, a moment still in the future but drawing steadily nearer, and from castigation of them for their stubborn disbelief to comfort and assurance to the small group of faithful believers, for whom the appointed time had come at last, but who, perhaps now for the first time contemplating the project in all its stark reality, with the numerous sacrifices which it was sure to entail and the countless obstacles which must be surmounted, were dismayed and even affrighted.

Not improbably too, as has been suggested, the opposition of the large mass of unbelieving exiles, probably marked by steadily increasing derision of and open hostility to the little band of faithful believers, made the lot of the latter more and more difficult, and warranted the prophet's message, addressed to them specifically, of faith, reassurance and glowing promise. It is a reasonable presumption that the two final addresses of the prophet, with the apparent narrowing of the audience to whom they were directed, and with the marked change in their content and tone, were spoken by him after the promulgation of Cyrus' edict and the manifest lack of sympathetic reaction thereto by the overwhelming mass of the Jewish exiles. On the one hand, Cyrus' edict had proved that the prophet, speaking in the name of Yahweh, had foretold truly that the opportunity to return to ancestral land would come to these exiles through the agency of that monarch. But on the other hand, the mass of the exiles refused to be convinced or to conform to the will and purpose of Yahweh as announced by the prophet. Moreover, as has been suggested, this irritation and antagonism, stimulated by the prophet's insistent denunciation of and pleading with them, gradually turned to open and violent antagonism, directed against the small handful of believers in his word, but also, and in first degree, against himself in person.

It could be that the prophet died very suddenly, soon after he had delivered his final address, that in chapter 40, at, we may say, about 535 B. C. Inasmuch as he inaugurated his prophetic ministry, as we have seen, by reaffirming Ezekiel's doctrine of "for His name's sake," it is quite possible that he may himself have heard Ezekiel proclaim this doctrine, and that it appealed to him so strongly and lodged so firmly in his mind that it found reformulation and renewed expression by him some thirty years later. If we assume that he was born in Babylonia at about 595 B. C., i. e. as the son of a Jewish exile who had been among the first deportees, those of 597 B. C., or perhaps even that he had been born somewhat earlier in Palestine and was carried, as a boy or a youth, to Babylonia in that first deportation, he would have been at least in his middle twenties, certainly an impressionable age, at the moment when he heard Ezekiel proclaim his doctrine. He would have been then, when he delivered this final address, at least in his early sixties, certainly an age well advanced when measured by the standards of human longevity of that era. The assumption that he died a natural death, and that too perhaps rather suddenly, shortly after 535 B. C., is accordingly reasonable and altogether probable, and would account simply and effectively for the apparently abrupt termination of his prophetic ministry and the seeming failure on his part to develop further and announce at least some of the rich potentialities inherent in the role which he had proclaimed for Israel as the servant of Yahweh.[48]

On the other hand, an alternative hypothesis, there is a legend, once widely current in pseudepigraphic and rabbinic lore,[49] that the prophet Isaiah suffered death by violence at the hands of ruthless adversaries. All the sources represent this martyred prophet as the historic Isaiah and his executioner as King Manasseh of Judah. The earliest record of this legend is in the pseudepigraphic work, "The Martyrdom of Isaiah,"[50] dating in all likelihood from the first century A. D. That this legend was indeed current at that time may probably be inferred also from Josephus.[51] But a legend of the violent and untimely death of a prophet Isaiah may have been current even earlier than this, and may perhaps rest upon a historic basis. That

---

[48] On the other hand, the possibility must not be discounted that the prophet may have been born in Babylonia, but considerably later than 595 B. C., and that he may have become acquainted with and deeply impressed by the Ezekelian doctrine of "for His name's sake" either by hearing of it from his elders or by reading the written record of it. In such case he may have been still a fairly young man, in either his twenties or thirties, during the course of his prophetic ministry.

[49] Cf. Ginzberg, *The Legends of the Jews*, IV, 278 f.; VI, 373 ff.

[50] In Charles, *The Apocrypha and Pseudepigrapha of the Old Testament*, II, 155–162.

[51] *Ant.*, X, 3, 1 (so Ginzberg, *op. cit.*, V, 374, note 103).

the true Isaiah, the prophet of the second half of the eighth century B. C., should have become the central figure of this legend is not at all surprising, since from not later than the fourth century B. C. until the rise of modern Biblical science the entire so-called Book of Isaiah was regarded as the work of the historic figure of that name, and accordingly tradition knew of only one prophet Isaiah. But there is absolutely nothing in the entire Biblical record to indicate that the real Isaiah continued to function as a prophet after the death of Hezekiah, during the reign of Manasseh.[52] And still less is there any suggestion whatever in the Bible that the historic Isaiah suffered violent death at the hands of adversaries, of whom one was Manasseh, King of Judah.

But if this legend have any historic basis whatsoever and center about what may properly be called an Isaianic figure, then this figure may very well be that exalted, anonymous prophet of the third quarter of the sixth century B. C., whose extant addresses are preserved in Isa. 40–48 and whom, for convenience of citation, we have come to call Deutero-Isaiah, or the Second Isaiah. And inasmuch as, so we have inferred, the prophetic ministry of this man aroused steadily growing opposition and animosity on the part of a large body of Jewish exiles and apparently came to an abrupt end, we may perhaps account for that circumstance by the assumption that he suffered an untimely and violent death at the hands of bitter adversaries, deeply resentful of his strictures against them and of the implications of his message to them concerning the way of life which they had consciously chosen for themselves and their posterity. As has been said, this is only a conjecture, but one with at least a sufficient measure of probability to warrant responsible consideration.

And perhaps a slight measure of support may be found for it in the fact that Rabbinic tradition has attached to the figure of Isaiah, the martyred prophet, the typically Deutero-Isaianic title, "servant

---

[52] Inasmuch as Isaiah's prophetic ministry commenced in the year in which King Uzziah died (Isa. 6.1), i. e. in all likelihood in 737 B. C., while Manasseh did not come to the throne of Judah until 692 B. C., had his prophetic activity continued into the reign of Manasseh it would have meant that he functioned as a prophet for at least approximately fifty years. Moreover, the record of his consecration (Isa. 6.1–13) suggests that he was already a mature person at the moment when he inaugurated his prophetic mission. This would mean, in turn, that he would have been, at the very least, well in his seventies at the moment of his death, whether by execution by the king or otherwise, in the reign of Manasseh. These considerations establish the historical improbability of the tradition that Isaiah functioned as a prophet still in the reign of Manasseh and that he suffered a martyr's death through execution by that impious king.

of the Lord."[53] Moreover, in the assumption of this fate for Deutero-Isaiah and this application of this particular title to him as an individual, rather than to the people of Israel as a whole, the only form in which he himself employed it, we may perhaps see in him, at least in some slight measure, the forerunner and pattern of the later Suffering Servant, a consecrated individual, imbued with the divine spirit, who must suffer and die for the redemption and salvation of all mankind.[54] Certainly this second hypothesis is, to say the least, attractive.

But be all this as it may, it does seem reasonably assured that the prophetic ministry of Deutero-Isaiah terminated quite suddenly and unexpectedly, before he could carry his doctrine of Israel, the people, as the servant of Yahweh to its ultimate, logical conclusions and could define in more or less specific terms precisely wherein the service of Israel in the cause of Yahweh would lie and what particular functions it was destined to purposefully and actively perform in bearing witness of Yahweh as the one true world-God and the one divine Savior of all mankind unto all the nations of the world. And the most natural accounting for this circumstance is the assumption of the sudden and probably unanticipated death of the prophet, though whether in natural manner or as the result of violence we can of course not determine.

Such was, in its gradual unfolding, the message of this truly exalted prophet, and such were the circumstances under which it steadily expanded. Confirmation of the conclusions reached thus far will be found, at least in some measure, in the presentation, in Part II of this study, in the original, textual form recovered for them in the afore-mentioned seminar, together with such further commentary as may seem helpful, of the seven extant literary compositions of the prophet.

[53] Ginzberg, *op. cit.*, V, 381, note 2; VI, 147, note 880.
[54] Cf. above, note 24.

# PART TWO

## V

### THE TEXT OF ISAIAH 40–48

## Isa. 48

CAREFUL examination of this chapter discloses first of all that two short passages, each the equivalent of a half-verse in length, have no relevance whatever to the theme of the address here recorded and are obviously displaced fragments, or perhaps quotations, from elsewhere in Biblical, prophetic literature. V. 22 occurs also in Isa. 57.21 (with only one, inconsequential textual divergence from the form here), where, just as here, it brings the chapter to a close. There at least its thought is integrated in some slight measure with that of the v. immediately preceding. Under any condition we need not hesitate to expunge v. 22 from this address.

Quite similarly v. 16b, manifestly in itself an incomplete, fragmentary statement, not only has no thought-connection whatever with either what precedes or what follows, but also it disturbs the natural thought-sequence. It is plainly a quotation, here altogether meaningless, from Zech. 4.9b; 6.15aβ, inadvertently inserted here by some relatively late scribe or editor, and so should also unquestionably be omitted.

Furthermore, in v. 6aβ some persons or things are addressed in the second person plural, while in the adjacent portions of the address the second singular is employed, manifestly with reference to the Jewish audience to whom the prophet is speaking. This suggests that v. 6aβ may well have been displaced in some way from its original position in the address. This seems to be the case also with v. 13b; for it can hardly be the earth and the heavens, which, so v. 13a affirms, Yahweh's hands had at the very beginning of the world brought into being and set in place, which are now summoned, or even challenged, by Yahweh to stand by together, seemingly in order to testify before or to debate with Him. Apparently this passage too is no longer in its proper position in the address. And this suggests, in turn, the possibility of displacement of other passages within the chapter. Under any condition some textual rearrangement of the address, as it lies before us in *MT* form, is unavoidable. But the task is not too difficult. And when completed, the prophet's address in its original form will have been recovered, with its logical thought-development and its cogent, irrefutable argument readily comprehensible.

| | | |
|---|---|---|
| 3/3/3 | שמעו זאת בית־יעקב / הנקראים בשם ישראל / וממעי יהודה יצאו | I |
| 3/3/3 | הנשבעים בשם יהוה / ובאלהי ישראל יזכירו / לא באמת ולא־בצדקה | |
| 3/3/3 | כי־ <בשם> עיר־הקדש נקראו / ועל־אלהי ישראל נסמכו / יהוה צבאות שמו | 2 |
| 3/3/3 | מ<אשר>־ידעתי כי־קשה אתה / וגיד ברזל ערפך / ומצחך | 4 |
| 3/3/3 | <מצחת> נחושה | |
| 3/3 | ואגיד לך מאז / בטרם תבוא השמעתיך | 5 |
| 3/3 | פן־תאמר עצבי עשם / ופסלי ונסכי צום | |
| 3/2 | קרא אני אליהם / יעמדו יחדו | 13b |
| | | 14a+ |
| 3/3/3 | הקבצו כלכם ושמעו / מי־בכם הגיד את־אלה / ואתם הלוא תגידו | 6aβ |
| 4/4/4 | קרבו אלי שמעו זאת / לא מראש בסתר דברתי / מעת היותה שם אני | 16a |
| 3/3 | אני־הוא אני ראשון / אף אני אחרון | 12b |
| 3/3 | אף־ידי יסדה ארץ / וימיני טפחה שמים | 13a |
| 3/3/3 | הראשנות מאז הגדתי / ומפי יצאו ואשמיעם / פתאם עשיתי ותבאנה | 3 |
| | | 6aα+ |
| 3/3 | שמע תחזה כלה / <אני> יהוה אהבו | 14b |
| 3/3 | יעשה חפצי בבבל / וזרעו מכשדים <תושיע> | |
| 3/3 | <> אני דברתי אף־קראתיו / הבאתיו ואצליח דרכו | 15 |
| 3/3 | השמעתיך חדשות מעתה / ונצרות לא ידעתן | 6b |
| 3/3/3 | עתה נבראו ולא־מאז / ולפני־יום לא שמעתם / פן־תאמר הנה ידעתין | 7 |
| 3/3 | גם־לא שמעת גם־לא־ידעת / גם־מאז לא־פתחתי אזנך | 8 |
| 3/3 | כי־ידעתי <כי־> בגוד תבגוד / ופשע מבטן קרא־לך | |
| 3/3/2 | למען שמי אאריך אפי / ותהלתי אחמל עליך / לבלתי הכריתך | 9 |
| 3/3 | הנה־צרפתיך ולא ככסף / בחנתיך בכור עני | 10 |
| 3/3/3 | למעני למעני אעשה / כי־איך יחל <שמי> / וכבודי לאחר לא־אתן | 11 |

| | | |
|---|---|---|
| 3/2 | שמע אלי יעקב / וישראל מקראי | 12a |
| 3/3 | כה אמר יהוה / גאלך קדש ישראל | 17a |
| 4/4 | צאו מבבל ברחו מכשדים / בקול רנה הגידו <זאת> | 20aαβ |
| 4/4 | השמיעה הוציאוה עד־קצה הארץ / אמרו גאל יהוה < > יעקב | 20aγb |
| 4/4/4 | ולא צמאו בחרבות הוליכם / מים מצור הזיל למו / ויבקע צור ויזבו מים | 21 |
| 3/3/3 | אני יהוה אלהיך / מלמדך להשכיל <מעשיך> / מדריכך בדרך תלך | 17b |
| 3/3/3 | לוא הקשבת למצותי / והיה כנהר שלומך / וצדקתך כגלי הים | 18 |
| 3/3/4 | והיה כחול זרעך / וצאצאי מעיך כמעותיו / לא יכרת שמך מלפני | 19 |

1   Hear ye this, O House of Jacob,
     Those who call themselves by the name of Israel,
      And have sprung from the loins of Judah,
   Who swear by the name of Yahweh,
     And acknowledge the God of Israel,
      But not in truth nor in sincerity.

2   For by the name of the Holy City they call themselves,
     And stay themselves upon the God of Israel,
      Whose name is Yahweh of Hosts.

4   Because I knew that thou art stubborn,
     That an iron sinew is thy neck
      And thy forehead a brazen plate,

5   I would foretell unto thee in advance;
     Before anything would happen I would let thee hear of it,
   Lest thou shouldst say, "My idol did them,"
     Or "My graven image" or "My molten image ordained
      them."

13b   I challenge them;
     Let them stand up together!

14a   Assemble, all of you, and hearken!
     Who among you hath foretold these things?

6aβ     Or you, do you not foretell?

16a   Draw near to Me; hear ye this!
     From the very beginning I have not declared My fiat
      secretly;
     From the moment when it (i. e. the world) came into
      being I was present.

12b   I, the Existent One, even I, am the first;
     Furthermore, I am the last.

13a   Moreover, My hand laid the foundation of the earth,
     And My right hand spread out the heavens.

3     The first things I foretold in advance;
     Yea, from My mouth they issued forth and I announced
        them;
     Of a sudden I acted and they came to pass.

6aα   Hearken, thou shalt behold the whole of it!

14b      I, Yahweh, love him;
     He will execute My purpose against Babylon,
     And his arm will bring deliverance from the Chaldaeans.

15    I have decreed; moreover, I have summoned him;
     I have made him come, and I shall make his course
        successful.

6b    I have let thee hear new things, of the present moment,
     Things concealed, which thou hast not known.

7     Now were they brought into being, and not of old;
     Yea, before today thou hadst not heard of them,
       Lest thou shouldst say, "Behold, I have known them."

8     Verily, thou hast not heard, nor yet hast thou known (them),
     Nor have I previously opened thine ear;
     For I know that thou art utterly faithless;
       Yea, rebellious one hast thou been called from birth.

9     For My name's sake I suspend Mine anger;
     Yea, for My repute have I compassion upon thee
      So as not to let thee be cut off.

10    Behold, I have refined thee, though not as silver;
     I have purified thee in the furnace of affliction.

11    For Mine own sake, for Mine own sake do I act;
     For how may My name be profaned?
      Nor will I yield My prestige to any other.

12a   Hearken unto Me, O Jacob,
     Yea, Israel, summoned by Me!

17a   Thus saith Yahweh,
     Thy Redeemer, Israel's Holy One;

20    Go forth from Babylon, flee from the Chaldaeans;
     With joyous shout announce this;
     Let it be heard, make it to go forth to the end of the earth;
      Say, "Yahweh hath redeemed Jacob;

21    Nor did they thirst in the waste places whither He brought
       them;

Water for them He made flow forth from the rock;
Yea, He split the rock and the water gushed forth."
17b   I, Yahweh, thy God,
Am He who teacheth thee to act with discernment,
Who guideth thee in the way thou shouldst go.
18    Wouldst thou but hearken to My commandments,
Then thy good fortune will be as the Euphrates,
And thy merit like the ocean waves;
19    And thy posterity will be like the sand,
And the offspring of thy loins like the grains thereof;
Thy name will not be cut off from before Me.

This address, quite plainly, the prophet directs to a Jewish audience
in Babylonia, manifestly a group of Jewish exiles resident there for
approximately a half century. He denounces them for their insincerity
and faithlessness. With their lips they profess loyalty to Yahweh, the
god of their fathers, to their ancient homeland and its sacred city,
Jerusalem, and to their ancestral traditions. In actual practice, however, they offer homage to idols or to the gods whom the idols represent, and credit them with everything which transpires in the
world, particularly as it affects them and their immediate environment. As an ardent devotee of Yahweh this disturbs the prophet
exceedingly. As the eager champion of the God of Israel, and that too
in the thought and spirit of his prophetic predecessor, Ezekiel, he
envisages Him as jealous of His reputation, particularly when
brought into comparison or, in a way, even into competition, with
other gods, and of course especially with the gods to whom these
faithless Jewish exiles are offering their true homage, the native
Babylonian deities, the gods of the land in which they are resident.
Accordingly he portrays Yahweh as prepared to act in order to
demonstrate, not merely His divinity as such, that He is as much a
god as is any other god, or for that matter all other gods together,
but more, far more, than this, that He surpasses all other gods in
divine character and power. And so he represents Yahweh as challenging these other gods to a debate or to the semblance of a court
trial in order to prove their divinity in comparison with His.

The true test of divinity, so the prophet proposes, not only here
but also in subsequent addresses, is ability to foresee and foretell
future events, to announce in advance what is destined to happen.
This a god is able to do, impliedly, just because he himself plans and
initiates these happenings and brings them to pass in execution of
his plan, when the proper moment for this comes. Accordingly in vv.

13b, 14a, 6aβ, 16a, 12b–13a, 3, arranged in this order, the prophet depicts Yahweh as issuing His challenge to these gods. The unity of this passage and its thought development, as thus reconstructed, are immediately self-evident. The plural forms of both pronouns and verbs, the latter in both the 2nd and 3rd persons, refer to the other gods or idols, specifically mentioned in v. 5b. It is they, and they alone, who in these vv. are directly addressed by Yahweh. Moreover, the appending of v. 6aβ directly to v. 14a produces a closely unified and very effective 3/3/3 tristich. The thought implicit in it is that, having in v. 13 challenged the other gods to stand up in debate and prove their divinity as compared with His, Yahweh puts to them the decisive question, "Who among you, which particular one of you, has foretold, has announced in advance, and then (by clear implication) has brought to pass these things?" "These things" are the incidents which are now happening and which, so the prophet intimates, are setting the world of that day in turmoil. Apparently the prophet then represents, by a brief halt in his own words, Yahweh as waiting silently for a moment, long enough for some one or even several of those so-called gods to speak up and claim, each for himself, the credit for, and with that the authorship of, these world-happenings; but of course not a single god speaks up or utters even a single word. Accordingly, with the biting sarcasm, of which, we shall in due time see, he is the supreme master, the prophet represents Yahweh as asking these assembled gods, as the alternative to his first interrogation, the decisive, self-condemnatory question, "Or you, do you not foretell?" Manifestly to this taunting question too there is no response.

And having thus proved conclusively the total lack of divinity and of divine power on the part of these spurious gods, the prophet proceeds to prove the true and unchallengeable divinity of Yahweh by affirming one of his distinctive doctrines, that Yahweh, and He alone, is the Creator of the universe. He was at the beginning and He will be until the very end; therefore He is the Eternally Existent One. Moreover, in the course of the creation of the universe, and that too creation by divine fiat, by the mere utterance of His creative word, before He brought anything into existence He would announce in advance just what He proposed to do. Then He would speak His divine command, would announce it aloud, so that it could be heard everywhere; suddenly He acted, and the thing or things came into being even as He had planned and announced them. Such was His divine procedure at the very beginning, and such has been His divine procedure ever since.

And as further evidence, the ultimate, decisive proof, of His divinity, and as further illustration of His normal procedure of announcing in advance, of foretelling, what is about to happen, what He is about to bring to pass, He, Yahweh, will now announce, through the medium of His prophet, His entire plan, new things, never before divinely announced or predicted, and therefore never heard previously by Israel or any other people, all the momentous things which are happening in the world at this very moment and their import, matters of concern for all mankind, viz. the advent of Cyrus, the Persian, and his uniform and widely expanding military successes to this present moment, together with their promise for the future. All this too is Yahweh's work, planned by Him for a specific purpose, and in due time to be brought to sure and complete fulfillment. And this divine purpose, to be mediated by Cyrus, is Israel's salvation, its deliverance from exile in Babylonia and its restoration to its ancestral land, its return thither through the intervening desert, with its innumerable obstacles and manifold, almost insurmountable hardships, in much the same miraculous manner as Yahweh had once before brought His people, following His deliverance of them from Egypt, through the then intervening desert to the goodly land which He had promised them. For this purpose He, and He alone, has called Cyrus, has brought him from his own native land, has prospered him and will continue to prosper him until this, His ultimate purpose, will be completely fulfilled.

The restoration by Yahweh of His exiled people from Babylonia to ancestral land had already been foretold by two Yahweh-inspired prophets, first Jeremiah and then Ezekiel, but only in broad, general terms and only for the vague, undetermined future. But now the time for this deliverance is drawing near. But the precise moment for and the manner of this all-important event, destined to transpire in the immediate future, Yahweh had not ventured to announce sooner, not even to Israel, His people. Instead He had perforce to withhold all this until this decisive moment; for, knowing full well Israel's utter untrustworthiness, particularly in relation to Himself, He realized that it would have deliberately misinterpreted, would have ascribed all this concatenation of events and the import thereof to some other god, who, so the further claim would have been, had foretold all this long before. And thus once again through Israel, His own people, Yahweh would have been discredited and, in comparison with these other presumptive gods, reduced to a position of disregard and shame.

But despite all this Yahweh could not dispense with Israel nor cast it off, as it unquestionably deserved. For the sake of His reputation as a god He had to retain Israel as His people; for a god without a people, through whom and for whom he might work, and thus demonstrate the measure of his divine power, and through whom he might be glorified in the sight of all mankind, was no true god at all, was completely lacking in divine quality and dignity, was unreal in every respect. Therefore for His own sake, Yahweh could not reject Israel as His people despite its manifest unworthiness, but must keep it, and must also restrain His amply justified wrath and bear with it. Accordingly He has sought to purify it, to purge it of its faithlessness to Him and of its hitherto constant disregard of His commandments and of the way of life He had enjoined for it. He had therefore sought to refine it in the furnace of affliction, i. e. through the suffering attendant upon military conquest, loss of national independence and exile to a distant land. This is of course in large measure a reaffirmation of Jeremiah's doctrine of מוסר, of the disciplinary character and purpose of the Babylonian conquest of Judah and the attendant Babylonian exile. All this Yahweh had wrought consciously and purposefully for His own sake; for under no condition could He permit His name to be profaned, nor that which was entirely to His credit and for His honor, and for His alone, to be accounted to some other being.

Accordingly He has no alternative. He must bear with His people and redeem it and restore it to its ancestral land; and the time for this is rapidly drawing near. This is the true import of what is now transpiring in the world. Through Cyrus, whom Yahweh has summoned as the agent of His ultimate purpose, Israel will be enabled to depart from Babylonia, and under Yahweh's protection will proceed safely through the desert, with its manifold hardships and dangers, and will at last attain its goal. And the nations, even unto the very end of the earth, beholding or hearing the report of this unparalleled deliverance of a conquered and exiled people and its restoration to and rehabilitation in its ancestral land, will at last recognize the true nature and transcendent, divine character and power of Yahweh and will render unto Him the homage which is His due and for which He is so solicitous.

Moreover, and with this alluring promise the prophet brings this address to a fitting and effectively climactic conclusion, since Israel is Yahweh's people and He, and He alone, is its true god, its true teacher of life's ways and its guide upon its entire course, if only it would hearken to His commandments, then it could confidently look forward to a safe and happy future, with its material well-being assured and with its population steadily increasing in such measure that its existence as Yahweh's own people would never cease.

Such is the steadily and logically unfolding argument of this address in the form in which we have in the aforementioned seminar reconstructed it. Instead of overhastily labelling almost one half of this chapter, actually the equivalent of ten out of twenty-two verses, as glosses, as was the procedure of the majority of earlier and highly regarded commentators, with the result that what little that would remain as the actual utterance of the prophet known as Deutero-Isaiah would convey no unified and adequate thought whatsoever, by the rearrangement of a few obviously dislocated but nonetheless thoroughly genuine passages, six verses in all, and their restoration to their seemingly original and certainly logical positions we have not only saved the entire chapter, with the exception of two brief passages, each the equivalent of approximately only a half-verse, for the prophet, but have recovered an address with a single, closely unified and cogent theme, logically and consistently developed, and singularly appropriate and meaningful for the particular audience to whom it was directed.

In discussing the textual emendations which we have found it necessary to make in order to recover as nearly as possible what we believe to have been the original form of this address, we shall of course here, and likewise in our treatment of the other addresses of Deutero-Isaiah, follow the order of vv. as we have re-arranged them.

1. The emendation of וממי to וממעי, proposed long ago and accepted by practically all commentators, is so obvious and necessary that it needs no argument to support it.

2. It is necessary for מעיר to read, with G, בשם עיר. The 'מ of מעיר undoubtedly resulted from the preservation of the final letter of the original בשם. The supplying of בשם recovers the thought originally set forth in v. 2a, the thought which alone is integral with that of the remainder of the v. The supplying of this word compels, for metrical considerations, the interpretation of עיר־הקדש as a by-name of Jerusalem, and therefore the reading of the two words together as a single beat. This is apparently the earliest instance in all Biblical literature of the designation of Jerusalem by this meaningful epithet (cf. also 52.1). It would seem then that this term was coined by Deutero-Isaiah. This suggests that already at the very commencement of his prophetic ministry Jerusalem, and with it of course the Temple, loomed large in the thought and vision of the prophet, though their specific part therein was as yet plainly undefined. For the ultimate role of Jerusalem and the Temple in the prophet's message cf. the note to 44.28 (incorporated into the address in Isa. 45, between vv. 19 and 20a).

4. For מדעתי read with D(ead) S(ea) I(saiah)a (=DSIa) מאשר־ידעתי. In the MT text the parallelism of v. 4c with v. 4b is imperfect, since v. 4c has no word which in thought conforms to גיד of v. 4b. Moreover, metrically a word is certainly missing in v. 4c. By supplying מצחת, "a plate (of armor)" (cf. I Sam. 17.6), obviously lost by haplography with ומצחך, both the proper 3-beat meter and a very effective parallelism and also play on words are recovered.

5. V. 5aβ defines precisely מאז of v. 5aα, viz. "in advance (of a coming event)"; so also in vv. 3, 8; however, in v. 7aα, where it contrasts with מעתה, מאז must be translated "of old; in former times." Probably with Torrey (*The Second Isaiah*, 375)

we should vocalize עָצְבִּי. In v. 5b the וי which links פסל ונסכי must be interpreted as
וי correlative (="or") rather than as וי connective (="and"); accordingly the
verb of which the two nouns are the subject should be read, as does *MT*, as a 3rd,
sing., masc., צָוָם. The prophet's representation here of these faithless Jews speaking
of their objects of worship and media of divination as "my idol, my image, etc."
rather than as "my god" is a very effective expression of that satire, of which, as we
shall see, he was a master.

14a. Since the whole of v. 14a is obviously a challenge directed to the idols
mentioned in v. 5b, and since also within this tristich three verbs and two pronouns are in the 2nd plu., and since accordingly a 3rd plu., masc. pronoun would
be utterly meaningless and decidedly confusing here, there can be little question
that, following *S* and also some forty manuscripts, בהם should be emended to בכם.

12b. For אני־הוא, "I, the Ever-Existent One," as a name of Yahweh, coined by
Deutero-Isaiah, cf. Morgenstern, "Deutero-Isaiah's Terminology for 'Universal
God'," *Journal of Biblical Literature*, LXII (1943), 269–280; Mowinckel, *He That
Cometh*, 77.

16. There can be no question that, as maintained by Oort, Duhm, Cheyne and
Torrey, v. 16b is a gloss. On the one hand, the second half, what would be the second
stichos of a 3/3 distich, obviously lacks two words, with the result that it expresses
no complete thought. And on the other hand, the half-verse, as it stands in *MT*, has
absolutely no thought-connection either with v. 16a or with the theme of the entire
address. Just as in Jer. 25.17; 26.12, 15, so here also the 1st per. pronominal suffix
can refer only to the prophet. But in v. 16a the 1st per. refers to Yahweh. Undoubtedly, just as in Zech. 2.12, 13, 15; 4.9; 6.15, where the clause, which voices
practically the same thought as here, disturbs the sequence of thought and is manifestly a gloss, so also here.

3. We must, quite obviously, with Duhm and Marti, emend the *MT* vocalization to וְאַשְׁמִיעָם].

6aα. Certainly for שמעת חזה we should read שמע תחזה, transferring the final letter
of the first word to the beginning of the second word. This altogether minimal
emendation recovers a simple and natural meaning for the stichos and makes it the
proper and very effective introduction to the thought of the vv. which follow in the
address, as we have reconstructed it, in which the "new things," viz. Yahweh's
plan with regard to Cyrus, are disclosed.

14b. In v. 14ba a word has unquestionably been lost, a word indispensable to
the thought and likewise to the very probable 3/3 meter of the distich in its original
form, as we have reconstructed it by linking v. 6aα with v. 14ba. Certainly the most
natural word here would be אני, with reference to Yahweh. And inasmuch as very
close at hand, at the beginning of v. 15, there are two אני's, one of which is, where
it stands, clearly superfluous for the thought and certainly disturbing of the meter,
it seems altogether likely that this אני stood originally at the beginning of v. 14ba
and was transposed to its present, improper position through scribal carelessness or
confusion. The *MT* vocalization, אֲהַבְו, should certainly be emended to אֹהֲבוֹ, which
may be interpreted either as an impf. *qal*, 1st sing. (cf. Hos. 11.1; 14.5; Mal. 1.2)
or as an act. part. *qal*, more probably the latter. The *MT* reading, חפצו, would
mean that Cyrus would, through Yahweh's favor, execute his own purpose against
Babylon, viz. its conquest, certainly not an unnatural thought here. However, inasmuch as the passage clearly records Yahweh's plan and purpose, of which Cyrus
was merely the agent, it seems altogether justifiable to emend, with Duhm, חפצו
to חפצי, "My purpose." And indeed DSIa does read חפצי (cf. De Boer, *Second Isaiah's*

*Message: Oudtestamentische Studien* XI [1956] 76). This reading brings out the thought which seems to animate the prophet in this, his initial address, that Yahweh's primary purpose with Cyrus is to effect the deliverance of Israel from the land of its exile and its restoration to its ancestral land. Apparently as yet he sees no larger world-purpose contemplated by Yahweh and to be achieved through Cyrus as the divinely appointed agent thereof. Certainly both the thought and meter of v. 14bγ in its *MT* form are incomplete; in fact the two words which at present constitute this verse-section convey no complete meaning at all. Obviously a word has been lost, and that too at the end of the line (cf. Morgenstern, "The Loss of Words at the Ends of Lines in Manuscripts of Biblical Poetry," *HUCA* XXV [1954], 41–84). And since the vss. offer no suggestion whatever in this connection, the missing word can be supplied only by conjecture. The context suggests that the missing word must be a verb, of which זרעו would be the subject. The verb which in this setting suggests itself most naturally is תושיע (cf. Isa. 53.1; 59.16; 63.5; Ps. 44.4; 98.1; Job 26.2). The supplying of this verb necessitates further the emendation of כשדים to מכשדים. Thus reconstructed, an effective parallelism is established within the two stichoi of the distich in v. 14bβγ, a parallelism which suggests quite forcibly that Yahweh's purpose in making Cyrus victorious over the Chaldaeans was in order to effect Israel's deliverance from Babylonia.

15. As has already been stated, the one אני in v. 15a is both superfluous to the thought and overloads the meter. Whether transposed to v. 14ba, as proposed, or not, it should under all conditions be omitted here. While והצליח is readily translatable and comprehensible as a perf., 3rd sing., masc., with Cyrus as the subject, the context would seem to require the first person, for certainly the natural continuation of the thought of הביאתיו, "I (i. e. Yahweh) have caused him to come," is "And I shall make his course successful." Cheyne, Duhm, Marti and Torrey, following *G*, would emend ואצליח to ואצליח. However, realizing that this is Deutero-Isaiah's initial prophetic address and that in all certainty it was delivered quite some time, several years in all likelihood, before Cyrus' conquest of Babylon, the climax of his military program, it seems best to interpret the verb as referring to the future, and so read ואצליח.

6b. For ולא read, with DSIa and *V*, לא, and for ידעתם, with DSIa, ידעתן. With this latter reading the pronominal suffix of the verb agrees in gender and number with its antecedent, נצורות. However, this latter emendation of *MT* is not at all vital, since, as v. 7 illustrates graphically, either the masc. or the fem. plu. suffix may be used here.

7. For יום, without the article, with the connotation, "today," cf. Isa. 43.13; Ezek. 48.35.

8. The *MT* vocalization, פָּתְחָה, "thine ear was not wide open," is by no means impossible (cf. Isa. 60.11; Cant. 7.13). However, the continuation of the thought in v. 8b, giving Yahweh's motivation for action on His part, makes the reading of *G*, פָּתַחְתִּי, preferable to that of *MT* (so also Duhm and Marti). After ידעתי insert, with DSIa, the almost absolutely indispensable כי, probably lost by haplography with the preceding כי. For the precise connotation of בגד here cf. De Boer, *op. cit.*, 52.

9. For ותהלתי it is of course absolutely necessary to read ולתהלתי; cf. Zeph. 3.19, 20; also Deut. 26.19; Jer. 13.11; 33.9. For תהלה with the connotation, "repute", cf. Ps. 48.11; 66.2; 102.22; 111.10. For אחטם־לך read, following Graetz, Cheyne and Marti, אחמל עליך. The consideration that this would be the only occurrence of the stem, חטם, in the entire Bible, and that its connotation here would be extremely uncertain, supports this emendation strongly.

10. The context plainly requires that בכסף be emended to ככסף. For בחרתיך read, with DSIa, בחנתיך.

11. Contextual, grammatical and metrical considerations establish with certainty that in v. 11b a word has been lost, a word which would be the proper subject of יחל, and which would likewise complete the necessary 3-beat meter of the stichos. The manifest parallelism of this missing word with וכבודי of the following stichos establishes further that this missing word can be only שמי (so also Torrey). For the import of the thought of Israel's profanation of Yahweh's name, here developed, but originating in Ezekiel's doctrine of "for His name's sake," cf. Ezek. 36.20–23; cf. also 20.39; 39.7; likewise Lev. 18.21; 19.12; 21.6; 22.2, 32 (all these passages are from the Holiness Code, and therefore are later than and in considerable degree directly reflect the thought of Ezekiel); Jer. 34.16; Amos 2.7 (a post-exilic gloss).

20. This v., linked with v. 21, constitutes a distinct thought-unit or strophe within this poetic address. The theme of the two vv. is the impending departure from Babylon and journey of the redeemed exiles to their ancestral land through the desert which intervenes between it and Babylonia, a journey distinctly reminiscent of redeemed Israel's traditional journey from Egypt through the desert to its eventual homeland. Accordingly these two vv. are cast very effectively in 4-beat measure, v. 20 as 4/4 double-distich and v. 21 as a 4/4/4 tristich. It is then obvious at a glance that metrical confusion exists in the *MT* of the second stichos of the first distich of v. 20, which has only three beats, while the stichos immediately following, the first stichos of the second distich of the v., has five beats. Furthermore, since הגידו is a transitive verb, it must have an object; but this is at present lacking. This difficulty is easily cleared up by transferring זאת from its position in *MT* to follow הגידו and by emending השמיעו to השמיעוה and thus bringing it into perfect parallelism with הוציאוה. Quite probably the final ה' of השמיעוה was lost by haplography with the next letter of the original text, the initial ה' of הוציאוה, and then זאת was transposed from its original position in order to provide an object for both verbs, הגידו and השמיעו. Similarly the second stichos of the second distich of v. 20 has five beats, i. e. again one beat too many for the prevailing four-beat meter. Certainly one word must be omitted here. The only possible choice lies between עבדו and יעקב. And inasmuch as the context requires the specific mention of יעקב here, while nowhere in this address is there any intimation whatsoever that Yahweh had chosen Israel to be His servant, to perform a particular service for Him, there can hardly be any question that עבדו is the word to be elided here. Quite plainly it was interpolated here by some careless scribe or by some editor who remembered that in other addresses, which we have shown to be later than this address, Deutero-Isaiah did apply to Israel repeatedly the very meaningful title, עבד יהוה, and so assumed that it should have stood here also.

17b. This is quite plainly a 3/3/3 tristich; but in *MT* the second stichos has only two beats, and likewise in its present wording certainly does not express a thought consonant with or worthy of the theme of this address. Plainly the difficulty lies in the verb, להועיל. This verb has only one connotation, "to derive profit," and is never used transitively, so that it might be followed by a direct object or some other dependent word, which, if supplied here, would provide the stichos with its missing third beat. Plainly we need here a transitive verb of fitting meaning, a word of which להועיל would be a natural corruption, together with its object. Now ע is quite frequently a corruption of an original ש (for an unmistakable instance of this cf. ודשתי of Jud. 8.7 with וידע, the corruption of the original וידש, of v. 16 of the same chapter), while the combination of letters ון, which exists in להועיל, lends itself even more readily to corruption from an original ש. Accordingly in the seminar להועיל was emended to להשכיל, while, as the missing object of this verb, מעשיך was supplied; for השכיל מעשים, "to act with discernment," cf. Deut. 29.8; I Kings 2.3; Ps. 64.10.

18. The use of וַיְהִי both here and, in altogether similar manner, in v. 19 occasions not a little difficulty. This *MT* reading permits only one translation, viz. "If only thou hadst (in former times) hearkened to My commands, then thy good fortune would have been ———, and thy seed would have been ———" (cf. Judg. 13.23; I Sam. 14.30; also Judg. 8.19). However, v. 19c, so both the tense of the verb and the dominant thought of the address indicate, deals with the future, and so must be translated as voicing the promise, "Thy seed will not be cut off," rather than a circumstance commencing in the past and continuing into the present, "Thy seed would not have been cut off." Actually for both ויהי's we would expect either ויהיה or והיה (ו consecutive). And DSIa actually reads והיה for the ויהי in v. 18, although it does read ויהי in v. 19. Accordingly it seems proper to emend each ויהי to והיה, and thus achieve that unity of thought and promise which this strophe, and with it the entire address in its original form unquestionably conveyed. Certainly כַּנָּהָר, in *MT* correctly vocalized with the article, must be interpreted as meaning, not merely "like a river," as most of the vss. and also modern translations render it, but rather "like the Euphrates," as Targ. and perhaps also *S* render it. For these Judaean exiles in Babylonia, dwelling, at least in large part, as ample evidence indicates, in Southern Babylonia, in reasonable proximity to the Euphrates, the simile here employed, which set the River in parallelism with the Ocean, would have been vivid and meaningful indeed.

19. Unquestionably it is well to read, with *G*, שמך for שמו. Unquestionably too in v. 19c at least the first לא is emphatic and so should be stressed by being read as a full beat. But this, in turn, would yield five full beats for v. 19c, something which the rules of Biblical Hebrew metrics forbid. Moreover, while כרת, in the *nif.*, is occasionally used with שם as its subject (Isa. 55.13; 56.5), שמד is never so employed. Accordingly it seems best to expunge ולא ישמד from the text. Its presence here may well be due to dittography with the next ensuing word of the original text, שמך. Certainly with this elision the thought-formulation becomes decidedly more vigorous and effective. However, even with this elision the stichos still contains four beats, and the entire metrical unit, a tristich, the final and climactic metrical unit of the entire address, is a 3/3/4. However, this metrical form for an emphatic, and especially for the final, metrical unit of a poem or an address in metrical form is not uncommon in Biblical Hebrew usage (cf. Isa. 42.13; 45.22; 49.6). I hope to show also, in due time, that the address of Amos, delivered at Bethel, likewise ended on a 3/3/4. (This metrical form was brought to my notice by my good friend and highly esteemed colleague, Professor Robert Gordis, in commenting, in a personal communication, upon my own incorrect metrical arrangement of the above-cited v. in my article, "Isaiah 42.10–13," in *To Do and To Teach — Essays in Honor of Charles Lynn Pyatt* 1953, 27–38). Certainly the drawing out of the final stichos of a poem or address in poetic form by giving it an extra beat adds force to it and thus imparts a powerful, climactic effect to the poem or address. Such is certainly the case with this address in Isa. 48.

## Isa. 47

Before attempting to interpret this chapter and to solve the various problems, some of them rather complex, which the task involves, it will be well to present its text, as reconstructed in the seminar.

| | | |
|---|---|---|
| 3/2 | רדי ושבי על־עפר / בתולת בת־בבל | 1 |
| 3/2 | שבי לארץ אין־כסא / > < / רכה וענגה | |
| 3/2 | שבי דומם > < / בחשך / בת כשדים | 5 |
| 3/2 | כי־לא תוסיפי יקראו־לך / גברת ממלכות | |
| 3/2 | ותאמרי לעולם אהיה / גברת עד | 7 |
| 3/2 | לא־שמת אלה על־לבך / לא־זכרת אחריתה | |
| 3/2 | ועתה שמעי־זאת עדינה / הישבת לבטח | 8 |
| 3/2 | האמרה בלבבה אני / ואפסי עוד | |
| 3/2 | לא אשב אלמנה / ולא־אדע שכול | |
| 3/2 | ותבאנה־לך שתי־אלה רגע / > < / שכול ואלמן | 9 |
| 3/2 | כתמם יבאו עליך / > < / בעצמת חבריך > < | |
| 3/2 | ותבטחי ברעתך אמרת / אין מיראני | 10 |
| 3/2 | חכמתך > < / היא שובבתך / >ודעתך התעתך< | |
| 3/2 | ובאה עליך רעה / לא־תדעי שחרה | 11 |
| 3/2 | ותפל עליך הוה / לא־תוכלי כפרה | |
| 3/2 | ותבא עליך פתאם / שאה לא־תדעי | |
| 3/2 | עמדי נא בְּחֲבָרַיִךְ / וברב כַּשָּׁפַיִךְ > < | 12 |
| 3/2 | אולי תוכלי הועיל / אולי תַּעֲצִי | |
| 3/2 | נלאת ברב יעציך / יעמדו־נא ויושיעוך | 13 |
| 3/2 | ברי השמים > < / המודיעים־לך / חדשים אשר־יבאו > < | |
| 3/2 | הנם היו כקש / אש שרפתם | 14 |
| 3/2 | לא יצילו את־נפשם / מיד להבה > < | |
| 3/2 | כן היו־לך סחריך / באשר־יגעת מנעוריך | 15 |
| 3/2 | איש לעברו תעו / אין מושיעך | |

| | |
|---|---|
| 1 | Get down and sit in the dust, |
| |     O virgin daughter of Babylon; |
| | Sit upon the ground throneless, |
| |     O tender and delicate one. |
| 5 | Sit in silence in the darkness, |
| |     O daughter of the Chaldaeans; |

> For never again shall they call thee
>> Mistress of kingdoms.

7 But thou didst say, "Unto eternity shall I exist,
>> Mistress forever."
>
> Thou didst not lay these things to heart;
>> Thou wast not mindful of her end.

8 But now hear this, O pleasure-seeking one,
>> Who art dwelling in security,
>
> Who sayest in her heart, "I am,
>> And besides me there is none.
>
> I shall not abide as a widow,
>> Neither shall I experience loss of children."

9 But both of these shall befall thee in a (single) moment,
>> Bereavement of children and widowhood.
>
> In their fullest measure shall they befall thee,
>> Through the effect of thy sorceries.

10 For thou didst put thy faith in thy science; thou didst say,
>> "Nothing frightens me."
>
> Thy sapience betrayed thee
>> (And thy science led thee astray).

11 So that misfortune shall come upon thee,
>> Whose blackness thou dost not know;
>
> And disaster shall befall thee,
>> Which thou canst not avert;
>
> And suddenly there shall overtake thee
>> Catastrophe, of which thou hast no foreknowledge.

12 Take now thy stand amidst thy magicians,
>> Yea, among thine innumerable sorcerers;
>
> Perhaps thou mayest find some help,
>> Perhaps thou mayest gather counsel.

13 Thou hast exhausted thyself with thy host of counsellors;
>> Let them now stand up and save thee,
>
> The scanners of heaven, who make known unto thee
>> New things, which are about to happen.

14 Behold, they are like stubble;
>> Fire consumes them;
>
> They can not save themselves
>> From the flame's grasp.

15 So are unto thee thy soothsayers,
>> With whom thou hast busied thyself from thy youth;
>
> They have gone astray, each one on his own course;
>> There is not one who might save thee.

1. V. 1a bids Babylon descend, of course from her lofty throne, which, figuratively, she occupied as mistress of the world (vv. 5, 7). בת־כשדים כי־לא תוסיפי. יקראו־לך occurs again and verbatim in v. 5. There it is decidedly in place, both as to thought-connection and meter, since it makes of v. 5 the expected 3/2 double-distich, whereas here it both disturbs the thought and makes of v. 1, altogether unnecessarily and with decidedly weakening effect, a 3/2 triple-distich. And inasmuch as in the original poem v. 5 followed immediately upon v. 1, the repetition of this clause here is manifestly the result of dittography. Furthermore, the omission of this clause here restores the thought-unity and the parallelism between the two original distichs of the v., heightens the vividness of the picture here, and likewise establishes close affinity with the picture set forth in Deut. 28.56a.

5. V. 5, with its initial word, שבי, "sit", continues directly the thought of v. 1b. Moreover, the command in v. 5a to conquered and humiliated Babylon, to sit in silence in the darkness, does not accord at all with that in vv. 2–3a, to cross over rivers, and thus go into exile or captivity. This is merely the initial evidence that vv. 2–4 are an extremely disturbing gloss, and that in the original poem v. 5 was the immediate continuation of v. 1. ובאי confuses both thought and meter and is definitely superfluous, and so should be omitted. Its omission restores the expected 3/2 meter.

7. Just as v. 5 continues immediately the thought of v. 1, so does v. 7 continue immediately the thought of v. 5; accordingly, like vv. 2–4, so v. 6 must likewise be a disturbing gloss; for further evidence thereof cf. below, pp. 18 ff. Appreciation of the fact that v. 7, like the entire remainder of the poem, is cast in 3/2 meter enables us to readily grasp its true meaning; for certainly גברת must be the initial word of the second stichos of the first 3/2 distich, and accordingly עד must be linked with it in order to complete the two-beat stichos, with the connotation "eternity" (cf. Isa. 9.5; 45.17; 57.15). Were אחריתה emended to אחריתם, the antecedent of the pronominal suffix would be אלה of the preceding stichos, and the resultant thought would be, "Thou wast not mindful of their outcome." This emendation would establish perfect parallelism between the two stichoi, and may for this reason be preferable to the MT reading. Also the possibility must not be lost sight of that the emendation might be to אחריתך, "thy end." All in all, however, since the MT reading offers a very reasonable thought, "her end," i. e. the inevitable end of a nation which deludes itself with the vain thought that it will remain world-mistress forever, it seems best to retain MT. Metrical considerations necessitate that לא־שמת be read as one beat.

8. Here also appreciation of the 3/2 meter enables us to readily grasp the thought of the v., and especially of 8b, in its true and full import.

9. ביום אחד disturbs the meter, is unnecessary to the thought, and so is plainly a gloss which defines רגע, and therefore should be omitted. For באו read, with V, Targ., and probably also G, יבאו. Certainly either בעצמת חבריך or ברב כשפיך is superfluous as to thought and overloads the meter. The same combination of terms occurs again in v. 12, where, however, both expressions are essential to both thought and meter. And inasmuch as there the full expression, ברב כשפיך, occurs again, it is in all likelihood secondary here, and so is the phrase to be omitted. Likewise מאד, at the very end of the v., should be omitted because where it stands it is absolutely meaningless, is syntactically without connection, and also overloads the meter.

10. Just what the precise import of ותבטחי ברעתך, "But thou didst put thy faith in thine evil," might be it is difficult to imagine. Unquestionably instead of ברעתך a word must have stood here which would be an effective parallel of חכמתך, in the corresponding position in the second and parallel distich of this double-distich, a word of which ברעתך would be an obvious corruption. Duhm emends to

בְדַעְתֵּךְ; and this emendation finds confirmation in the presence of this same word in the second stichos of the parallel distich as reconstructed. The דעה, the "science," of Babylon, was of course, as the context indicates, its extensive practice of divination and magic. Certainly אין ראני is meaningless here, for for Babylon, in the role of world-mistress, to say, "No one sees me," would be incomprehensible. Accordingly read אין מיראני, "Nothing frightens me." This relatively simple emendation supplies a thought natural and appropriate at just this stage of the unfolding theme of the poem. Because of her deep faith in her divinatory and magical practices Babylon fears nothing. Unquestionably v. 10aβb is in disorder and needs recasting. In the first place, inasmuch as the thought of the whole of v. 10b has already been expressed, and that too in practically identical wording, in v. 8aβ, where it accords with both thought and meter far better than it does here, it should certainly be omitted here. Furthermore, v. 10aβ must be the first stichos of the distich which parallels the distich of v. 10aα and so completes the double-distich. Moreover, this second distich, like the one which precedes it, must be a 3/2. But in its *MT* form there is one word too many in this stichos, while the second stichos of the distich is, particularly after the elision of the whole of v. 10b, completely lacking. Furthermore, the wording in the 3rd sing., היא שובבתך, of v. 10aβ indicates unmistakably that only one of the two nouns at present standing there can be the antecedent of היא, and so be original in this position. And this, in turn, suggests the ready solution of the problem of the missing second stichos. ודעתך must have been the first word of that two-beat stichos. This leaves only one word actually missing. And inasmuch as ודעתך in this second stichos is the complete parallel of חכמתך of the first stichos, this missing word must have been a verb which in thought paralleled closely שובבתך of the first stichos. With considerable confidence we propose התעתך (cf. Jer. 50.6). And inasmuch as this word and ודעתך end in the same three consonants, we can readily imagine that התעתך was lost through haplography. For שובב with the connotation, "to deal treacherously, to betray," cf. Ps. 60.3.

11. For ובא read, with DSIa, and also as the syntax requires, וּבָאָה. For שַׁחֲרָה of *MT* read שָׁחֳרָהּ (cf. Lam. 4.8). Whether v. 11c is original or an editorial addition it is impossible to determine with assurance. Certainly this third distich, which makes the metrical unit a triple-distich, with its repetition of לא־תדעי, and this too without any amplifying noun as its object, as in the first distich, is rather weak and its total effect is somewhat of the nature of a bathos. On the other hand, the possibility must not be dismissed that תדעי here has a specific meaning, suggested by its setting, viz. "to know through the use of Babylon's דעה, science (v. 10)," i. e. its divinatory techniques. The stichos would then say that even with all its divinatory practice Babylon can not possibly foresee the dread catastrophe impending over it. This thought would pave the way effectively for what the remaining portion of the poem has to say. Under any condition a definitive decision as to whether the distich is original or a gloss can not be reached, and so it seems best to retain it.

12. It seems proper to vocalize here בַּחֲבָרָיִךְ, "among thy magicians" (literally, "thy binders of knots" [for magical effect]), and כַּשָּׁפַיִךְ, "thy sorcerers." The reading of DSIa, בחובריך, apparently construing this word as an act. part. *qal*, supports this interpretation. Inasmuch as v. 12aβ is metrically disturbing here, adds nothing to, and even interrupts somewhat the sequence of, the thought, and particularly since it occurs again and practically verbatim in v. 15aβ, where it fits perfectly both as to thought and meter, with Duhm, it should unquestionably be omitted here as a dittograph. Certainly תערוצי, "thou shalt inspire terror" or "thou shalt be terrified," can not be the proper word here. DSIa omits the whole of v. 12b, while *G* omits אולי תערוצי. Both Σ and *V* seem to have read תעצומי, "thou mayest find

strength," for תערוצי. However, in consideration of the thought of the very next distich, and a simple emendation indeed, for תערוצי read תִּנָעֵצִי. This reading integrates this double-distich very closely with what follows.

13. For עצתיך read, with Duhm, Marti and Kittel, יֹעֲצַיִךְ, "thy counsellors." This comparatively minor emendation establishes a very close thought-unity between vv. 12 and 13 and in fact throughout all of vv. 12–15; for certainly these "counsellors" are the magicians and sorcerers of v. 12 and the soothsayers of v. 15, to whom, with biting sarcasm, the poet bids, in v. 12, Babylon turn in desperate hope that they may be able to offer her counsel which may perchance help her in some way. החזים בכוכבים overloads the meter and is plainly a gloss, which attempts, though mistakenly, to define the two preceding words. הברי שמים should certainly be emended to ברי השמים. The reference is to the Babylonian *bârû*-priests, the professional diviners, who foretold the future, not by observing the stars, as the defining gloss here states, but rather by hepatoscopy or extispicy (cf. Zimmern, *Beiträge zur Kenntniss der Babylonischen Religion*, 81–121; Haupt, *JBL*, 1900, 66 f.; also Isa. 44.25 and perhaps Jer. 50.36). V. 13b is manifestly unintelligible in its *MT* reading and likewise defies metrical arrangement. The reconstruction which we propose is so readily apparent and restores the expected meter so perfectly that it scarcely needs detailed exposition or further justification. Under any condition, with לך following המודיעים, as we have reconstructed the distich, עליך after יבאו becomes completely superfluous, and, since it likewise disturbs the 3/2 meter, should be omitted.

14. It seems well to emend הנה to הנם, for this would clarify the thought and make the statement more emphatic. לחמם should certainly, following DSIa, *V* and *S*, be vocalized לְחָמָם. However, here the question arises again whether the third distich of this v. is integral to the thought and so is original. Actually its precise meaning in this setting is not clear, and under any condition adds little to the vigor of the thought here expressed. Moreover, it seems to disturb what would be without it a very close thought-connection between vv. 14ab and 15. Furthermore, v. 14c reads better as a 3/3 than as a 3/2, for, in order to permit the latter reading, it becomes necessary to read לשבתי-נגדו as one beat, which, while not impossible, is certainly neither natural nor easy. All in all therefore it seems best, with Duhm, Marti and Cheyne, to regard v. 14c as an editorial gloss, based perhaps largely upon the graphic and effective picture in 44.14–20.

15. As the context demands, סחריך must be the subject of היו and so should follow immediately after לך. This rearrangement, confirmed by the gloss in v. 12aβ, restores the expected 3/2 meter. However, since יגע is used regularly with the preposition 'ב, it is necessary to read, as in the dittograph in v. 12aβ and also with some fifteen mss., באשר. For metrical reasons and other considerations as well, this reading is preferable here to the retention of אשר of *MT* and the supplying of בם after יגעת. For סוחר with the connotation "magician, soothsayer" cf. Meissner, *Supplement zu den Assyrischen Wörterbüchern*, 71a. The use of specifically Accadian terms both here and in v. 13 suggests strongly that the author of this poem was a Jewish resident of Babylonia and thoroughly familiar with his cultural environment, in other words either a Jewish exile himself or the offspring of such a one. The final two words of this final distich of the poem constitute a powerful climax to the entire poem.

We have omitted vv. 2–4 and also v. 6 from the reconstructed poem on the ground that they are glosses, and this for various and cogent reasons. In the first place, it should be noticed that we are dealing here, not with what is essentially a prophetic address, directed to a specific group of people, but what is rather a poem of elegiac form and character, apostrophized to, or rather at, Babylon. Its theme is the narrowly impending downfall and eternal doom of Babylon as a nation. Accordingly, just as might have been expected, the entire poem is in 3/2 meter, the characteristic meter of Biblical elegiac poetry, as Budde has demonstrated (*ZATW* II [1882], 1 ff.; XI [1891], 234 ff.). But vv. 2–4, 6 are in altogether different meter. Vv. 2–3 are in the four-beat meter, while v. 4 is in either 4/2 or 3/3 meter, depending upon whether שמו is to be construed with what precedes or what follows. V. 6, in its *MT* form, seems to consist of one 4/2 and one 3/3 distich; actually, however, as we shall see, the v. was originally a 4/4/4 tristich.

Certainly v. 4 can not be integral in the poem. It, and possibly also the altogether unintelligible v. 3b, and also v. 6, all passages which we hold to be interpolations, make specific mention of or reference to Yahweh. On the other hand, in the poem itself, as we have reconstructed it, there is no direct mention nor even suggestion of Yahweh, although there is every reason to believe that in the mind of its Jewish author Yahweh is the primary source of the impending downfall of Babylon. Furthermore, there is no explicit antecedent of the pronominal suffix of גאלנו in v. 4, although unquestionably Israel, the author's people, is the implicit antecedent. Likewise in this v. Yahweh is referred to in the 3rd person, while apparently in v. 3b and certainly in v. 6 He is the speaker. The passage has close thought-affinities with five other passages in Isa. 40–48 (41.14; 43.14; 44.6, 24; 48.17), at least one of which (43.14), however, seems, as we shall learn in due time, to be a gloss. But it has equally close, or even closer, thought-affinities with six passages in Isa. 49–66 (49.7, 26; 54.5, 8; 60.16; 63.16), and of these one (54.5) repeats the thought here set forth in practically identical form and wording. It is accordingly a reasonable, and in fact an almost certain, inference that v. 4 is a gloss. Various hypotheses as to how it might have found its place here readily suggest themselves.

Just what the meaning of v. 3b may be and also what its true metrical form defy all possible conjecture. The various reformulations of the half-verse proposed by earlier commentators help little, if at all. The one thing sure is that, however scholars may emend them, the two verbs are both imperfects in the 1st sing., with Yahweh obviously the speaker. But, as has already been intimated, there is in this poem itself no place whatsoever for Yahweh to play such a role as this half-verse seems to suggest, whatever it may have been. Unquestionably v. 3b, regardless of however it be emended and interpreted, does not fit in any way into this poem, and so it too must be a gloss.

In v. 6 also Yahweh is quite obviously the speaker. The thought of the v. is plain and is somewhat reminiscent of Isa. 10.5–11 and also of Zech. 1.15. Furthermore, if the altogether superfluous חללתי נחלתי be omitted as a disturbing scribal or editorial gloss, the v. stands out as an effective 4/4/4 tristich. The assumption that חללתי נחלתי is a gloss is confirmed by the fact that the antecedent of the pronominal suffixes of ואתנם and להם is certainly not נחלתי, the noun immediately preceding, but the more remote עמי. This natural connection of pronoun and antecedent the intervention of the two words which we would omit disturbs greatly.

When we turn to vv. 2–3a we find that together they constitute a 4/4 double-distich and as a unit present a very graphic and effective picture of some conquered nation, presumably Babylon, being carried away into exile or captivity in some foreign land or lands, lands between which and Babylonia rivers intervene. What rivers these may be, whether the Euphrates and Tigris or other streams, is not indicated, and so it is impossible to determine in which direction and to what foreign lands, and therefore by what foreign conqueror, the passage envisaged the conquered nation being transported. But while the picture is graphic indeed, it accords not at all with either the metrical form or the dominant thought of the poem proper.

That is, as we have seen, couched throughout as an elegy over conquered Babylon in the regular elegiac 3/2 meter. Moreover, the poem proper seems not to envisage conquered Babylon as being carried away into captivity in some distant land, but rather as remaining in her native land and there reduced to the most abject conditions of conquest, subjection and national humiliation. Accordingly it seems best, as was already intimated in the discussion of v. 5, to regard vv. 2–3a, along with v. 6, as not parts of the original, elegiac poem, but rather, in view of their unquestionably high, literary merit and the effectiveness of the denunciation of Babylon in v. 6, as a fragment, or rather as two fragments, of a prophetic address, the remainder of which has apparently been lost. These two fragments we would reconstruct thus:

| | | |
|---|---|---|
| 4/4 | קחי רחים וטחני קמח / גלי צמתך חשפי שוליך | 2abα |
| 4/4 | גלי שוק עברי נהרות / תגל ערותך נם־תראה חרפתך | 2bβ–3a |
| | קצפתי על־עמי < > ואתנם בידך / לא שמת להם רחמים / | 6 |
| 4/4/4 | על־זקן הכבדת עלך מאד | |

2abα   Take millstones and grind flour;
        Open thy veil, draw up thy skirt;
2bβ–3a Lay bare the thigh, cross over rivers;
        Let thy nakedness be revealed, yea thy shame become visible.
6       I was angered at My people, so I gave them into thy possession. Thou didst not show them mercy;
      Upon the aged thou didst make thy yoke exceedingly heavy.

2ab. The command to grind flour is here put first, since impliedly this flour will be the food upon which conquered Babylon will subsist upon her journey into exile. The rivers which she will have to ford upon this enforced journey will be so deep that she will have to draw up her garments to the utmost and bare her nakedness completely to her utter shame. Despite G. R. Driver's lucid and inviting interpretation of שבל (in *Studies in Old Testament Prophecy in Honor of T. H. Robinson*, 58), inasmuch as DSIa reads שוליך here, and also in the light of Jer. 13.26, it seems best to, with Nötscher (in *VT* I [1951], 300), adopt the DSIa reading.

It seems altogether probable, in view of the use of the four-beat meter throughout, that these two fragments, vv. 2–3a and v. 6, belonged to the same original address, although there, in all likelihood, they did not stand in immediate juxtaposition. Whether this original address was the work of Deutero-Isaiah or emanated from some other prophetic source it is of course impossible, for lack of adequate evidence, to determine with certainty. But the manifestly high, literary quality of these two fragments and also the bitterly hostile attitude of the author of at least v. 6 to Babylon because of its ruthless treat-

ment of conquered and exiled Israel, and likewise the fact that the
two fragments both represent Yahweh as the speaker and the downfall
of Babylon, as depicted in v. 6, as brought upon it by Yahweh in
retribution for what it had done to Israel, together with the further
fact that in these vv., just as in the elegiac poem itself, Babylon is
addressed directly, a literary or hortatory procedure employed absolutely nowhere else in Isa. 40–48, or for that matter in all of Isa.
40–66, suggest very strongly that Deutero-Isaiah may well have been
the author of the lost prophetic address, of which these vv. are a very
small fragment. It is likewise quite probable that the thought implicit
in the two final words of v. 1 is what induced the interpolation of
vv. 2–3a in just this position.

A much more difficult question is whether the elegiac poem itself,
which constitutes the nucleus of this chapter, should be ascribed to
Deutero-Isaiah or to some other, unknown literary figure. The poem
is scarcely prophetic in character. It suggests nowhere that the
pending conquest and subjugation of Babylonia, here portrayed,
would be the work of Yahweh or that Israel might have any concern
therewith. Also there is nowhere in the poem the slightest suggestion
that the conquest of Babylon would be by Cyrus, and especially by
Cyrus called by Yahweh for this explicit purpose, and accordingly
supported by Him in all his military projects. In fact, a matter to
which Torrey has already called attention (*op. cit.*, 370), v. 8 implies
clearly that at the time of composition of this poem no national
danger confronted Babylon and she felt completely secure in her
position as world-mistress. This suggests that this poem must have
been composed at a time when Cyrus, even though perhaps already
King of Anshan, did not as yet seem to present any threat to Babylon.

Furthermore, none of the distinctive doctrines or arguments of
Deutero-Isaiah find expression or even the slightest suggestion in this
poem, neither the doctrine of "for His name's sake," which, as we
have learned, he had taken over from Ezekiel and which he employed
extensively in the initial stages of his prophetic ministry and of the
evolution of his total prophetic message, nor yet his bitter antipathy
to idols, nor that the true test of divinity is ability to correctly foretell
future events, nor his universalistic conception of the world, nor any
other. Also, unlike in the assured addresses of Deutero-Isaiah, whose
oft-recurring theme is denunciation of exiled Israel for its faithlessness
to Yahweh, here there is no reference to nor suggestion of Israel
whatsoever, but only denunciation of Babylon and announcement
of its impending doom. On the other hand, the very high literary
quality of the poem is manifest in every line, as is also the author's

uncompromising hostility to Babylon. Moreover, the author's intimate familiarity with the military and political aspirations of Babylon and also with its religious practices, and particularly its techniques of priestly divination and magic, indicate beyond all possibility of challenge that its author was definitely a Babylonian Jew, one who had the utmost contempt for Babylonian religion and its priestly officiants, and, by quite probable implication, also for the Babylonian deities in whose service these futile diviners functioned. All this would accord well with the thought and message of Deutero-Isaiah. Linguistically too the poem smacks somewhat of Deutero-Isaiah; cf. שים עלי־לב (v. 7; cf. 41.22; 42.25); אחרית (with the connotation, "outcome"; v. 7; cf. 41.22); אפס (v. 8; cf. 40.17; 41.12, 29; 45.6, 14; 46.9); כקש (v. 14; cf. 40.24; 41.2). And the biting satire of vv. 12–15 reminds us strikingly of the various satiric utterances of the prophet in his different addresses, and particularly of the magnificently satiric passage in 44.9–20, one of the classic examples of satire in all world-literature, in which the prophet ridicules both idols and their makers and worshipers. That the prophet was a real master of satire is self-evident. And beyond all question this passage, 47.12–15, is in every respect worthy of him.

All in all then it seems altogether reasonable to ascribe this poem, in conformity with tradition, to Deutero-Isaiah, but to a relatively early moment in his life, before Cyrus had as yet appeared clearly upon the historic scene and likewise before the prophet's distinctive doctrines had begun to evolve, or at least to find concrete expression, or even before he had, as we have learned, initiated his actual, momentous prophetic career by reaffirming Ezekiel's doctrine of "for His name's sake." The poem would fit well into this early, pre-prophetic period of the prophet's life, when he had as yet no awareness of a call by Yahweh to become His spokesman and the medium of His revelation unto His people of His divine purpose for it and for all mankind, the period when, presumably still a relatively young man, endowed with literary power of high degree, the future prophet could give vivid expression to his deeply rooted hatred of Babylon, its government, its people and its religion in this powerful and stirring elegiac poem. Accordingly we may with reasonable assurance regard this poem as the earliest literary utterance of Deutero-Isaiah, the forerunner of his later, entire, prophetic career, earlier then even than his initial prophetic address, in Isa. 48.

## Isa. 46

The text of this address is in a decidedly better state of preservation than that of any other of the prophet's extant addresses. No shifting whatsoever of the order of the vv., or even of portions thereof, is required, while the necessary textual emendations are relatively few and for the most part simple and readily discernible.

| | |
|---|---|
| | כרע בל קרס נבו / היו עצביהם לחיה ולבהמה / נשאתיהם עמוסות 1 |
| 4/4/4 | משא לעיפה |
| 3/3/3 | קרסו כרעו יחדו / לא־יכלו מלט נפשם / משם בשבי הלכו 2 |
| | שמעו אלי בית יעקב / וכל שארית בית ישראל / העמסים מני־בטן 3 |
| 4/4/4 | הנשאים מני־רחם |
| 3/3 | ועד־זקנה אני אשא / ועד־שיבה אני אסבל 4 |
| 3/3 | אני אעמס ואני־אשא / ואני אסבל ואמלט |
| 3/3 | למי תדמיוני ותשווני / ותמשילוני ונדמה 5 |
| 3/3 | הזלים זהב מכיס / וכסף בקנה ישקלו 6 |
| 3/3 | ישכרו צורף ויעשהו־אל / יסגדו אף־ישתחוו <אליו> |
| 3/3 | ישאהו על־כתף יסבלהו / ויניחהו תחתיו ויעמד < > 7 |
| 3/3 | אף־יצעק אליו ולא־יענה / מצרתו לא יושיענו |
| 3/3 | זכרו זאת והתבוננו / השיבו הפושעים על־לב 8 |
| 3/3/3 | זכרו ראשנות מעולם / כי־אנכי אל ואין־עוד / האלהים ואפס כמוני 9 |
| 3/3 | מגיד מראשית אחרית / ומקדם אשר לא־נעשו 10 |
| 3/3 | אמר עצתי תקום / וכל חפצי אעשה |
| 3/3 | קרא ממזרח עבדי / מארץ מרחק איש־עצתי 11 |
| 3/3 | < > דברתי אף אביאנה / יעצתי אף אעשנה |
| 3/2 | שמעו אלי אבירי־לב / הרחוקים מצדקה 12 |
| 3/3 | קרובה צדקתי לא־תרחק / ותשועתי לא תאחר 13 |
| 3/3 | ונתתי בציון תשועה / לישראל תפארתי <אשיב> |

1  Bowed down is Bel, toppled over is Nebo.
   Their images have passed over to beasts and cattle.
      Carried aloft (by men) or borne (upon animals), they
      are a burden unto exhaustion.
2  Toppled over, bowed down together,
   They are unable to rescue themselves;
   From there they go into captivity.

3   Hearken unto Me, O House of Jacob,
      Yea, the entire remnant of the House of Israel,
         Ye who have been borne from birth, have been carried from the womb;

4   Yea, even unto old age will I carry;
      Yea, unto hoariness will I transport;
   I will bear along and I will carry,
      Yea, I will transport and I will rescue.

5   To whom would ye liken Me, or contrast Me,
      Or compare Me, so that we might seem alike?

6   They pour forth gold from the purse,
      And silver by scales they weigh out.
   They hire a goldsmith, and he fashions it into a god,
      Unto which they bow down, yea, prostrate themselves.

7   They lift it upon their shoulders, they transport it;
      Then they set it in its place, and it stands still;
   Moreover, should one cry unto it, it would not answer;
      From his distress it would not save him.

8   Remember this and consider,
      Ye rebels, recall it to mind;

9   Remember the very first things from of old,
      That I am God, and none other;
         God (am I), and there is none like unto Me.

10   (I), who from the beginning foretell the outcome
      And from the past things not yet transpired;
   Who say: My plan shall persist,
      Yea, My entire purpose will I perform;

11   Who summon My servant from the East,
      From a far-off land My agent.
   I have decreed, and I will indeed bring it to pass;
      I have planned, and I will surely perform it.

12   Hearken unto Me, ye stubborn ones,
      Who are far from deliverance;

13   Close by is My deliverance, it is not far off,
      And My salvation will not delay;
   And in Zion will I establish salvation;
      Unto Israel My glory will I restore.

1. This v. abounds in difficulties of manifold character, some of them not easily resolved, nor always with complete certainty. Despite this, however, when interpreted in its close integration with vv. 2–7, the thought which the v. aims to convey becomes both clear and

certain. Cheyne would interpret vv. 1–2 as picturing the carrying off
of these Babylonian idols as booty by the conqueror; and indeed
v. 2b does seem to affirm that such would be their fate. It may well
be therefore that at the time this address was spoken, manifestly
before Babylon had been taken by Cyrus, the prophet did anticipate
that the Persian monarch, conforming to a long-established practice,
(cf. I Sam. 4–6), would carry off the images of the Babylonian gods
to his native land as trophies of victory and of his complete subjection
of hitherto all-powerful Babylonia. Actually Herodotus (I, 183) does
record that Darius I failed in an attempt to carry away the golden
image of Marduk from his temple in Babylon, but that his son,
Xerxes, succeeded in so doing. But while this thought is definitely
present in the prophet's message, it is here plainly only incidental.
The dominant theme of this section of the address is the manner in
which the images of the Babylonian gods must be carried by their
worshipers, of course in the sacred procession of the Akîtu Festival,
and this to the complete exhaustion of their bearers, contrasted with
the meaningful fact that Yahweh, Israel's god, not only need not be
carried by His worshipers, but also that He carries them Himself
throughout life, from birth, or even from conception, until hoary
old age. Implicit in this graphic contrast of Yahweh with the
Babylonian gods is undoubtedly the fact that they are represented
by idols, whereas Yahweh is represented by no idol. And implicit also
is one further contrast, all to Yahweh's distinct advantage, viz. that
the Babylonian gods, unable to protect their people from conquest,
must soon be carried away, along with their people, into captivity
in a foreign country, whereas Yahweh is about to restore His exiled
people to their ancestral land and bring about the restoration there
of His ancient sanctuary, the seat of His glory. The v. seems then to
go on to say that, after having exhausted their human carriers, the
images of the Babylonian gods must be transferred, still, impliedly,
in the course of the festival procession, to the backs of animals, both
domestic and wild, and even these, natural burden-bearers though
they are, are likewise exhausted by the weight of their loads. The
implication of the v. seems to be that in the sacred procession of the
annual Akîtu Festival, starting at Esagilla, the Marduk temple in
the city of Babylon, and proceeding thence down the sacred highway,
Ai-ibur-šabum, to the wharf on the bank of the Euphrates, where
they were loaded upon boats, to be transported to the sacred mountain, where the resurrection of Marduk was scheduled to take place
on the third day thereafter, to be followed by the return of the idols,
with the image of the resurrected Marduk at their head, still in the

sacred procession, to Esagilla, there to be restored to their former places (v. 7aβ; cf. Thureau-Dangin, *Rituels accadiens*, 146–148), the images of the gods were carried a part of the way, presumably on both the outgoing journey and the final stage of the return, i. e. then the two portions of the sacred procession which immediately contacted the sanctuary, upon the shoulders of the priests or official bearers, only, however, since the burden of them was far too exhausting to be borne all the way by human carriers, to be transferred at the proper place and moment to animal carriers. The mention of חיה here is, to say the least, a bit surprising, since its normal connotation is "wild beast," particularly as contrasted with בהמה, "domestic animal." Marti, however, holds that חיה may occasionally have the connotation, "beast of burden"; and his contention may well be borne out by Num. 35.3. In this connection also attention may be directed to the representation of the procession of Assyrian gods upon the rock-relief of Maltaya.[1] In this procession eight deities, each represented by its idol, participate, all borne along on the backs of animals, five of which are definitely wild beasts, probably sacred to the gods whose idols they carry, while three are distinctly domestic animals. The determination of the precise import of לחיה here is one of the difficulties inherent in the v. which can not be resolved with certainty. But this circumstance in no way qualifies the general interpretation of the v., and with it that of the entire address, proposed above.

The consecution of the perf., בָּרַע, by the part., קֹרֵס, is impossible. Inasmuch as all the verbs which follow in vv. 1–2 and continue the picture are perfects, and since all the versions interpret it as a perf., we should certainly read קָרַס. Unquestionably the connotation for היה ל', "to pass over to; to be transferred to," is a bit extreme; and yet היה ל' has such a wide range of meanings, occasionally approximating quite closely that here proposed (cf. Jer. 3.1; Hos. 3.3; Ruth 1.12), that we need hardly question this interpretation of the phrase here, particularly since it alone accords with the plain import of the v. as a whole and also with the main theme of the entire address. The suffix of נשאתיכם of *MT* has no antecedent in the text, nor can it refer to the members of the prophet's audience. The only possible antecedent is עצביהם; and certainly it was these idols which were carried along upon the shoulders of human beings in the Akîtu Festival procession; accordingly emend to נשאתיהם (so Blank, *Prophetic Faith in Isaiah*, 50). Here and in vv. 2–4, 7 נשא has the specific connotation, "to carry (upon the shoulders by a human being)" (cf. v. 7 and also 45.20b), whereas עמס connotes specifically "to load upon a beast of burden." סבל too has much the same meaning as נשא; cf. סָבָל, "a porter." Accordingly נשאתיהם here can mean only "their (images thus far) carried aloft (by men)." Dill-

---

[1] Cf. Gressman, *Altorientalische Bilder zum Alten Testament*², (1927), 95f. and picture #335.

mann, followed by Torrey, would interpret לְעֵיפָה, "for a weary beast"; however, inasmuch as in Biblical Hebrew a fem. adjective frequently expresses an abstract concept (cf. Davidson, *Hebrew Syntax*, 16, §14), the word may very well be translated here "unto exhaustion."

2. This v. resumes the specific thought of v. 1a and advances it a stage further. Certainly the subject of the verbs in this v. is the Babylonian gods mentioned in v. 1a. A textual confusion, one, however, easily resolved, is almost self-apparent at the end of the second and the beginning of the third stichos. Obviously the parallelistic thought-contrast between these two stichoi can imply only that these gods could not save even themselves, much less their people, and that in consequence both gods and people must go into captivity. Certainly the expression מלט משא is meaningless in every way. Instead in v. 2b we expect beyond all question the very common expression, מלט נפשם. And actually ונפשם does stand at the beginning of the third stichos, where it is plainly the subject of הלכה; but these two words, joined as subj. and pred. are senseless. On the other hand, משא, following immediately after מלט is, in part at least, a dittograph of the same word in the third stichos of v. 1, most probably in the original manuscript written immediately above. Accordingly נפשם, of the third stichos here, omitting, however, the ו of *MT*, should be transposed to the second stichos and follow immediately after מלט, as its natural object. But this leaves the third stichos lacking an essential word and beat. We suggest that the missing word is משא, and that, in part at least, the impossible משא of the second stichos is a corruption and displacement of this word. Obviously the final verb of the sentence was הלכו, like the other verbs of the sentence in the third plu. and with the same subj. as they, viz. the Babylonian deities. The thought of v. 2c then is that "from there," i. e. from the spot where, in the course of the festal procession, their images have toppled over, as the very next and the climactic stage in the demonstration of the total impotence and lack of divinity of the so-called gods whom they represent, they must go off into captivity before their conqueror.

3. This v. is a 4/4/4 tristich. It may be noted here that the first three metrical units, in which the theme of this address is set forth, are all tristichs. In the second stichos of this tristich וכל must receive a full beat in order to provide the requisite four beats for the stichos; accordingly the word voices an emphatic thought, "yea, the entire, etc." Manifestly, as the very obvious parallelism implies, stichoi one and two of this tristich envisage practically the same group; consequently the second stichos deals only with the Judaean exiles in Babylonia, the prophet's regular, and in fact his only, audience, and does not contemplate the exiles from the Northern Kingdom (so Kimchi), carried off by Sargon of Assyria almost two centuries earlier and settled by him far to the north; nor yet does it seem to contemplate, as Duhm and Marti suggest, the Jewish community remaining in Palestine.

4. הוא Torrey would translate "the same," i. e. "the changeless One." But the obvious and very effective parallelism of v. 4a, and in fact of all four stichoi which comprise the double-distich, suggest compellingly that הוא is a corruption of an original verb which paralleled אסבל; accordingly emend to אשא. V. 4b repeats the various verbs used in vv. 1–4a, and specifically and in the same relative positions the two verbs used in v. 4a, to describe the carrying operation; thus it affirms that all that which the impotent Babylonian gods could not do for their people Yahweh can and will do for His people. But of these various verbs עמס is in *MT* conspicuous for its absence, while, on the other hand, עשיתי here is an expression somewhat surprising and even disturbing; accordingly emend to אעמס.

5. Certainly the context suggests, or even demands, that for ותשוו we read, with *S*, ותשווני.

Duhm, Marti, Cheyne and others hold that vv. 6–8 interrupt the natural consecution of thought from v. 5 to vv. 9 ff. and that they must therefore be an interpolation from some non-Deutero-Isaianic source. But such is not at all the case. Plainly these scholars have failed to grasp the true import of these vv. in this setting. They assume, altogether mistakenly, that these vv. contemplate the making of an image of Yahweh by faithless Jewish exiles in Babylonia and its then being carried from the workshop of the goldsmith who fashioned it by the Jew or Jews who had ordered it made, to his or their home, where it is set down in the place appointed for it, there to function as the household god. However, were this so, it would be difficult indeed to explain the use of the plural form of the seven verbs in vv. 6–7 to describe the action of a single person or even of a single household. Still less would there be justification for the affirmation of v. 7b, regardless of who its author might be, that if one cried to Yahweh for help, even though Yahweh were represented by a household idol, He could not respond. Moreover, in v. 8 these Babylonian Jews, whom the prophet is addressing, are called specifically "rebels; faithless ones." This certainly implies a much more radical departure from the true cult of Yahweh than the mere making an image of Him, grave though such an offense might have been regarded. This term implies specifically that these "rebels" have forsaken Yahweh more or less completely (cf. 48.1 f.) and have gone over, at the very least in considerable measure, to the positive worship of the Babylonian gods. Accordingly vv. 6–8 must be integral in this address, for they voice a thought essential to the main theme. They also express once again and in a manner quite characteristic of Deutero-Isaiah, the prophet's contempt for the Babylonian gods and for the idols which represent them, and for their unreality, their non-existence and their absolute impotence, and thus their complete antithesis to Yahweh, as He is depicted in vv. 9–10. In the light of these considerations it can scarcely be questioned that vv. 6–8 are integral in this address and essential to its thought. In fact vv. 6–7 give the immediate answer to the question stated so forcibly in v. 5, and, in turn, lead directly to the charge expressed with equal force in vv. 8–9. They say that, in significant contrast to Yahweh, Bel, Nebo and all the other Babylonian deities are naught but lumps of metal fashioned by a goldsmith into particular shapes, which are borne along in the festival procession, of course upon the shoulders of their devotees, and which, when the sacred procession is ended, are set down once again, each in its customary place in the sanctuary, where it remains stationary, unable to move itself from this position and, much more to the point, unable to respond to any appeal to it for help or to bring its worshipers deliverance from danger or distress. All this vv. 8–9 bid these faithless Jews bear in mind and ponder over whenever they would compare Yahweh with other gods, and particularly with the Babylonian gods.

6. V. 6a implies graphically that, as the most precious metal, gold was regularly carried in a purse or pouch, presumably in small pieces, the value of each of which was practically self-apparent, whereas silver was carried in bars or large lumps, the value of which could be determined only by weighing (cf. Morgenstern, "Two Prophecies from 520–516 B. C.," *HUCA* XXII [1949], 370, note 6). V. 6 constitutes quite obviously a 3/3 double-distich, in the second stichos of the first distich of which ותמשילוני, a long, four-syllabled word, with a conjunctive ו prefixed and a pronominal suffix at the end, must be read as two beats, and in the second stichos of the second distich of which a word is certainly missing, a word indispensable to both the thought and the meter; accordingly insert, with *S*, אליו after ישתחוו, a word essential to the thought of both this verb and of יסגדו. It is manifestly another instance of the loss of a word at the end of a line of Biblical poetry (cf. Morgenstern,

"The Loss of Words, etc.," 67 f.). As has already been indicated, the antecedent of the participle, הזלים, and therefore the subj. of the seven verbs in the third, plu. in vv. 6–7, can not possibly be the renegade Jews, who are addressed directly in the second plu. in vv. 5 and 8, for, in addition to other considerations, already cited, this sudden transition from second plu. to third plu. would have been inexplicable and its import incomprehensible. Had the thought of vv. 6–7 been that it was these renegade Jews who were having the image or images in question made, there would not only have been no reason whatsoever for not continuing to employ the second plu. for the seven verbs in vv. 6–7, now in the third plu., but there would have been every reason for so doing; for certainly the charge against these renegade Jews would then have been more direct, specific and condemnatory. Unquestionably then the two vv. contemplate the manufacture of an idol or idols upon commission by Babylonians, by their priests or other religious authorities, and for use in the official temple cult. For the making of such images, two images in fact, made of both wood and gold, for use in the ritual of the Akîtu Festival cf. Zimmern, *Das babylonische Neujahrsfest*, 148; Thureau-Dangin, *op. cit.*, 132 f., ll. 190–216.

7. This v. consists of the customary two metrical units, of which the first, in v. 7a, is in *MT* a 3/3/3 tristich, while the second in v. 7b, is a 3/3 distich. Inasmuch as from v. 4 to this point the 3/3 distich has been the only metrical unit employed, and inasmuch too as v. 7 is definitely a close thought-unit with v. 6, and also since the third stichos in v. 7a actually merely defines the precise meaning of ויעמד at the end of the second stichos, "and it stands fast," i. e. "it does not move from its place," but adds nothing essential to the thought, it seems quite probable that this third stichos is an editorial, explanatory gloss; however, of this we can not be altogether certain. In the second stichos of the second distich, that in v. 7b, metrical considerations require that לא receive a full beat; and this, in turn, makes the word emphatic, "it can not ever save him." This brings this significant theme into the foreground as a basis of comparison of Yahweh with the Babylonian deities and paves the way effectively for the climactic thought of this address, set forth in its closing utterance, v. 13, the assurance and the promise that, in significant contrast to the inability of the Babylonian gods, whom these faithless Jews are strongly inclined to worship, to work salvation in any manner, salvation even for themselves and their own people, Yahweh's salvation of His people is near at hand and is constantly drawing closer. And this is, in turn, further and definitive evidence that vv. 6–8 are indeed an essential and integral part of this address.

8. Despite the efforts of Gesenius, Duhm and other scholars to read a meaning into והתאששו, a hapaxlegomenon, there can hardly be any question that a textual corruption lurks here, and that accordingly some textual emendation is necessary. Klostermann, Cheyne and Marti would emend to והתאשמו, "and acknowledge yourselves guilty," certainly a minimal textual emendation. However, since the *hitpaʻel* of אשם occurs nowhere else, the emendation is questionable. *V* seems to have read והתבששו, "and be ashamed of yourselves," obviously an equally minimal emendation. But the *hitpôlel* of בוש occurs only in Gen. 2.25, and so it too may perhaps be questioned here. *S* reads והתבוננו, "and consider"; and since this reading continues directly the thought of the preceding verb, זכרו, and with it the first stichos of the v. would voice a perfect thought-parallelism with the second stichos, this reading, approved by Ryssel and Dillmann, is decidedly preferable. Inasmuch as these faithless Jews are being addressed directly, it is necessary to read, in the second stichos, הפושעים, as a vocative. Certainly the thought-antecedent of זאת in the first stichos of this v., all that which these rebellious Jewish exiles are bidden to remember,

to ponder over and to recall to mind, is not merely what is told in vv. 1–5, but also and more immediately that which is stated directly and forcefully in vv. 6–7. Furthermore, זכרו as the first word of the distich in v. 8, parallels exactly זכרו as the first word of the tristich in v. 9. Accordingly this charge in v. 8, to remember all that which is presented so vigorously and convincingly in vv. 1–7, leads on well and with heightening effect to the charge in v. 9, to remember the true nature of Yahweh, that He is the one, universal God, the sole Creator of the world, all of whose acts are the fulfillment of wisely and benevolently conceived purpose. This consideration is final and definitive proof that vv. 6–8 must be integral in this address.

9. This v. is obviously a 3/3/3 tristich. The third stichos must therefore commence with אלהים. אל and אלהים here are manifestly synonyms and have the connotation, "God," i. e. the one, sole world-God. However, whereas Deutero-Isaiah employs אל frequently with the connotation, "God," i. e. the one world-God (43.12; 45.21, 22; note also האל in 42.5), with him אלהים seems to connote "a god," rather than "God" (cf. 44.6; 45.5, 21). On the other hand, he employs האלהים once (45.18) to express the concept, "the God," i. e. "the God par excellence; the one world-God." Accordingly it seems proper to read האלהים here. This reading establishes between the second and third stichoi complete and perfect thought-parallelism. ראשנות מעולם can refer only to the successive stages of Yahweh's creation of the universe, Deutero-Isaiah's oft-cited proof that Yahweh is the one and only world-God, positively affirmed here in the second and third stichoi of this tristich; cf. 48.12b–13a, 3; 45.7, 12, 18; 42.5, 8 f.; 43.9, 18; 41.22.

10. The subject of the three participles, each the first word of the three successive distichs in vv. 10–11a, is of course אנכי of v. 9. This consideration establishes the close unity of vv. 9–11 and defines the full content of the thought which the prophet bids, in vv. 8–9, these renegade Jews to remember.

11. The distich in v. 11a refers quite obviously to Cyrus. The designation of him as עיט, "a vulture," would be appropriate indeed in view of the rapidity and invariable success of his military operations (cf. 41.2 f.) and also of the likening of Nebuchadnezzar to an eagle, in Jer. 49.22; Ezek. 17.3 (so Dillmann and others). However, as Torrey has indicated, עיט hardly provides an effective parallelism with איש עצתי of the second stichos, where such parallelism is plainly required. איש עצתי here certainly does not have the connotation, "man of My counsel," i. e. "My counsellor," the human being with whom Yahweh counselled, but rather, as the following distich, especially in its reconstructed form, clearly implies, "the man of My purpose." Accordingly Torrey would emend עיט to עבדי, an emendation which we accept. Certainly the emendation is of minor range and, with the specific connotation, "My agent," rather than "My servant," provides the expected perfect and effective parallelism to איש עצתי. If this emendation be correct, it would be the very first instance in the several addresses of the prophet thus far of the use of the term, עבדי, with the pronominal suffix referring specifically to Yahweh (note that on quite independent and cogent grounds we have eliminated עבדו from 48.20). In this particular instance the term refers to Cyrus rather than to Israel. However, it may well be that, once employed by him, it had subconsciously such rich meaning and appeal for the prophet that in his very next address, approximately a year later, and constantly thereafter, he applied the term, עבדי, no longer to Cyrus, but only to Israel, as Yahweh's servant, the agent of His purpose of universal salvation (45.4; 44.1, 2, 21, 26; 43.10; 42.19; 41.8, 9). In v. 11b the first אף is disturbing in several respects. Certainly the second and third אף, each immediately preceding a verb in the impf., first, sing., and each standing in the same respective position in

its own stichos, are in parallelism and are essential to the thought of the v. But this first אף, standing before a verb in the perf., first, sing., is meaningless and likewise overloads the meter, and also weakens the effect of the two אף's which follow. Certainly it is the result of dittography and, with G, should be omitted. Each of the two authentic אף's must receive a beat in order to bring out the essential 3/3 meter; accordingly each must be interpreted as emphatic. Unquestionably יצרתי, a word whose use here would be not a little confusing and even disturbing, should, with *Duhm*, be emended to יעצתי, "I have planned." This word, representing a relatively minor emendation, accords well with the basic theme of the v., and even makes the parallelism between the two distichs of the v. perfect in every respect.

12. Many eminent scholars, following G, would emend אבירי to אבדי, but inasmuch as Jer. 4.9 indicates that אבדי לב means "ye who have lost courage; ye cowardly ones," a term which would certainly not fit these faithless Jews whom, in v. 8, the prophet has termed "rebels," it is far better to abide by the reading of *MT*. אבירי לב occurs also in Ps. 76.6, where it stands in parallelism with אנשי חיל, and apparently means "stouthearted." The term may well be compared with חזקי לב (Ezek. 2.4) and קשי לב (Ezek. 3.7), and, like those two terms, have the connotation, "stubborn ones." Such a denunciatory term would, in the prophet's mouth apply well to these Jewish renegades, who steadfastly refuse to be influenced by his argument and plea. צדקה here has unquestionably the same connotation as in v. 13aα, where it is plainly in parallelism with תשועה, "salvation; deliverance" (so also 51.6; cf. 45.8 and also 56.1). The verb, צדק, was primarily a term describing legal or court procedure. Its primary connotation is "to be innocent"; *hif.*, "to declare (some one) innocent." And inasmuch as a person pronounced innocent by the court was immediately released from custody, the derivative noun, צדקה, whose primary meaning was "innocence, right, righteousness," quickly acquired the secondary connotations, "vindication" and "release; setting free." This last seems to be the particular meaning of the word both here and in v. 13, with specific reference to Yahweh's promised release or deliverance of His people from exile in Babylonia and their restoration to their ancestral land. With this particular connotation Yahweh's צדקה is indeed a perfect parallel to His תשועה.

13. For קרבתי read, with DSIa, קרובה, "near." This reading heightens considerably the parallelism of the two stichoi of the first distich of the double-distich which constitutes the v. Certainly a word, necessary to complete the expected, or even the required, 3/3 meter, is missing at the end of the second distich of the v. This word was unquestionably a verb, one which would provide a fitting parallelism to ונתתי at the beginning of the first stichos, and, coming at the very end of the second stichos, would establish a very effective parallelistic and chiastic relationship between the two stichoi; accordingly supply אשיב (cf. Morgenstern, "The Loss of Words, etc.," 66 f.). תפארתי "My glory," i. e. undoubtedly "My glorious presence," in other words, "Myself."

The v. provides a climactic conclusion of overwhelming power to this address, for it sums up in potent and irrefutable manner the utter contrast of Yahweh with Marduk, Nabu and all the Babylonian gods whom these renegade Jewish exiles would accept and worship while rejecting Him. For while not only must the idols of the

Babylonian gods be carried in the festival procession to the utter exhaustion of their bearers (v. 1), and, when, at the close of the entire festival ritual, they are once again set down in their normal places in the temple, they can never move therefrom nor answer the appeals for help and salvation from danger and distress directed to them by their worshipers (v. 7), and in fact can not even save themselves and their people from conquest by a foreign power, manifestly Cyrus, but must eventually be carried off, along with the Babylonian people, into captivity in a foreign land (v. 2), Yahweh not only is represented by no idol, and so need not be carried, but instead carries His people throughout all existence (vv. 3 f.), but also is about to save His people, to deliver them from exile and bring them back to their ancestral land, and will even reestablish Himself in His ancient sanctuary in His sacred city in the midst of His restored people. In every respect Yahweh, Israel's god and savior, is the complete and positive antithesis to the altogether negative, unreal and completely impotent Babylonian gods. The effective climax thus reached establishes beyond all question that vv. 6–8 are integral in this address.

## Isa. 45

As has already been said,[1] Isa. 45 is in many respects the climactic address of our prophet. In it he has completely, or almost completely, outgrown Ezekiel's doctrine of "for His name's sake" and arrived at his own distinctive doctrine and message. This message is that Yahweh is the one and only God, the true, universal God, the sole Creator of the world, that, moreover, He has created the world for dwelling, to be inhabited by men, that Cyrus and, impliedly, his posterity after him, is His appointed world-ruler, His "Anointed King," selected by Him for a specific purpose, viz. to conquer and govern and, again impliedly, to thus unify the entire world, to bring all nations and peoples under a single ruler, and through this medium pave the way for them to achieve that salvation for which they had sought so long and so eagerly, but hitherto all in vain, the termination forever of all warfare, destruction and devastation, and resultant world-peace, unity and security. But world-conquest and attendant world-unification by Cyrus, stimulated to this task by Yahweh, are merely the initial steps in the fulfillment of Yahweh's universal purpose and plan.

[1] Cf. above, pp. 40 ff.

For before the nations can achieve world-peace through such unification, and thus ultimately find salvation, they must first come to recognize Yahweh as the one and only world-God, to render unto Him the homage which is His due, and to live the life which, so He has purposed from the beginning, all men should, or even must, live together. They must become a world-unit in the recognition and worship of Him as the one world-God as well as in acknowledgement of and obedience to a single world-king. Accordingly, in order to bring unto the nations and unto all mankind this understanding of Yahweh and of His real nature and universal, benevolent purpose for them, Yahweh has chosen Israel, His own people from of old, as His servant, His agent unto them, had in fact chosen it for this service from its very birth as a people. And that it may now perform this service truly and effectively, Yahweh will cause Cyrus to send Israel back from exile in Babylonia to its ancestral land, will bring about the restoration of Jerusalem and the Temple, and will again establish Israel there as His people. And the nations, and even Cyrus himself, beholding all this, beholding Israel's salvation by Yahweh, its own particular and sole god from ancient times, will come to realize that He alone is the one, true world-God, therefore their God also, and accordingly for them too the only possible source of salvation, the one and only Savior. And thus at last the world will come to be inhabited by men, by nations and peoples united in recognition and worship of the one world-God, and dwelling together amicably instead of destroying one another in endless warfare; and thus Yahweh's ultimate purpose will be brought to eventual fulfillment.

Very interestingly, many authoritative commentators, and particularly Kittel, Duhm, Marti, Cheyne and Torrey, make this address commence at 44.24, largely because כה אמר יהוה there suggests the inauguration of a new message, and also because the mention of Cyrus by name in 44.28 and again in 45.1, the only passages in Isa. 40–48 where, despite numerous other references to him in these chapters, his name is cited, suggests that the closing portion of Isa. 44 constitutes a literary unit with Isa. 45. But 44.28 we shall interpolate into this address, immediately following 45.19, where, as we shall see, it fits perfectly and carries the thought a logical stage onward. Vv. 24–26a we shall retain as an integral part of the full address in Isa. 42–44, as we shall reconstruct this. Isa. 44.26b–27 we shall transpose to chapter 41. Accordingly the entire address with which we are now dealing is contained within the limits of chapter 45 plus 44.28. However, in addition to some comparatively slight textual rearrangement within the chapter, v. 8 must be omitted as either a doxological or an editorial interpolation, while v. 14 must be transposed to Isa. 60, where, following immediately upon v. 11, it fits perfectly and effectively expands the thought of that passage.

The address falls into three distinct sections, in each of which the thought and message of the prophet are carried a logical and significant step forward. Section I (vv. 1–7) is formally addressed to Cyrus himself. In it the prophet represents Yahweh as, through him, speaking directly to Cyrus, whom He hails as His "Anointed One," i. e. as His appointed king, chosen by Him and in close and constant association with Him, and by Him made world-conqueror and world-ruler. In all this Yahweh has been motivated by a threefold purpose (vv. 4, 6–7), (a) that Cyrus himself may come to realize that it was Yahweh, and He alone, and no other god whatsoever, who had called him, called him by his own name, had prospered him and raised him to his present exalted and responsible position; and this He had done (b) primarily for the sake of Jacob, His servant, and Israel, His chosen one; and all this, Yahweh's calling Cyrus, His choice of Israel as His servant or agent, and Cyrus' impending, benevolent action with regard to Israel, all for the fulfillment of His, Yahweh's, ultimate and largest purpose, (c) that all the world, all mankind, from the extreme east to the remotest west, might come to comprehend that Yahweh alone is God, the one world-God, the sole Creator of the entire universe, the only possible Savior of mankind, and that besides Him there is no other god at all, not even Cyrus' own, native Iranian deities, Ormuzd and Ahriman, the gods of light and darkness, of good and evil.

It needs but a moment's thought to realize that under no condition could the prophet have addressed this message directly to Cyrus in person. It is inconceivable that the prophet might under any circumstance have been permitted to approach the person of the great king and speak to him directly in this challenging manner. Moreover, second thought must reveal that these vv., with their statement of Yahweh's threefold purpose, are integral to the address as a whole, and, further, that this entire address is a distinct, hortatory unit and is spoken to Israel alone, to an audience of Jewish exiles in Babylonia, Jewish exiles who, though not actually rejecting Yahweh, their ancestral deity, had to a very considerable extent lost faith in Him and had accordingly gone over in varying measure to the worship of the Babylonian gods.

In Section I of this address the prophet graphically represents Yahweh as fulfilling the initial stage of His threefold purpose, viz. convincing Cyrus himself that it was He, Yahweh, and He alone, who had called him by name, had given him victory and success in all his undertakings, and had finally, as the fulfillment of his highest aspirations, elevated him to this exalted position, made him to be sole ruler of the entire world, His own Anointed One. Plainly the prophet is here attempting to refute Cyrus' own statement, undoubtedly widely publicized quite early in his reign, in order to strengthen the allegiance to him of the native Babylonians, that it was Marduk, the head of the Babylonian pantheon, who, seeking for his people a just and righteous ruler, one pleasing unto him, had called him, Cyrus, king of Anshan, by name, had made him victorious in all his military program, and, as the culmination thereof, had given Babylon itself to him, and this too without the slightest resistance.[1] That the prophet was personally acquainted with the public proclamation of Cyrus, of which this inscription is an incidental record, may be safely inferred from the prophet's specific statement that it was Yahweh, and no other god whatsoever, who had called Cyrus by name, had accompanied him upon his expeditions and regularly given him victory, and who had shattered bronze doors and broken iron bars, i. e. had opened city gates, before him, undoubtedly a reference to the surrender of Babylon to Cyrus with no resistance whatsoever. Moreover, the prophet's reference to the ungirding of kings and the girding of Cyrus in their stead unquestionably has in mind specifically Cyrus' capture and disposal of Nabunaid, the last native king of Babylon, and his assumption of the Babylonian kingship in the latter's stead. All this is practically self-evident. And equally apparent is it that the theme of Section I of this address is the first stage of Yahweh's threefold purpose, viz. Yahweh's demonstration to Cyrus personally that He, and He alone, and not at all Marduk, as Cyrus had officially proclaimed, nor yet his own ancestral gods, Ormuzd and Ahriman, as he may have told himself in his own innermost thoughts, had wrought all this for him, but only He, Yahweh, Israel's god, the one true world-God, He and none other.

Section II, vv. 9–17+v. 20b (and excluding v. 14) is addressed in its entirety directly to Israel, to the doubting, questioning and even faithless Jewish exiles in Babylonia. Its theme, or, perhaps more precisely, its motivation, is the response of Yahweh, uttered through the prophet, to the people's doubting and challenging reaction to the prophet's statement of the second stage of Yahweh's ultimate purpose with Cyrus, viz. that what He had done for Cyrus and the high position of world-King to which He had elevated him were ultimately

---

[1] Cf. the Cyrus inscription in Pritchard, *Ancient Near Eastern Texts Relating to the O. T.*, 315 f.

for the sake of His servant, Jacob, of Israel, His chosen one. Apparently his audience had challenged, and perhaps even ridiculed this statement of the prophet; for manifestly they could not forget that but some fifty years earlier this same Yahweh, their national deity, had, so it seemed to them, been completely unable to protect them from the conquering Babylonians, and had thus demonstrated that He was altogether inferior in power and authority to the Babylonian gods, in whose land they were now quite happily settled. In vv. 9–13 the prophet rebukes, but in purely objective and argumentative manner, these Jewish exiles for their doubts and challenge of Yahweh's purpose in their behalf and His ability to enforce this. He asks (v. 11b), "Do you question Me concerning coming events with regard to My children, and with regard to the work of My hands would you give Me directions?" But apparently v. 15 records the sneering, and even contemptuous, evaluation of Yahweh by some outspoken member of the prophet's Jewish audience, a comment which the prophet immediately takes up, repeats verbatim, and makes the text of his scathing denunciation of disbelieving, faithless Israel in the remainder of Section II, vv. 20b, 16–17, of this address.

Then in Section III of the address, vv. 18–19; 44.28; vv. 20a, 21–23, the prophet represents Yahweh as announcing, in some, though by no means elaborate, detail, the third and final stage of His universal purpose, the restoration of Israel to its ancestral land and the rebuilding of Jerusalem and the Temple by Cyrus, and then the salvation of all mankind and the bringing of all men to recognize and acknowledge Him as the one, sole God of the entire universe, the one potential Savior, and to accord to Him, and to Him alone, all their homage. The passage implies very much that is basic to the prophet's message in its ultimate form. The eventual purpose of Yahweh, as the one universal world-God, is the salvation of all mankind, His creatures. This salvation will be achieved by the unification of all nations into one world-state, under the beneficent rule of a single world-king, chosen by Yahweh from all mankind to be the agent of His supreme world-purpose. As the practical result of this unification of all peoples into a single world-kingdom all warfare and its attendant destruction will cease forever, all men will dwell together in peace and unity, and the world will then indeed be inhabited by men, even as Yahweh, the world-God, had intended from the very moment of creation. And all men will then come to recognize Yahweh as their true, divine Savior and as the one and only world-God, and so will spontaneously render unto Him their grateful homage.

And all this will be achieved through the mediation of Israel, Yahweh's particular people and His chosen servant or agent. Restored by Yahweh to its ancestral land, Israel will there resume a normal way of life, in full accord with Yahweh's purpose for it, and will worship Him truly and Him alone. For the proper worship of Yahweh the Temple in Jerusalem is indispensable. Accordingly, as an early stage in the fulfillment of that portion of Yahweh's purpose allotted to him, Cyrus will send exiled Israel back to its native land and will also restore Jerusalem and rebuild the Temple. And thus beholding redeemed Israel living once more in its native land and quietly and happily worshiping its own ancestral god and living the life which He had instituted for it, the nations will at last come to realize that He, and He alone, is the one true God and Savior, not only for Israel but also for all mankind, that in Him must they put their trust, unto Him must they render their homage in a positive manner, and from Him, at His sanctuary, must they learn the way of life which He would have all men live together, the way of life exemplified by restored and now faithful Israel.

Such was the salvation which, according to our prophet, Yahweh proposed for all mankind, His creatures; such was the way of life which from the very beginning He had intended that all men should live together; and such was the specific service which Israel, His people and His servant, was to perform, in order that Yahweh's ultimate, universal purpose might be brought to fulfillment.

Actually this entire message is not presented directly and positively in coordinated form in the prophet's own words in this or in any other subsequent address; but it is all certainly implicit in Section III of this address. And unquestionably it became the immediate inspiration of the Universalist party in the Jewish community of Palestine, with its active program of conversion of foreigners to Judaism, during the brief period of the second Temple, 516–485 B. C.[1] And it found graphic and effective expression, though, not at all surprisingly, with es-chatological reinterpretation, in the message of a later, anonymous prophet, a message so vivid and so appealing that it came to be ascribed, in practically identical form, to two pre-exilic prophets, Isa. 2.1–4 and Mic. 4.1–4. Beyond all question in both passages, with the omission of the introductory, eschatological setting, we can hear the echo of Deutero-Isaiah's own message, ringing on through the ages unto eternity.

Such is the thought and such the organization of this closely unified, logically unfolding and manifestly powerful address.

But while this address is distinctly unified in thought, while the

---

[1] Cf. Morgenstern, "Jerusalem — 485 B. C.", *HUCA* XXVII (1956), 161 f.

theme of Section II flows directly out of that of Section I and that of
Section III, in turn, directly out of that of Section II, it is questionable
whether the prophet had contemplated this entire address, with its
widely ranging message, in advance. Rather it seems altogether
probable that, when he began to speak, he planned, or perhaps felt
divinely inspired, to say no more to his audience of Jewish exiles than
what is contained in Section I. However, the doubting, and even
challenging, attitude of his hearers, or at least of a considerable
portion of them, impelled him to utter the first portion of Section II,
vv. 9–13, in which he mildly and patiently rebuked his audience for
their manifest disbelief in the truth of the message which he had just
proclaimed. And then, in turn, the sneering comment of one of his
still disbelieving listeners, taken up by the prophet and repeated
verbatim in v. 15, prompted, or even provoked, him to the much
more scathing denunciation, in vv. 15, 20b, 16–17, of those faithless
ones in his audience who had manifestly rejected Yahweh more or
less completely and gone over to the worship of the Babylonian gods.
And, so it seems, during the course of this brief but positive denunciation of faithless Israel a new vision and a new and larger message,
hitherto not clearly conceived, suddenly opened up in his mind, a
true manifestation of divine inspiration, the vision of the real nature
and import of Yahweh's universality, of His being the sole Creator
of the universe, the one world-God, the vision of the unity of all
mankind under this one world-God, its only potential Savior, and
the positive purpose of this one world-God to bring unto His creatures,
unto all mankind, the salvation so long, so desperately and so vainly
sought by them. And then, in recognition of His manifold beneficence
unto them, all men would spontaneously seek Him and become united
in positive worship of Him. Such seems to be the manner in which
this monumental and decisive address of this inspired prophet, with
its significant advance over the message previously proclaimed by
him, evolved.

That this address was delivered after Cyrus' conquest of Babylon
and his assumption of the Babylonian kingship is obvious both from
the prophet's hailing him, in v. 1, as Yahweh's Messiah and also
from the manifest dependence of the wording of the prophet's personal
message to Cyrus, i. e. Section I, upon the latter's proclamation to
the Babylonian people, issued undoubtedly very soon after his ascension of the Babylonian throne. Cyrus himself records[1] that he entered
Babylon on the 3rd of Marcheshvan, some three and a half months

---

[1] Schrader, in *KB* III, part 2, pp. 134/5, ll. 18 f.

after the capture of the city by Gobryas, his lieutenant, and promptly issued his proclamation to the native population of the city. This was accordingly in October or November of 539 B. C. This address of the prophet could have been delivered not too long thereafter, in all likelihood, as has already been suggested, early in 538 B. C.

Perhaps we can date the address even more precisely. The references, in v. 5, to Yahweh's girding of Cyrus[1] and, in v. 4, to Yahweh's addressing Cyrus by a particular title,[2] probably the title, King of Babylon, or else perhaps "Mine Anointed" (v. 1) or "My Shepherd" (44.28a), suggest strongly that the particular occasion for this address was Cyrus' formal ascension of the Babylonian throne. This would have been during the closing days of the Akîtu Festival; for it was then that the Babylonian king, after, to some degree at least, enacting the role of the dying and resurrected sun-god, Marduk, formally assumed, or reassumed, the kingship and reascended the throne. That accordingly Cyrus formally and with appropriate ceremony became King of Babylon at the Akîtu Festival in 538 B. C., i. e. some five months after his entrance into the city, is reasonably certain. And that the celebration of this festival was the occasion for this address by the prophet, while not definitively evidenced, is at least strongly supported by these considerations, finds some corroboration in the scathing denunciation of the idol-carriers and worshipers in V. 20b; for, as we have already learned,[3] the carrying of idols in the sacred procession was one of the distinctive ceremonies of the Akîtu Festival. Moreover, the celebration of this festival, with many Jewish exiles participating therein to varying extent, would have readily provided the prophet with the audience which he needed for this address. While therefore we may not affirm with absolute certainty that this address was delivered by the prophet towards the close of the Akîtu Festival in 538 B. C., it does seem reasonably probable that such was the case. And if so, then this address would have followed the address in Isa. 46 by exactly one year. It would have been for the prophet a momentous year indeed, one in which he would have witnessed the fulfillment of his earlier predictions to his Jewish fellow-exiles with regard to Cyrus, an experience which must naturally have contributed much to the crystalization of his distinctive prophetic doctrine and message, as it is set forth in this address.

The address, in the form in which we have reconstructed it, reads thus:

---

[1] Cf. the reference in v. 1 to Yahweh's ungirding of kings in Cyrus' favor.
[2] אכנך; cf. the commentary upon the v., below, pp. 110–111.
[3] Above, pp. 92 ff.

| | | |
|---|---|---|
| 3/3 | כה־אמר יהוה למשיחו / לכורש אשר־החזקתי בימינו | I |
| 3/3 | לרד לפניו גוים / ומתני מלכים אפתח | |
| 3/3 | לפתח לפניו דלתים / ושערים לא יסגרו | |
| 3/3/3 | אני־יהוה ואין עוד / זולתי אין אלהים / אאזרך ולא ידעתני | 5 |
| 3/3 | אני לפניך אלך / והדרכיך אישר | 2 |
| 3/3 | דלתות נחושה אשבר / ובריחי ברזל אגדע | |
| 3/3 | ונתתי־לך אוצרות חשך / ומטמני מסתרים ‹אגלה› | 3 |
| 4/4 | למען תדע כי־אני יהוה / הקורא בשמך אלהי ישראל | |
| 4/4 | למען־עבדי יעקב וישראל בחירי / אקרא־לך בשמך אכנך ולא־ ידעתני | 4 |
| 4/4/4 | למען ידעו ממזרח שמש / וממערבה כי־אפס בלעדי / אני יהוה ואין עוד | 6 |
| 4/4/4 | יוצר אור ובורא חשך / עשה שלום ובורא רע / אני־יהוה עשה כל אלה | 7 |
| 3/3 | הוי רב את־יצרו / חֶרֶש אֶת־חַרְשׁ אדמה | 9 |
| 3/3 | היאמר חמר ‹ › מה־תעשה / ופעלו אין־ידים לך | |
| 3/3 | הוי־אמר לאב מה־תוליד / ולאם מה תחילין | 10 |
| 3/3 | כה אמר יהוה / קדוש ישראל ויוצרו | 11 |
| 3/3 | הָאתיות תשאלוני על־בני / ועל־פעל ידי תצוני | |
| 3/3 | אנכי עשיתי ארץ / ואדם עליה בראתי | 12 |
| 3/3 | אני־ידי נטו שמים / וכל צבאם צויתי | |
| 3/3 | אנכי העירתיהו בצדק / וכל דרכיו אישר | 13 |
| 3/3 | הוא יבנה עירי / וגלות ‹עמי› ישלח | |
| 3/3 | לא במחיר ולא־בשחד / אמר יהוה צבאות | |
| 3/3 | אכן־אתה אל מסתתר / אלהי ישראל מושיע | 15 |
| 4/4 | לא־ידעו הנשאים את־עץ פסלם/ומתפללים אל־אל לא יושיע | 20b |
| 4/4 | בושו וגם־נכלמו כלם יחדו / הלכו בכלמה משרתי צלמים | 16 |
| 3/2 | ישראל נושע ביהוה / תשועת עולמים | 17 |
| 3/2 | לא תבשו ולא־תכלמו / עד־עולמי עד | |
| | כי־כה אמר יהוה | 18 |
| 4/4 | בורא השמים הוא האלהים / יצר הארץ ‹ › הוא כוננה | |
| 4/4 | לא־תהו בראה לשבת יצרה / אני יהוה ואין עוד | |
| 3/2 | לא בסתר דברתי / במקום ‹ › חשך | 19 |
| 3/2 | לא־אמרתי לזרע יעקב / בתהו בקשוני | |
| 3/2 | אני־יהוה דבר צדק / מגיד מישרים | |
| 3/2 | האמר לכורש רעי / וכל־חפצי ישלם | 44.28 |
| 3/2 | האמר לירושלם תבנה / וההיכל יוסד | |

| | | |
|---|---|---|
| 3/3 | הקבצו ובאו התנגשו / יחדו פליטי הגוים | 20a |
| 3/3 | הגישו >אלהיכם< והגידו / אף יועצו יחדו | 21 |
| 3/2 | מי השמיע־זאת מקדם / מאז הגידה | |
| 3/2 | הלא אני יהוה / ואין > < מבלעדי | |
| 3/2 | אל צדיק ומושיע / אַיִן זולתי | |
| 3/3/3 | פנו אלי והושעו / כל אפסי ארץ / כי־אני אל ואין־עוד | 22 |
| 4/4 | בי נשבעתי יצא מפי / צדק הדבר ולא ישוב | 23 |
| 4/4 | כי־לי תכרע כל ברך / תשבע כל לשון > < ביהוה | |

1. Thus saith Yahweh to His Anointed,
   To Cyrus, whose right hand I have grasped,
   In order to subdue nations before him,
   And that the loins of kings I may ungird,
   To open before him double-doors
   And gates, which shall not be closed.

5. I, Yahweh, and none other,
   Besides Me no god,
   Engirdle thee, even though thou dost not know Me.

2. I go before thee
   And thy ways I guide aright.
   Doors of bronze I shatter,
   And bars of iron I cut asunder.

3. And I give unto thee the treasure-stores of darkness,
   Yea, the hidden hoards of secret places I lay bare,
   So that thou mayest know that I am God,
   That He who calleth out thy name is Israel's god.

4. For the sake of my servant, Jacob, yea, of Israel, Mine elect,
   I call unto thee by thy name, I hail thee by title, even
   though thou dost not know Me;

6. So that (men) may know from the place of sunrise,
   And also from the place of its setting, that there is none
   besides Me;
   I am God, and there is none other;

7. Fashioner of light and Creator of darkness,
   Maker of good and Former of evil,
   I, Yahweh, am the Maker of all these.

9. Woe unto that which contends with its fashioner,
   A sherd with him who works with earth!
   Should the clay say: What wouldst thou make?
   Or his handiwork: Hast thou not hands?

10. Alas for him who says to a father: What wouldst thou beget?
    Or to a mother: With what art thou in travail?

11. Thus saith Yahweh,
    The Holy One of Israel, yea, its Fashioner:
    Do you ask of Me concerning My children coming events,
      And with regard to Mine own handiwork would you give
        me instructions?

12. Me, who have made the earth
    And mankind upon it have created,
    Me, whose hands spread out the heavens
    And who regulates all their host?

13. I have incited him with a purpose,
    And all his projects do I guide aright.
    He shall rebuild My city,
      And Mine exiled people shall He send back,
    Neither for compensation nor for advantage,
      Sayeth Yahweh of Hosts.

15. Verily Thou art a god who hideth himself!
    The god of Israel is a savior?

20b. Those who carry their wooden idol do not comprehend,
    So they pray to a god who can not save.

16. They are put to shame, yea, are humiliated, all of them
      together;
    They who minister unto images move along in disgrace.

17. Israel is saved by Yahweh,
    Salvation everlasting;
    Ye shall not be put to shame, neither shall ye be humiliated
    Unto all eternity.

18. For thus saith Yahweh:
    The Creator of the heavens, He is God;
      The Fashioner of the earth, He has set it in operation.
    Not as a void did He create it; to be inhabited did He fashion it,
      I, Yahweh, and none other.

19. Not in concealment did I utter My decree,
    In a place of darkness.
    I did not say to the posterity of Jacob,
    For no purpose seek me!
    I, Yahweh, decree purposefully,
    Announce things which are true,

44.28. Who say of Cyrus: My shepherd (is he),
    And all My purpose will he fulfill;
    And who say of Jerusalem: She shall be rebuilt,
    And My sanctuary shall be established anew.

20a. Assemble and come hither, draw near,
    Together, ye remnants of the nations;

21.    Bring near your gods and let them predict;
       Let them even take counsel together.
       Who proclaimed this from of yore,
       From ancient times predicted it?
       Was it not I, Yahweh,
       Than whom there is none other?
       A god purposeful, yea, a deliverer,
       Besides Me there is none.

22.    Turn unto Me and find salvation
       All ye ends of the earth,
       For I am God, and there is none other.

23.    By Myself have I sworn; from My mouth hath it gone forth;
       Purposeful is the decree, and it shall not turn back;
       Verily unto Me shall every knee bend,
       Every tongue shall swear by Yahweh.

1. Certainly לרד requires correction, and various commentators have proposed quite a wide range of emendations. Unquestionably of all these the simplest and readiest to hand is to read, with Hitzig, לָרֹד, the inf. const. qal of רדד (cf. Ps. 144.2; also Isa. 41.2, as we shall emend it). For דלתים DSIa reads דלתות, while all the vss. translate simply "doors," without any indication that they had a dual form before them. However, inasmuch as the doors or gates within a city wall were regularly indicated by the dual form (cf. Deut. 3.5; I Sam. 23.7; II Chron. 8.5, *et passim*), it seems wise to retain the word here. In his afore-cited inscription (l. 12) Cyrus tells that Marduk both grasped his hand and pronounced his name, and likewise went at his side as a friend (l. 15; cf. v. 2 here) in connection with his conquest of Babylon and the appointment of him as ruler of the world (cf. McCurdy, *History, Prophecy and the Monuments*, III, 410, 423 f. for Deutero-Isaiah's citation of Cyrus' inscription, or at least of a public proclamation by him, in this passage). Certainly the v. implies that Cyrus' conquest of nations and walled cities and deposition of their kings lie in the past. The historic setting of this address is manifestly later than the settings of Isa. 46-48.

5. Where it stands now in *MT* v. 5 is obviously misplaced. This is evidenced by various considerations. In the first place, it disturbs the unity and the thought-sequence of vv. 3b-4, 6-7 (cf. below, pp. 44 f.). Furthermore, vv. 4b and 5c express practically the same thought, and that too with the last two words of each v. identical. These two words manifestly voice a thought of considerable importance, and their very identity might seem at first glance to establish a definite parallelism between the final stichoi of these two adjacent metrical units. Actually, however, the thought expressed by these two words, though important, is not primary in either stichos and therefore the impression of parallelism resulting from this identity would be misleading. And unquestionably the effect of the repetition of these two words in such close proximity to each other would be, from both a literary and a hortatory standpoint, decidedly unpleasant and disturbing. Still another consideration; vv. 3b-4, 6-7 have not only a positive thought unity but also, as is decidedly appropriate and effective, a distinct metrical unity in that together they consist of two 4/4 distichs followed by two 4/4/4 tristichs. Inserted midway in this metrical, as well as thought, unit, v. 5, a 3/3/3 tristich, disturbs the meter seriously.

On the other hand, inserted between vv. 1 and 2, v. 5 fits perfectly both as to metrical form and unity of thought. Vv. 1–3a are all 3/3 distichs, while v. 5 is a 3/3/3 tristich. Inserted immediately after v. 1, it comes exactly midway in this group of six 3/3 distichs, and thus, from a metrical standpoint, provides an effective balance for the strophe. Moreover, after Yahweh's direct and challenging declaration to Cyrus, in v. 1, that He is the god who has grasped Cyrus' right hand, has made him victorious over the nations of the world, and particularly over Babylonia, and has ungirded kings in his favor, we would expect a statement to follow almost immediately identifying this god for Cyrus; and precisely this is what v. 5 does. Certainly this introduction of Yahweh to Cyrus is far more appropriate and effective following immediately after v. 1 than it is in its present position, four vv. later. And certainly too the אני with which v. 2 begins becomes far more meaningful and effective when following immediately upon Yahweh's introduction of Himself to Cyrus, in v. 5, than it would be without this identification of Yahweh in His relationship with Cyrus which v. 5, thus interpolated, provides.

One additional consideration confirms this insertion of v. 5 immediately after v. 1. V. 1bβ tells that it was Yahweh who had ungirded kings, impliedly of course in Cyrus' favor. V. 5c completes this thought by its statement that Yahweh was the god who had girded Cyrus, and this even though Cyrus did not as yet know Him. The full import of this statement, following so closely upon that of v. 1bβ, becomes clear when we realize that donning the royal girdle and sword seems to have been, along with mounting the throne and putting the crown upon the head, the distinctive ceremonial procedure by which a Persian king was formally installed in the royal office (cf. the *Shah Nahmeh* of Firdousi; French translation by Mohl, I, 55, 77, 105). Manifestly the prophet had immediate acquaintance with this ancient, Persian insititution, probably because he had himself just witnessed it. And certainly the fact that v. 5c actually thus completes the thought of v. 1bβ is almost definite proof that originally v. 5 followed immediately upon v. 1. Moreover, now separated by five distichs, the repetition of ולא ידעתני in v. 4b (where the two words must be read together as a single beat, i. e. not with the same emphasis as in v. 5c, where they must be read as two beats; cf. our metrical arrangement of the Hebrew text), after its initial use in v. 5c, becomes decidedly meaningful and effective.

2. As all the vss. indicate, והדורים here is certainly a corruption. And inasmuch as in v. 13a the statement occurs, with Yahweh as the subject, ודרכיו אישר, we may with reasonable assurance change והדורים to ודרכיך, certainly a fairly minimal emendation. For ישר דרכים, "to make successful; to prosper," cf., in addition to v. 13, Ps. 5.9; Prov. 3.6; 11.5.

3. Supply אגלה at the end of the first distich, thus recovering the expected 3/3 meter and likewise providing an effective chiastic parallelism between the two parts of the distich (cf. Morgenstern, "The Loss of Words etc.," *HUCA* XXV [1954], 67). It should be noted that in his above cited inscription (l. 12) Cyrus affirms that Marduk pronounced his name, thereby heralding him as his appointed ruler of the entire world.

4. Unlike in vv. 3b and 6, where it is a conjunction, and as such may be pronounced as a full beat, here למען is a preposition, and so must be linked closely with its object, and so be read as a single beat. Certainly we must, with *G*, omit the ו of ואקרא, in conformity with the rules of Hebrew syntax.

6. It is necessary to read וממערבה. Only מערב, and never מערבה, is used as the antithesis of מזרח (cf. Isa. 43.5; 59.19; I Chron. 12.15). The antecedent of the pronominal suffix of וממערבה is of course שמש. While שמש is usually a masc. noun, not infrequently, just as here, it is a fem. (cf. Deut. 24.15; II Sam. 2.24; II Kings 3.22;

Jonah 4.8, *et pass*.). וממערבה must be read as two beats for the sake of the meter; this is easily possible, since it is a polysyllabic word with two prefixes and a pronominal suffix.

7. Since כל must obviously receive a full beat, it should of course be read כֹּל; so also in vv. 13, 22, 23.

9. For חרשי read, with Torrey, חָרַשׁ, the construct of חָרָשׁ; parallelism with the first stichos of the distich makes this reading imperative. The חרש was the skilled worker in stone (Ex. 28.11; II Sam. 5.11), iron (I Sam. 13.19; Isa. 44.12; II Chron. 24.12), wood (II Sam. 5.11; Isa. 44.13, *et pass*.), plaster (I Chron. 14.1); so here חרש אדמה, "the skilled worker in earth or clay," a term practically synonymous with יצר of the first stichos. In v. 9bα there is one word too many for the meter; accordingly ליצרו, which in this context is altogether superfluous, should be omitted as an explanatory gloss. The manifest close parallelism between the two stichoi which constitute the distich of v. 9b demands that in the second stichos the two pronominal suffixes be inverted, so that for ופעלך we read, with the majority of the earlier commentators, ופעלו and for לו we read לך.

10. For ולאשה read, with *G*, ולאם; this establishes a perfect parallelism with לאב of the first stichos of the distich. The subject of אמר can be only the as yet unborn babe. Thus understood, the parallelism of the distich which constitutes v. 10 with the double-distich of v. 9 is self-apparent. In fact vv. 9–10 together constitute a very effective triple-distich, which voices one single, general thought. And inasmuch as הוי in v. 9 received a full beat, this second הוי, with which the third distich begins, may be readily slurred over and so be read with אמר as a single beat, thus preserving the uniform 3/3 meter, not only of this triple-distich, but also of the entire strophe, vv. 9–13.

11. V. 11b certainly voices the challenge which disbelieving and faithless Israel levels at Yahweh, and which, so the prophet represents it, is here repeated by Him in the form of a question. Accordingly vocalize הָאֹתִיּוֹת (ה interrogative), and for שאלוני read תשאלוני (the ת lost by haplography). This emendation establishes the expected parallelism with תצוני in the second stichos of the distich. V. 11b plainly refers back to vv. 9–10 and makes their import in this setting perfectly clear. Yahweh, here the יוצר ישראל, corresponds to the יוצר and the חרש אדמה of v. 9, and likewise to the father, and even to the mother, of v. 10; while Israel, and of course especially Israel in exile, is the creation of Yahweh, and specifically the broken sherd which challenges the potter, "Have you no hands (to make me aright, strong and un-breakable)?" In fact Israel, here likened to the broken sherd, is, beyond all question, that section of the Jewish nation which, carried off into exile some fifty years earlier, was indeed a sherd broken off from the vessel of which it was originally a part. (This interpretation was first proposed by my colleague, Professor Sheldon H. Blank, in the afore-mentioned seminar quite some years back.) Impliedly Israel in exile, hearing the prophet's message, spoken in the name of Yahweh, that Yahweh was the one, single, and therefore all-powerful world-God, who alone had elevated Cyrus to his present position as world-ruler, and that He had done this primarily for the sake of Israel, His servant, and Jacob, His chosen one, challenges the prophet's statement with the quite natural question, why, if Yahweh, Israel's god, is indeed all that the prophet claims Him to be, did He, a half-century earlier, permit His people to be conquered and carried away into exile, a sherd broken off, as it were, and cast away, far away indeed.

12. Inasmuch as אני merely anticipates the pronominal suffix of ידי, the two words may easily be read together as one beat; thereby the uniform 3/3 meter of

this strophe is preserved. צבאם here designates, not the angels or other heavenly creatures, those who normally constitute the heavenly host, but rather the heavenly bodies, the sun, moon and stars. Accordingly צויתי here may well be translated, "I regulate; I control; I direct" (cf. Gen. 1.14 f.; Ps. 104.19).

13. For בצדק (also in vv. 19, 23) connoting "with (divine) purpose," cf. Blank, *Prophetic Faith in Isaiah*, 152–156. For ונלותי we should certainly read, with G, ונלות עמי, both for the sake of the meter, which requires a third word in the stichos, and also for clarity and forcefulness of expression. אמר יהוה צבאות at the end of the v. indicates the conclusion of the strophe, consisting of vv. 9–13, and supports our conclusion that v. 14 is an intrusion here.

14. As has already been indicated, v. 14 can not possibly be integral in this address. The picture which it presents is totally unrelated to the theme of this address, while the sudden introduction of the 2nd, fem., sing. in the six pronominal suffixes in the sentence, with no possible antecedent whatsoever, would be inexplicable indeed. On the other hand, the v. fits perfectly in Isa. 60, following immediately after v. 11, both as to its thought and its use of the 2nd, fem., sing.

15. Klostermann and Duhm, compelled to regard v. 14 as an integral part of this address, since they knew not how otherwise to dispose of it, would emend אתה to אתך. But the transposition of v. 14, as suggested above, enables us to retain v. 15 in its *MT* form. The precise import of the v. and also the grounds for transposing v. 20b to follow immediately after v. 15 have already been presented.

20b. A moment's thought must make clear that where it stands in *MT* v. 20b is definitely out of place, for it destroys completely the perfect thought-unity between vv. 20a and 21; note the succession of impv., 2nd plu., masc., all addressed to the idolatrous nations, in vv. 20a and 21. On the other hand, with v. 20b interpolated between vv. 15 and 16, note the significant antithetic parallelism between vv. 15b and 20bβ, and that in fact the statement of v. 20bβ, that these idol-bearers pray to a god who can not save, is the direct answer to the sneering question of v. 15b, "the god of Israel is a savior?" Similarly, though perhaps not quite as obviously, v. 20bα, with its statement that the bearers of idols do not comprehend the true nature, and therefore the absolute powerlessness, of these presumptive gods which they worship, is the close and effective parallel of v. 15a, with its sneering statement that Yahweh is a god who conceals himself, i. e. does not reveal himself completely nor make his true purpose fully clear and comprehensible to his worshipers. Accordingly not only is the total lack of unity of v. 20b with v. 20a thus convincingly established, but also and even more positively the close and complete thought-unity of v. 20b with v. 15.

16. With the interpolation of v. 20b between vv. 15 and 16 a subject is provided for the two verbs in v. 16a and an antecedent for the pronominal suffix of כלם. Accordingly there is no necessity whatsoever to emend כלם יחדו, and this too in rather drastic manner, as many of the earlier commentators felt compelled to do. Inasmuch as in vv. 20b–16 it is unquestionably not the professional idol-makers nor yet the Babylonian worshipers of the gods whom the idols represent, but rather the idol-worshipers among the Jewish exiles, who are denounced so scathingly, it is probably well for חרשי to read, with Targ., משרתי. While שרת normally connotes professional, priestly ministry to a god, here, as also in Isa. 56.6, it may well mean "to worship devotedly." Accordingly the משרתי צלמים in this v. would be identical with הנשאים את־עץ פסלם of v. 20b; and this is, in turn, further corroboration of our interpolation of v. 20b between vv. 15 and 16. And still further support of this new verse arrangement may be found in the fact that quite obviously vv. 20b and 16 together constitute

a 4/4 double-distich. Inasmuch as it is doubtful whether in Biblical Hebrew there was actually a word, ציר, with the connotation, "image," it is well, with Cheyne and Marti, to read צלמים for צירים.

17. If it be correct that in v. 16 it is those among the Jewish exiles in Babylonia who had been faithless to Yahweh and had gone over to the worship of the Babylonian gods who are denounced, then it follows almost necessarily that the Israel here referred to, for whom a safe and happy future is assured, can be no longer the entire nation or people of Israel, nor yet the entire body of Jewish exiles, but only a section of the latter body, a distinct minority no doubt, the true Israel, as it were, the Israel whom Yahweh had chosen as His servant, the agent of His universal purpose. The faithless ones among the former Israel are doomed to shame and humiliation. But the true Israel, so the prophet affirms, is destined by Yahweh for eternal salvation and dignified and happy existence. This is apparently the very first time that the prophet has drawn this distinction between the false and the true Israel and centered his interest in the latter. It is manifestly this true Israel, and it alone, which is destined to be saved by Yahweh, to be restored to its ancestral land, and to function as Yahweh's servant. The importance of this new stage in the gradual unfolding of the prophet's message can not be emphasized too strongly.

18. Inasmuch as the body of this v. is manifestly a 4/4 double-distich, the opening clause, כי־כה אמר יהוה, which, were it to be read metrically, would have only three beats, and so would disturb the meter greatly, should be regarded, as is not infrequently the case, as standing outside the meter and as uttered by the prophet in order to introduce the new, final and climactic strophe of this address. Plainly in v. 18aγ there is one word too many for the meter; and inasmuch as ועשה is utterly superfluous, adds nothing to, and even weakens the expression of, the thought, it should be omitted, thus restoring the 4/4 meter of the distich.

19. This v. is quite obviously a 3/2 triple-distich. But granting this, then the second stichos of the first distich plainly contains one word too many; and this word can be only ארץ. Actually the presence of this word here is disturbing, not only metrically but also in relation to the thought which the prophet obviously seeks to express. As Job 10.21 indicates, the ארץ חשך, "the land of darkness," was the netherworld, the place of abode of the dead. Certainly the prophet did not mean to represent Yahweh as saying that He did not utter His decree in some place in the netherworld. Rather we expect some fitting parallelism to בסתר in the first stichos; and by omitting ארץ, with its altogether misleading import, and reading simply במקום חשך, "in a place of darkness," we acquire a parallelism to בסתר fitting and effective indeed. In v. 19b it seems necessary to read בתהו for תהו and to interpret it as meaning "for naught; for no purpose"; the 'ב was undoubtedly lost by haplography.

44.28. Note that this v., which, where it stands in MT, is certainly out of place, fits in perfectly here both as to metrical form and thought, agreeing, as it does, with and supplementing the thought of v. 13b. In fact some such utterance as this with regard to Cyrus and the fulfillment by him, in his role as Yahweh's appointed world-administrator, of Yahweh's purpose, that Israel, the true Israel of course, be sent back to its ancestral land, Jerusalem be restored and the Temple be rebuilt, is almost indispensable here. Furthermore, the reference to Jerusalem and the Temple just here, in this particular place, clearly implies that in the prophet's concept of Israel as the servant of Yahweh, charged with the task of mediating the salvation of all the nations and bringing them to acknowledgment of Yahweh as the one and only world-God, the one, true Savior of mankind, and positive worship of Him, the resumption of dwelling by Israel in its ancestral land, and particularly in Jerusalem, and of its own worship of Yahweh there in the Temple, His distinctive sanctuary, are absolutely essential. Certainly in this v. we must read the same word, either האמר or לאמר, at the beginning of each distich; and inasmuch as both G and V seem to have read האמר in both places, this reading seems preferable. Furthermore, since both Cyrus and Jerusalem are referred to in the 3rd person, the Temple should likewise be so referred to; accordingly emend תוסד to יוסד; likewise for והיכל we should read, with V, ולהיכל.

21. With the disturbing v. 20b shifted to a different position, the very close unity between vv. 20a and 21a becomes immediately apparent. In both passages the "remnants of the nations," i. e. all the nations conquered by Cyrus and now incorporated into his vast empire, all those nations which had looked eagerly and vainly each to its own god or gods for salvation from conquest and subjection by the irresistible foe, are addressed in the 2nd pers., plu. So close is the relationship in both thought and metrical form between these two distichs that we naturally expect them to constitute a double-distich. Accordingly, since v. 20a is a 3/3 distich, we expect v. 21a to be the same. Actually, however, one word seems to be missing in what should constitute the first stichos of the distich of v. 21a. But remembering that הגישו is a transitive verb and so must have an object, we realize immediately that this object is wanting here, and that it must be the missing word required to complete the expected three-beat first stichos of this distich. Moreover, it is associated with הגידו, "foretell, prognosticate"; and in Deutero-Isaiah these prognosticators have always been the gods, either of the foreign nations, who have prognosticated falsely or not at all, or Yahweh, the sole, true prognosticator. And inasmuch as the remainder of the v. indicates that once again, as so often in these addresses of our prophet, the theme is a contest between Yahweh and the gods of the foreign nations, in order to determine who alone among them foretold the conquest of the world by Cyrus and his benevolent intentions for exiled Israel, there can be no doubt whatsoever that the missing object of הגישו must be אלהיכם. Moreover, since these gods must first be present, if they are to attempt to answer the challenge, the present order of the two verbs should be reversed (cf. Isa. 41.22). Accordingly the text should read: הגישו אלהיכם והגידו; with of course אלהיכם, thus supplied, as the subj. of both והגידו and יועצו in the second stichos of the distich. V. 21bcd obviously constitutes a triple-distich; and inasmuch as b and d are plainly in 3/2 meter, we naturally expect c to also be in the same meter. Unquestionably v. 21cβ is overloaded, has two words too many. However, the omission of the altogether superfluous עוד אלהים restores the expected meter and likewise establishes a perfect parallelism between cβ and dβ. Whether in dβ the Massoretic reading, אין, should be retained, no doubt for emphasis (cf. Hos. 13.4), or אן be read, as in cβ and as is customary, is an open question, but one of no import whatsoever insofar as the thought of the passage is concerned. For מאז, "from ancient times," cf. Isa. 48.3, 5, 7, 8; 44.8.

22. V. 22 is plainly a 3/3/3 tristich. The second stichos indicates that the prophet is no longer directing his message to only "the remnants of the nations," but to all mankind, even unto the very ends of the earth, and is bidding them, in Yahweh's name, to turn to Him, the sole, universal God, and through Him find that salvation which until now they had sought so long, so eagerly and so vainly. In the third stichos of the tristich אל is, in a way, a proper name, has the connotation, "God," the one, sole God of the universe (so also in 40.18; 43.12; 45.14; 46.9). It may well be that in this usage of אל there is, as has been suggested by var-

ious scholars, a faint reminiscence of the name and figure of 'El, the supreme deity of the Ugaritic pantheon a thousand or more years before our prophet's time. But if so, we can hardly imagine that the prophet himself was at all conscious of this. But unquestionably, since the prophet is here addressing, not Israel specifically, but all the nations together, אל, rather than יהוה, or even than אלהים, is the proper term by which to designate the one world-God. After this positive affirmation that Yahweh is God, and also after the equally positive statement of v. 21cβ and dβ, that there is no God other than He, ואין־עוד no longer possesses primary emphasis, and therefore it may be read as a single beat.

23. The v. is obviously a 4/4 double-distich, and so constitutes a dignified and effective, climactic conclusion to this very meaningful and theologically momentous address. Certainly the utterly incomprehensible צדקה דבר דבר is the result of incorrect word-division; we should accordingly read צדק הדבר. For צדק with the connotation, "divine purpose," cf. the note to v. 13. Yahweh's דבר is His decree which, through the divine purpose inherent in it, automatically, irresistibly and effectively brings to fulfillment the purpose for which He had uttered it; for a fuller and more explicit statement of this same thought cf. Isa. 55.11. It is readily apparent that the second stichos of the second distich is incomplete both as to thought and metrical form. Plainly a word is missing; and that word can be only the name of the god by whom the person in question swears; in this case Yahweh. And the expected ביהוה we find, with G and also with Rom. 14.11, where this v. is quoted, as the second word of v. 24. There the word is absolutely meaningless and should be transposed, with the omission of the intervening אך, to the end of v. 23, where unquestionably it stood originally. There, as the final word of the second stichos of the distich, it completes an effective chiastic parallelism with בי, the first word of the first stichos of the first distich of the v. The obvious implication of the passage is that, since Yahweh is the sole God of the entire world, only by Him, by the use of His name, and His name alone, can men swear. In fact, and quite obviously, would He Himself for any reason swear an oath, He too can swear only by Himself; therefore בי נשבעתי at the beginning of this v. Moreover, inasmuch as Deutero-Isaiah was unquestionably the very first to affirm that Yahweh was the one, sole, existent God and that all other presumptive gods were non-existent unrealities, it follows with certainty that all passages in the Bible which speak of Yahweh as swearing by Himself must be later than Deutero-Isaiah (cf. Gen. 22.16; Isa. 62.8; Jer. 22.5b; 49.13; 51.14; Amos 4.2; 6.8aα; 8.7).

24. Just what v. 24a may mean, after the omission of אך and the transposition of ביהוה to the end of v. 23, it is impossible to tell; nor do any of the vss. offer the slightest help here. The half-verse must be dismissed as hopelessly corrupt. V. 24b is translatable, especially if, with DSIa and practically all the vss., we emend יבוא to יבאו, recognizing that the final ו must have been lost, either by transposition to precede the א or by haplography with the ו at the beginning of the next word. But who or what the antecedent of the pronominal suffixes of the two prepositions in v. 24b might be, whether Yahweh or Israel, it is impossible to determine. However, the half-verse has decided thought affinities with 41.11a. Under any condition the half-verse does not accord in any way with the theme of this address and is beyond all question an intrusion here, perhaps transposed in some manner from some other utterance of the prophet.

25. It seems altogether probable that אך, now standing at the beginning of v. 24, immediately preceding ביהוה, stood originally at the beginning of v. 25, where it would still immediately precede ביהוה. In all likelihood it was this immediate

proximity which, through a not unnatural scribal error, brought about its transposition to its present place. Thus reconstructed, the v. becomes a 3/3 distich, either thus:

אך ביהוה יצדקו/ויתהללו כל־זרע ישראל

or thus:

אך־ביהוה יצדקו ויתהללו/כל זרע ישראל

The issue between these two metrical arrangements is whether אך voices an emphatic thought, and so should be stressed and thus receive a full beat, or not. This it is impossible to determine; for it is difficult to believe that v. 25, thus reconstructed, could have followed originally after v. 23, and so have served as the conclusion of this exceedingly momentous address. V. 23, both through its thought and its metrical form, constitutes, as has already been said, a most effective, climactic ending of the prophet's message to both Israel and the nations at large. With v. 25 appended, the resultant sudden transfer of theme from the nations at large and their conversion to Yahweh and consequent salvation, to Israel and its vindication and praise would be, from the standpoints of both thought and metrical form, a decided bathos. Moreover, the Israel of this v. is "all the seed of Israel," i. e. the entire former Israelite, or at least Judahite, nation or people, whereas in v. 17 and throughout the latter portion of the address proper it is rather the true Israel, the minority section of the Babylonian Jewish community still faithful to Yahweh. Accordingly v. 25 is certainly not an integral part of this address. There is no reason whatever to question its Deutero-Isaianic authorship. But where it may have stood originally, in which address of the prophet, it is utterly impossible to determine. Not at all improbably it may have been a unit with v. 24, in the latter's original form, and both vv. together a part of some utterance by the prophet which unfortunately has not been preserved.

## Isa. 42–44

These three chapters are interpreted by practically all scholars as containing a number of addresses by the prophet, three at least, or even more. We shall endeavor to show that these three chapters, with the elision of a few, brief passages which have quite plainly been interpolated, and likewise with considerable textual rearrangement, constitute a single, well integrated address, probably the most extensive single, prophetic address recorded in the Bible.

It has long been recognized by the vast majority of scholars that 42.1–4, 6–7 are a fragment of the Suffering Servant document. 42.10–13 are a psalmodic fragment,[1] probably inserted here for doxological purposes connected with the reading of selections from the prophets in the ritual of the Synagogue of the early post-Exilic period.[2] Also

---

[1] Cf. Morgenstern, "Isaiah 42.10–13," in *To Do and To Teach: Essays in Honor of Charles Lynn Pyatt* (1953), 27–38.

[2] Cf. Morgenstern, "The Origin of the Synagogue," in *Studi Orientalistici in onore di Giorgio Levi Della Vida* (1956), II, 200 ff.

42.21; 43.14; 44.23 are, or at least strongly seem to be, interpolations of similar character. 42.14 and 19b seem likewise to be interpolations, totally unrelated to the overall theme of the address. And finally 44.28 we have transposed to come between 45.19 and 20a. In the same manner we shall transpose 44.26b–27 to the address in Isa. 41. With the elision of these passages, totalling fifteen vv. in all, what remains constitutes a single address, one of the most significant of all the extant addresses of this exalted prophet.

As we have reconstructed it in the oft-mentioned seminar, this address reads as follows:

| | | |
|---|---|---|
| 3/3/3 | כה־אמר האל יהוה / בורא השמים ונוטֶהם / רקע הארץ וצאצאיה | 42.5 |
| 3/3 | נתן נשמה לעם־עליה / ורוח להלכים בה | |
| 3/3/3 | אני־יהוה הוא שמי / וכבודי לאחר לא־אתן / ותהלתי לפסילים | 8 |
| | הראשנות הנה באו / וחדשות אני מגיד / בטרם־תצמחנה אשמיע | 9 |
| 3/3/3 | אתכם | |
| 3/3 | אחריב הרים וגבעות / וכל עשבם אוביש | 15 |
| 3/3 | ושמתי נהרות לאיים / ואגמי ‹מים› אוביש | |
| 4/3 | והולכתי עורים בדרך לא־ידעו / בנתיבות לא־ידעו אדריכם | 16 |
| 4/3 | אשים חשך לפניהם לאור / ומעקשים למישור ‹אתן› | |
| 4/3 | אלה הדברים אעשה ‹להם› / ולא אעזבם ‹לעד› | |
| 3/3/3 | הוצא עם עור / ועינים יש ‹ועורים› / וחרשים ואזנים למו | 43.8 |
| 3/3 | העורים הביטו לראות / והחרשים שָׁמְעו ‹להקשיב› | 42.18 |
| 3/3 | מי עור כעבדי / וחרש כמלאכי אשלח | 19a |
| 3/3 | רָאות רבות ולא־ישמר / פָּקוֹחַ אזנים ולא־ישמע | 20 |
| 4/3/3 | והוא עם בזוז ושסוי / הָפֵחו בחורים כלם / ובבתי כלאים החבאו | 22 |
| 4/3 | היו לבז ואין מציל / למסשה ואין־אמר השב | |
| 4/3 | מי נתן למשסה יעקב / וישראל לבוזים ‹אותו› | 24 |
| | הלוא יהוה זו חטאו־לו / ולא־אבו בדרכיו הָלוך / ולא שמעו | |
| 4/3/3 | בתורתו | |
| 4/4 | וישפך עליו בחמה אפו / ועברתו כלהבה ‹עליו שלח› | 25 |
| 4/4 | ותלהטהו מסביב ולא ידע / ותבער־בו ולא שם על־לב | |
| 4/4 | ועתה כה אמר יהוה / בראך יעקב ויצרך ישראל | 43.1 |
| 4/4 | אל תירא כי־גאלתיך / קראתי בשמך לי אתה | |
| 4/3 | כי־תעבר במו־מים אתך אני / ובנהרות לא ישטפוך | 2 |
| 4/3 | כי־תלך במו־אש לא תכוה / ולהבה לא תבער־בך | |
| 3/3 | כי־אני יהוה אלהיך / קדוש ישראל מושיעך | 3a |

| | | |
|---|---|---|
| 3/3 | מאשר יקרת בעיני / נכבדת ואני אהבתיך | 4 |
| 3/3 | ואתן אדם תחתיך / ולאמים תחת נפשך | |
| 3/3 | נתתי כפרך מצרים / כוש וסבא תחתך | 3b |
| 3/3/2 | אל־תירא כי־אתך אני / ממזרח אביא זרעך / וממערב אקבצך | 5 |
| 3/3 | אמר לצפון תני / ולתימן אל תכלאי | 6 |
| 3/3 | הביאי בני מרחוק / ובנותי מקצה הארץ | |
| 3/3 | כל הנקרא בשמי / ולכבודי / > < / יצרתיו אף־עשיתיו | 7 |
| 3/3 | כל הגוים יקבצו / ויאספו אלהיהם  >יחדו< | 9 |
| 3/3 | מי בהם יגיד־זאת / וראשנות ישמיעֻנו | |
| 3/3 | יתנו עדיהם ויצדקו / וישמעו ויאמרו אמת | |
| 3/3/2 | מי יצר אל / ופסל  >ומסכה<  נסך / לבלתי הועיל | 44.10 |
| 3/3/3 | > <  / עץ לא־ירקב יבחר / חרש חכם יבקש־לו / להכין פסל לא־ימוט | 40.20 |
| 3/3/3 | הפסל נסך חרש / וצרף בזהב ירקענו / ורתוקות כסף יצרף | 19 |
| 3/3 | איש את־דעהו יעזר / ולאחיו יאמר חזק | 41.6 |
| 3/3 | ויחזק חרש את־צורף / מחליק  > < / את־הולם פטיש | 7 |
| 3/3 | יאמר לדבק טוב־הוא / ויחזקהו במסמרים לא־ימוט | |
| 4/3 | יצרי פסל כלם תהו / וחמודיהם בל יועילו | 44.9 |
| 4/3 | בל יראו ובל ידעו / ועדיהם המה  >עשיהם< | |
| 3/3 | הן־כל חברָיו יבשו / וחרשים המה מאדמים | 11 |
| 3/3 | יתקבצו כלם יעמדו / יפחדו יבשו יחד | |
| 3/3/3 | חרש ברזל יעצב / > <  / במפֶה ובמקבות יצרהו / ויפעלהוּ בזרוע כחו | 12 |
| 3/3 | גם־רעב ואין־כח  >לו< / לא־שתה מים וייעף | |
| 4/4 | חרש עצים נטה קו / > <  / בשרד > <  / במקצעות ובמחוגה יתארהו | 13 |
| 4/4 | ויעשהו  >בחרט<  כתבנית איש / כתאר אדם לשבת בית | |
| 3/3 | יכרת לו ארז / ויקח תדהר ואלון | 14 |
| 4/4 | וימצא לו עץ מיער / נטע אל ונשם יגדל | |
| 3/3/3 | והיה לאדם לבער / ויקדח  >אש<  וַנחם / אוּ־ישיק ואפה לחם | 15 |
| 3/3 | אף־יפעל אל / וישתחו / יעשה פסל ויסגד־לו | |
| 3/3/3 | חציו שרף במראש / על־גחליו בשר > <  / יצלה > <  / ויאכל > <  / צלי וישבע | 16 |
| 3/3 | אף־יחם ויאמר האח / חמותי ראיתי אור | |
| 3/3 | ושאריתו  > <  / יעשה לפסל / ויסגוד לו וישתחו | 17 |
| 3/3 | ויתפלל אליו ויאמר / הצילני כי־אלי אתה | |
| 3/3/3 | לא יֵדעו ולא־יבינו / כי־טחו מראות עיניהם / מהשכיל לבתם  >כבדו< | 18 |

| | | |
|---|---|---|
| 3/3 | ולא ישיב אל־לבו / ולא־דעת־לו ולא־תבונה לאמר | 19a |
| 3/3/3 | חציו שרפתי במו־אש / ואפיתי על־גחליו לחם / אצלה בשר ואכל | |
| 3/3/3 | ויתרו לתועבה אעשה / לבול עץ אסגוד / >אשתחוה ואליו אתפלל< | 19b+20aα |
| 3/3/3 | לב הותל הטהו / ולא יציל את־נפשו / ולא־יאמר הלוא־שקר בימיני | 20aβb |
| 4/4 | נסגו אחור >< / הבטחים בפסל / האמרים למסכה אתה אלהינו | 42.17 |
| 3/3 | זכר אלה יעקב / וישראל כי־עבדי אתה | 44.21 |
| 3/3 | יצרתיך עבד לי / אתה >< / לא תנשני | |
| 3/3 | כה אמר יהוה / גאלך ויצרך בבטן | 24 |
| 3/3/3 | אנכי־יהוה עשה כל / נטה שמים לבדי / רקע הארץ ואין־אתי | |
| 3/3 | מפר אתות בדים / ומְסמיהֹם יהולל | 25 |
| 3/3 | משיב חכמים אחור / ודעתֹם יסכל | |
| 3/3 | מקים דבר עבדו / ועצת מלאכיו ישלים | 26a |
| 3/3 | אתם עדי נאם־יהוה / ועבדי אשר בחרתי | 43.10 |
| 3/3 | למען־תדעו ותאמינו לי / ותבינו כי־אני הוא | |
| 3/3 | לפני לא־נוצר אל/ /ואחרי לא יהיה | |
| 3/3 | אנכי אנכי יהוה / ואין מבלעדי מושיע | 11 |
| 4/4/4 | אנכי הגדתי והשמעתי והושעתי / ואין בכם >אל< זר / ואתם עדי >< ואני אל | 12 |
| 3/3/3 | גם־מיום אני הוא / ואין מידי מציל / אפעל ומי ישיבנה | 13 |
| 3/3 | אני יהוה קדושכם / בורא ישראל מלככם | 15 |
| 3/3 | מי בכם יאזין־זאת / יקשיב וישמע לאחור | 42.23 |
| 3/3/3 | כה אמר יהוה / הנתן בים דרך / ובמים עזים נתיבה | 43.16 |
| 3/3 | המוציא רכב וסוס / חיל ועזוז יחדו | 17 |
| 3/3 | ישכבו בל יקומו / דעכו כפשתה כבו | |
| 3/3 | אל תזכרו ראשנות / וקדמניות אל תתבננו | 18 |
| 3/3 | הנני עשה חדשה / עתה תצמח אף־תדעוה | 19 |
| 3/3 | >< אשים במדבר דרך / בישימון נתיבות >אתן< | |
| 3/3 | תכבדני חית השדה / תנים ובנות יענה | 20 |
| 3/3 | כי־אתן במדבר מים / נהרות בישימון >אשים< | |
| 3/3/2 | להשקות עמי בחירי / עם־זו יצרתי לי / תהלתי יספרו | 20bβ+21 |
| 4/3 | ולא אותי קראת יעקב / כי־יגעת בי ישראל | 22 |
| 4/3 | לא הבאת לי >< / עלתיך / ובזבחיך לא כבדתני | 23 |
| 4/3 | לא העבדתיך במנחה / ולא הוגעתיך בלבונה | |
| 4/3 | לא קנית לי >< / קנה / וחלב זבחיך לא־הרויתני | 24 |
| 4/3 | אך העבדתני בחטאותיך / הוגעתני בעונתיך | |

| | | |
|---|---|---|
| 3/3 | הזכירני נשפטה יחד / ספר אתה למען־תצדק | 26 |
| 3/3 | אביך הראשון חטא / ומליכך פשעו בי | 27 |
| 3/3/2 | ואחלל שרי הקדש / ואתן לחרפה יעקב / וישראל לגדופים | 28 |
| 3/3/3 | כה אמר יהוה / מלך ישראל וגאלו / יהוה צבאות ⟨שמו⟩ | 44.6 |
| 3/3 | אני ראשון ואני־אחרון / ומבלעדי אין אלהים | |
| 3/3 | ומי כמוני יקרא / ויגידה ויערכה למו | 7 |
| 3/3 | משמיע מעולם אתיות / ואשר תבאנה יניד ⟨ ⟩ | |
| 3/3/3 | אל תפחדו ואל־תיראו / הלא מאז השמעתי / והגדתי ואתם עדי | 8 |
| 3/3 | היש אלוה מבלעדי / ואין עוד זולתי | |
| 3/3/3 | אנכי אנכי הוא / מחה פשעיך למעני / וחטאתיך לא־אזכר עוד | 43.25 |
| | מחיתי כעב פשעיך / וכענן חטאתיך ⟨העברתי⟩ / שובה אלי | 44.22 |
| 3/3/3 | כי־גאלתיך | |
| 4/3 | ועתה שמע יעקב עבדי / וישראל בחרתי בו | 44.1 |
| 4/3 | כה אמר יהוה עשך / ויצרך בבטן עזרך | 2 |
| 4/3 | אל תירא עבדי יעקב / וישרון בחרתי בו | |
| 4/3 | כאשר אצק מים על־צמאה / ונזלים עַל־יבשׁה | 3 |
| 4/3 | ⟨כן⟩ אצק רוחי על־זרעך / וברכתי עַל־צאצאיך | |
| 4/3 | וצמחו בניך כחציר ⟨על־הרים⟩ / כערבים על־יבלי מים | 4 |
| 4/3 | זה יאמר ליהוה אני / וזה־יְקָרא בשם יעקב | 5 |
| 4/3 | וזה יכתב בידו ליהוה / ובשם ישראל יְכַנה | |

42.5    Thus sayeth God, Yahweh,
> He who created the heavens and stretched them out,
>> He who spread out the earth and that which cometh
>> forth from it,
> Who giveth breath to the people upon it
>> And spirit to those who walk thereon,

8    I, Yahweh, the Existent One is My name,
> And My homage to any other I will not yield
>> Nor My praise to idols.

9    The former things, behold, they have come to pass,
> And new events I foretell.
>> Before they will spring forth I shall announce them.

15    I shall make desolate mountains and hills,
> And all their herbage I shall parch;
> And I shall turn rivers into islets,
>> And pools of water I shall dry up;

16    And I shall make the blind to travel over a road they do
> not know,

By paths unfamiliar to them I shall guide them;
I shall turn darkness before them into light,
And the uneven places I shall make level.
These are the things which I shall do for them,
Nor shall I forsake them ever.

43.8    Bring forth the people that is blind;
Though they have eyes they are blind,
And they are deaf though they have ears.

42.18    Ye blind ones, gaze about in order to see,
Yea, ye deaf, listen in order to hear.

19a    Who is blind like my servant
And deaf like My messenger whom I send?

20    There is seeing of many things, but he does not observe;
There is opening wide of ears, but he hears not.

22    For he was a people despoiled and ravaged;
Ensnared in holes were they, all of them,
And in prison-houses were they hidden away.
They were for prey, with none to deliver,
For ravagement, with none to say: Stop!

24    Who gave Jacob to ravagement
And Israel to those who despoiled him?
Was it not Yahweh, He against whom they had sinned,
And in whose ways they were loath to walk,
And to whose revealed law they would not hearken?

25    So in indignation He poured out His wrath upon him,
And His anger He despatched like a cloud against him,
So that it burned all about him, but he would not give heed,
And it blazed against him, but he would not take
notice.

43.1    But now thus saith Yahweh,
Thy Creator, O Jacob, yea, thy Maker, O Israel;
Fear not, for I am about to redeem thee;
I have summoned thee, Mine art thou.

2    When thou passest through the sea, I am with thee,
And through the rivers, they shall not overflow
thee;
When thou walkest through fire, thou shalt not be burned,
And the flame shall not blaze against thee.

3a    For I, Yahweh, am thy God,
The Holy One of Israel is thy Savior.

4    Because thou wast precious in Mine eyes
Thou hast acquired dignity and I have loved thee.

So I gave up mankind in place of thee,
And peoples in thy stead.

3b    I gave Egypt as thy ransom,
Ethiopia and Sabaea in exchange for thee.

5    Fear not, for I am with thee;
From the East I will bring thine offspring,
And from the West will I reassemble thee.

6    I will say to the North: Give up!
And to the South: Hold not back!
Bring My sons from afar,
Yea, My daughters from the end of the earth,

7    Every one who calls himself by My name,
Whom I have formed, yea, have made, for My glory!

9    Let all the nations assemble,
And let their gods gather together!
Who among them might foretell this,
Or former things proclaim unto us?
Let them produce their witnesses, that they may be vindicated,
Or let them listen and say: (It is the) truth.

44.10    Who hath fashioned a god
And an idol, yea, a molten image, has poured out,
To no purpose whatsoever?

40.20    A tree which will not decay he selects,
An expert artisan he seeks for himself,
In order to fashion an image which can not move itself.

19    The artisan pours out the idol;
The smith plates it with gold
And joints of silver he moulds.

41.6    Each one helps the other,
And to his comrade he says: Be strong!

7    The artisan supports the smith,
The polisher him who wields the hammer.
He says of a joint: It is good.
And he fastens it with nails so that it may not slip.

44.9    The fashioners of idols are vanity, all of them,
And their precious objects are to no purpose.
They see not, neither do they comprehend;
And their witnesses are their makers themselves.

11    Behold all its fellow-associates are put to shame
And its artisans are made to blush.

Let all of them assemble; let them stand up,
Let them become worried, be put to shame together.

12    The worker in iron fashions an idol;
With bellows and with hammers he shapes it,
And he brings it to completion with his own strong arm;
Also he becomes thirsty, so that he has no strength;
He drinks no water, so that he becomes faint.

13    The worker in wood spreads a tape;
With chalk, with scrapers and with compass he shapes it,
And with graving-tool he makes it like the form of a man,
Like a human being in shape, in order to dwell in a sanctuary.

14    He hews for himself a cedar,
Or he takes a fir or an oak tree,
Or he finds for himself a tree in the forest,
Which a god has planted and the rain made grow.

15    And it serves the man for burning;
So he kindles a fire and warms himself,
Or he sets it ablaze and bakes bread.
In addition he makes (from it) a god and renders homage;
He makes an idol and prostrates himself to it.

16    Half of it he has burned as a fire,
Upon the coals of which he roasts flesh;
He eats roasted meat and becomes satiated.
Also he warms himself and says: Ah!
I have become warm, I see a light!

17    While of what remains of it he makes an idol,
And prostrates himself to it and renders homage;
And he prays unto it and says;
Deliver me, for my god art thou!

18    They do not perceive, neither do they understand,
For too glazed over are their eyes to see,
Too heavy are their hearts to comprehend;

19a    So that he does not take to heart,
Nor has he perception or understanding that he should say:
Half of it I burned as fire,
And upon its coals I baked bread;
I am roasting meat and am about to eat,

19b+20aα    While the remainder of it I am making into an abomination;

To a clod of wood I bow down;
I prostrate myself and to it I pray.

20aβb    A heart gone astray has misled him,
So that he can not rescue himself;
Nor yet would he say: Is not something false in
my right hand?

42.17    They are turned around, those who put their trust in an
idol,
Who say unto a molten image: Thou art our god.

44.21    Remember all this, O Jacob,
Yea, Israel, for My servant art thou.
I have fashioned thee as a servant unto Me;
Thou must never reject Me.

24    Thus sayeth Yahweh,
Thy Redeemer, yea, thy Fashioner in the womb:
I, Yahweh, am the Maker of everything,
Who stretched out the heavens all alone,
Who spread out the earth with no one with Me,

25    Who circumvents the portents of the seers,
And their magical acts brings to naught,
Who turns sages aback,
And their technique changes to folly;

26a    Who confirms the word of His servant,
And the counsel of His messengers He fulfills.

43.10    Ye are My witnesses, sayeth Yahweh,
Yea, My servant, whom I have chosen,
To the end that ye may understand and have faith in
Me,
And may comprehend that I am the Existent One;
Before Me no god was fashioned,
And after Me none will (ever) be.

11    I, I am God,
And besides Me there is no savior.

12    I foretell and I proclaim, and I work salvation;
And among you there is no strange god;
So ye are My witnesses, that I am God.

13    Moreover, from today on I am the Existent One,
And there is none who can wrest from My hands;
I act, and who can reverse it,

15    I, Yahweh, your particular possession,
The Creator of Israel, your King?

42.23    Who among you will hearken unto this,
Will give ear and hear of future events?

43.16 Thus sayeth Yahweh,
  He who sets a road through the sea,
    Yea, through the mighty waters a pathway,
17 Who bringeth forth chariot and horse,
    Army and troop all together;
  They lie prostrate, they do not rise;
    They are extinguished, like a wick they are quenched.
18 Recall not earlier events,
    And over former happenings do not ponder.
19 Behold, I am about to do a new thing;
    Now will it become real; moreover, ye shall recognize it.
  I shall set a road through the desert,
    Through the wilderness will I fix paths.
20 The beasts of the field shall pay homage to Me
  The jackals and the ostriches;
  For I shall put water in the desert,
    Streams will I set in the wilderness,
20bβ–21 In order to provide drink for My people, My chosen one,
  This people which I have fashioned for Myself,
    That they may recite My praise.
22 But upon Me thou didst not call, O Jacob,
    Verily thou didst grow weary of me, O Israel.
23 Unto Me thou broughtest not thy burnt-offerings,
    And with thy sacrifices thou didst not do homage
      unto Me.
  I did not demand that thou worship Me with grain-offering;
    Neither did I burden thee with incense-offering.
24 Thou didst not spend thy money for Me for cane,
    And with the fat of thy sacrifices thou didst not
      satiate Me.
  Instead thou didst belabor Me with thy sins,
    With thine iniquities thou didst weary Me exceedingly.
26 Recall to My memory; let us enter into judgment together;
    Speak up, thou, so that thou mayest find vindication.
27 Thy very first ancestor sinned,
    And thy kings transgressed against Me.
28 So I profaned the holy princes,
    And I gave Jacob over to reproach
      And Israel to insult.
44.6 Thus sayeth Yahweh,

Israel's King and its Redeemer,
>   Whose name is Yahweh of Hosts;
I am the first and I am the last,
>   And besides Me there is no god.
7   And who like Me makes proclamation
>   And foretells something and carries it through for
>   himself;
Who proclaims long in advance things to come,
>   And what will happen foretells?
8   Fear not and be not afraid!
>   Have I not proclaimed from earliest times
>   And foretold; and ye are My witnesses?
Is there a god besides Me,
>   Or is there any other than I?

43.25   I, I, the Existent One,
>   Blot out thy transgressions for Mine own sake,
>   And thy sins I remember no more.

44.22   I have blotted out thy transgressions like a mist,
>   And like a cloud I have caused thy sins to pass away;
>   Turn again unto Me, for I have redeemed thee.

44.1   So now hearken, O Jacob, My servant,
>   Yea, Israel, whom I have chosen.
2   Thus sayeth Yahweh, thy Maker,
>   Yea, He who fashioned thee in the womb, thy Helper:
Fear not, My servant, Jacob,
>   Yea, Yeshurun, whom I have chosen.
3   Even as I pour water upon the thirsty soil,
>   Yea, streams of water upon the dry ground,
So will I pour My spirit upon thine offspring
>   And My blessing upon thy posterity.
4   So that thy sons shall flourish as grass upon the mountains,
>   As poplars beside the water-brooks.
5   One shall say: I belong to Yahweh;
>   And one shall call himself by the name of Jacob,
And one shall write with his own hand: Yahweh's (posses-
>   sion),
>   And by the name of Israel shall he entitle himself.

The metrical form of this address is of particular interest. Appreciation of this fact is of immediate service in the task of textual reconstruction and rearrangement. The address consists of one hundred and ten metrical units, of which fifty-four are 3/3's, twenty-two are 4/3's, eight are 4/4's, nineteen are 3/3/3's, four are 3/3/2's, two are 4/3/3's, and one is a 4/4/4. This is an unusually large proportion of tristichs to distichs. The various meters are mingled quite indiscriminately, as might well be expected in a hortatory piece. Yet it is noteworthy how frequently a single tristich is followed by one, two or even three closely related distichs in the corresponding meter, 3/3's following a 3/3/3 or one 3/3/2 (43.5–7), and 4/3's following a 4/3/3 (42.22, 24a), with in each instance the tristich making a specific affirmation and the distichs amplifying it, usually with positive, but occasionally (44.15, 16) with contrasted, thoughts or statements. This technique is exceedingly effective. Also it should be noted that the address ends in a strophe consisting of eight 4/3's, a metrical form which imparts dignity and climactic effect to the conclusion of the address.

42.5. הָאֵל, as a title, "the God," i. e. the one, universal God; cf. Ps. 85.9 and frequently in Deutero-Isaiah. For ונוטיהם read, as a sing., ונוטהם; cf. Hos. 7.6. וצאצאיה designates all that springs forth from the earth, but particularly animals and men; it is in parallelism with להלכים בה of the next distich. Cheyne, Duhm and Marti would supply יוציא after וצאצאיה; but this would make this v. a 3/3/4, a rare and here an impossible meter. Vv. 5 and 8 together state graphically and effectively the primary theme of this address, the absolute oneness and universality of Yahweh as the sole world-God and the utter unreality and futility of other, supposed gods and of the idols by which they are represented.

8. For הוא as a name or title of Yahweh (so already Dillmann) coined by and characteristic of Deutero-Isaiah cf. 48.12b and the note to this v. The fact that DSIa reads ושמי indicates (a) that it, and no doubt the general public also, clearly understood הוא as a name or title of Yahweh, and also (b) that the scribe had no appreciation of the metrical character of this type of Hebrew literature; for, linking ושמי to what follows, as the conjunction would necessitate, would have made of this a 3/4/3 tristich, which is of course an unheard of meter. To achieve the 3/3/3 meter it is necessary to read אני־יהוה, as is regularly the procedure with Deutero-Isaiah, and also לא־אתן each as one beat, but, on the other hand, to read ותהלתי, a four-syllabled noun with prefix and suffix, as two beats.

9. The unusual position of הנה, as the second word in the stichos, makes it emphatic and necessitates its receiving a full beat. In contrast to הראשנות, "the former things," which is naturally determined and so requires the article, וחדשות, with *MT* and contrary to DSIa, does not need the article since it is as yet indeterminate, "new things." These "new events" can not be Cyrus' capture of Babylon, as Dillmann and Marti interpret it, for that had already taken place. Rather these "new things" can be only Yahweh's clearly contemplated deliverance of Israel from exile and its restoration to its ancestral land, as the address, in the form in which we have reconstructed it, clearly predicts. Correspondingly הראשנות can be only Yahweh's sending of Israel into exile in Babylonia some fifty years earlier, even as predicted by Yahweh through the mouths of earlier prophets. The v. implies clearly that Yahweh informs Israel of coming events before they transpire just because Israel is His servant, His agent, who, in order to function effectively in that role, must know in advance what Yahweh, as the divine source of all history, purposes to do and just when to expect it. Accordingly in this address Yahweh announces, or at least intimates, to Israel His purpose to deliver it from exile in Babylonia and to bring it safely through the desert back to the land of its fathers.

15. This v. is manifestly a 3/3 double-distich; accordingly in the second stichos of the first distich read וכל and give the word a full beat, and in the parallel position in the second distich for ואגמים read ואגמי מים (cf. 14.23). The expression, אחריב הרים here brings to mind the mountain, Horeb, "the Bare Mountain," devoid of vegetation; just this is the implication here, as the second stichos of this distich makes

clear. It is tempting to emend the second אוביש to אָשִׁית, a word quite similar in
form and synonymous in meaning. However, as Torrey brings to our attention, in
the two stichoi of the very next distich לא ידעו occurs twice in much closer juxtaposition than אוביש in this distich; accordingly it is probably wise not to emend the
word. Oort and Duhm would emend לאיים to לציות on the basis of Ps. 105.41 and
also on the basis of the contention that in Biblical Hebrew אי never connotes a
small islet in a river. However, the picture of a river drying up so much that patches
of earth, which may well be termed איים, "islets," appear, is so graphic that it seems
best to retain *MT* here. However, the vocalization, לָאִיִּים, is certainly preferable
to that of *MT*. The picture which this v. inaugurates is of course that of Israel's
return, under Yahweh's protection, from Babylon through the desert, with all its
hardships and dangers, to its ancestral land.

16. This v. is manifestly a triple-distich, but obviously in considerable textual
disorder. The first distich is a 4/3, while the second distich seems to be of the same
meter, though with a word lost at the end of the line. This word can be only אתן,
the word regularly used by Deutero-Isaiah in parallelism with אשים of the first
stichos of the distich. The supplying of this word not only restores the meter and
parallelism of the distich, but also recovers an effective chiasm of the two stichoi.
Likewise it seems best, with Marti, to regard the 'מ of מחשך, "a dark place," as a
dittograph of the 'מ of אשים, immediately preceding, and for it to read חשך,
"darkness," the natural antithesis to אור, "light." The third distich of the v. presents
many difficulties. In the first place, the two verbs in the perf., following the sequence
of impfs. in the first two distichs, are very disturbing. Unquestionably, with both *G*
and Targ., we should read both of these verbs as impfs. also. Furthermore, following
a hint from *V*, for the altogether impossible עשיתם, we should read אעשה להם; this
reading restores the expected, but missing, fourth beat of the first stichos of the
distich. In the second stichos, in addition to emending עזבתים to אעזבם, a word practically essential to the completion of the thought as well as to the meter is obviously
missing; accordingly supply לעד' (cf. Morgenstern, "The Loss of Words, etc."
*HUCA* XXV [1954], 56 f.). The "blind ones" are obviously the Jewish exiles in
Babylon. The statement of the first distich, that Yahweh would cause them to go,
impliedly upon their return journey to their ancestral land, by a road and by paths
"which they do not know," implies further that this return will not be by the same
route by which Nebuchadnezzar had brought them to Babylon, undoubtedly the
northern route, but that their return would be by the southern route, identical with
or paralleling that by which, but a few years earlier, Nabunaid, the last Babylonian
monarch, and his retinue travelled regularly between Babylon and Teima, the royal
residence in the western desert. It was altogether natural for Deutero-Isaiah, living
when he did, and for other prophetic writers after him to envisage the return of
exiled Israel to its ancestral land by this route (cf. Isa. 35; 40.3 f. and *passim*).

43.8. The reference to "the blind ones" is continued in vv. 18–20. But it is the
theme also of 43.8, a v. which, where it stands in *MT*, manifestly disturbs the
context and is out of place. On the other hand, 43.8 fits in perfectly here, between
vv. 16 and 18–20, while equally plainly v. 17 disturbs the context here and must be
transposed to a more suitable position; accordingly replace 42.17 by 43.8. This v.
seems to be a 3/3/3 tristich, but the second stichos plainly requires an additional
beat; accordingly, again with *G* and Targ., and as the context requires, supply
ועורים to follow יש; this not only restores the meter and completes the thought, but
it also establishes a perfect parallelism between the second and third stichoi of the
tristich. Also, with Marti, for הוציא read the impv., הוֹצֵא.

42.18. There can be no question that, following Haupt and other scholars, in their present arrangement in *MT* the two stichoi reverse the expected thought sequence of first seeing and then hearing, and that they should be inverted. This conclusion is confirmed by the fact that the v. is manifestly a 3/3, but that the present first stichos in *MT* manifestly lacks a beat; when transposed to function as the second stichos in the distich, this missing word would come at the very end of the line, the place where, as we have learned, in Biblical poetry words have been most readily and frequently lost. The parallelism of the two stichoi tells us immediately that the missing word must have paralleled לראות and must have continued the thought of שמעו, just as לראות continues the thought of הביטו; accordingly supply להקשיב as the missing word. Naturally, while supplying this word, we must read the impv., שְׁמָעוּ.

19. In v. 19b the first עור should certainly be changed to חרש. Likewise כמשלם presents almost insurmountable difficulties. It is in all likelihood a corruption of an original כמשלחי. But thus reconstructed, this second distich merely repeats in inverse order, and that too a bit awkwardly, the thought already set forth effectively in the first distich. It is undoubtedly the result of rather bungling textual expansion, and so should be omitted as a gloss. However, it does establish quite conclusively that for כי־אם־עבדי we should read כעבדי, and thus establish a perfect parallelism between the two stichoi of the first distich.

20. As the final 'ת of ראית indicates, the word should be read רָאוֹת, as an inf. const., used here as a verbal noun. Correspondingly we should vocalize פָּקוֹחַ, also as an inf. const. Also the here altogether meaningless 2nd sing. masc., תשמר, should be emended to the 3rd sing. masc., ישמר, to correspond to its parallel word in the second stichos, ישמע. The subj. of the two verbs is of course the servant and messenger of v. 19a. A glance at the reconstructed text shows that vv. 18, 19a and 20 together constitute a very effective 3/3 triple-distich, with the single theme, the blindness and deafness of the servant. Appreciation of this fact confirms our omission of v. 19b as a disturbing gloss.

21. Just what this v. actually means, and particularly in this setting, it is impossible to determine. Moreover, whatever its meaning might be, it certainly disturbs the continuity of the thought here and should be omitted as a gloss. It may be noted also that this is the only passage in the entire Bible where חפץ is followed by למען and where also אדר is used in the *hif'il*. This sentence may well be a doxological refrain inserted at just this point at the close of the reading of this passage from the prophets in the Synagogue liturgy.

22. This v. together with vv. 24–25 continues the thought of the triple-distich immediately preceding and defines wherein the blindness and deafness of the servant, Israel, consisted, viz. in failing, or even refusing, to see and realize who was the true author of Israel's conquest by Nebuchadnezzar and its present exile, that, by implication, it was not at all the, falsely presumed, more powerful Babylonian gods, who, as the address will subsequently establish, were not gods at all, but Yahweh alone, their own ancestral god and the sole, universal God, against whom they had sinned rebelliously and in whose way they had refused to walk. The v., stating historical facts of such grave import, is cast in the dignified 4/3 measure, a 4/3/3 tristich plus a 4/3 distich. For הָפֵּת, which is certainly meaningless here, we should undoubtedly read, in close parallelism with החבאו, חִפְּחוּ. Also the altogether meaningless and, as all the vss. indicate, misleading בַּחוּרִים, we should revocalize בְּחוֹרִים. Certainly also for משסה we should read, even as the recurrence of the word in v. 24

indicates, למשסה. Inasmuch as the preceding word ends in a ל', the ל' here was undoubtedly lost through haplography.

23. This v. seriously disturbs the thought-unity of this passage and has been displaced from its original position, probably between 43.15 and 16. We shall consider it in that position.

24. This v. is a 4/3, 4/3/3, and so is obviously the perfect, antithetical counterpart of v. 22, and with it constitutes a closely integrated thought-unit. Certainly in the second stichos of the initial distich a beat is lacking. Plainly once again a word has been lost at the end of a line; in this instance the missing word could have been only the object of לבוזים; accordingly, with G, supply אותו. For חטאנו read, with G, and in agreement with the two 3rd plu. verbs which follow, חטאו. אבה is followed regularly by the inf. const., usually, though not invariably, introduced by ל'; accordingly here read הָלוֹךְ.

25. This v. abounds in difficulties, particularly in its first half. The v. is manifestly a double-distich, and the second distich is a 4/4. The first stichos of the first distich likewise has, or seems to have, four beats; therefore it is to be expected that the first distich is likewise a 4/4, and that accordingly its second stichos should also have four beats. But in MT only two words constitute the second stichos, and by themselves express no complete or translatable thought. Obviously something has been lost from this second stichos, in the extent of at least two words. It should be noted also that the second distich speaks of something burning and flaming, but the distich does not say what it was. But since both verbs are 3rd fem. sing. it follows that a fem. sing. noun, the subj. of the two verbs, must have stood in the second stichos of the first distich. It could scarcely have been מלחמה, for a word connoting "warfare" could hardly have served as the subj. of the two verbs in the second distich. Accordingly Klostermann, followed by Cheyne and Torrey, have emended ועזו מלחמה to כלהבה ועזו. Granting that מלחמה might very well have been a corruption of כלהבה, nonetheless ועזו, a masc. noun, can certainly not be the subj. of the two 3rd fem. sing. verbs which follow. Accordingly, in considerable measure a conjecture, we propose, as the probable, original reading of this second stichos of the first distich, ועברתו כלהבה עליו שלח; for שלח עברה cf. Ps. 78.49. In the first stichos of the first distich חמה אפו is syntactically impossible; accordingly, with Isa. 66.15, read בחמה אפו. In the second stichos of the second distich, following a suggestion of G and to agree with the tense of ידע and with the general thought of the passage, for ישים read שם.

43.1. This v. is also quite obviously a 4/4. It inaugurates Yahweh's comforting reassurance to Israel that its discipline for its faithlessness is ended and that the moment of its deliverance from exile is nigh.

2. In order to provide an effective parallelism with ובנהרות and also with במראש in the corresponding position in the second distich, for במים read, with S, במורים; the prophet employs במו twice again in this address, in 44.16, 19.

3-4. Textually these two vv. are in perfect condition, but there seems to have been some disarrangement within them. V. 4 continues directly the thought of v. 3a, while v. 3b, in turn, fits perfectly after v. 4b. In fact vv. 3a and 4a together constitute one double-distich, while correspondingly vv. 4b and 3b constitute a second double-distich. Each double-distich voices a closely unified thought, with effective parallelism between its constituent distichs. Moreover, the second double-distich illustrates graphically the thought of the first by enumerating some of the peoples whom Yahweh gave up in order to take Israel as His own, chosen people, here specifically the peoples dwelling at the very ends of the then known world.

In v. 4b, just as in 45.12, אדם has the connotation, "mankind," and so is synonymous with לאמים, "peoples." The implication of this passage seems to be that from Creation on Yahweh, as the sole Creator of the entire universe, might well have functioned as the one and only universal world-God, recognized and worshiped as such by all peoples, and so might have stood in a single, uniform relation to all nations from the beginning of existence. However, from the very first He cherished an especial affection for Israel, and so took it as His particular people and centered His love and care upon it. But to do this He had to renounce His relations with and claims upon the other peoples and the rest of mankind as a whole. But the further thought is implicit here, that, even while retaining Israel in a special relationship to Himself, Yahweh is about to reassert His divine rule over the entire world and over all peoples within it. To do this He must first establish convincingly that the so-called gods of the other nations are impotent unrealities, nothings at all. And this only a few short sentences later He proceeds to do in highly effective manner. After this is accomplished there will follow the תשועה, the "salvation" of all the other nations and peoples, whom Yahweh had at first discarded, and their restoration to His just dominion and loving care, and with this true universalism. In this program, Israel, as the people beloved of Yahweh and knowing Him from of old, will have an especial role and will still be His chosen people, the agent of His universal purpose. Such is the theme of this entire address, of which in a way 43.3a+4+3b, supplemented by vv. 5–7 are the key.

5–6. The text of these two vv. is in perfect order and together they voice a closely unified thought. They picture Yahweh's reuniting all Israel, at present scattered in all directions. The exiles from the East are of course the group in Babylonia. Those from the West would then be those, such as Jeremiah, who, at the time of the fall of Jerusalem to the Babylonians in 586 B. C., had sought refuge in Egypt. Those from the South would be those who at the same time had fled into Arabia, certainly as far down the Red Sea coast as Medinah and Mecca, and perhaps even as far as Sheba. Those from the North would be the remnant of the exiles of the ten northern tribes, for the most part resident since 721 B. C. in Northern Mesopotamia. That in the early post-exilic period the hope of the restoration of these tribes and of the reunion thereby of Israel with Judah was ardently cherished is amply attested in the Biblical literature of that period (cf. Rosenau, "Ezek. 37.15–28: What Happened to the Ten Tribes," *HUCA Jubilee Volume* [1925], 79–88).

7. As it stands in *MT* this v. would have to be read as a 3/2/2 tristich, a scantily attested meter in Biblical Hebrew poetry. However, by the omission of one of the three synonymous verbs in the second stichos, preferably בראתיו, the v. becomes a normal 3/3 distich and likewise reads more smoothly and effectively than in its present form. In the first stichos in order to achieve the 3-beat measure כל must be given a full beat and so be regarded as emphatic. Also הנקרא must be interpreted as a reflexive, "Every one who calls himself, etc."

9. V. 9 is obviously a 3/3 triple-distich. But the first distich plainly has one word too many in the first stichos and one too few in the second stichos. This difficulty, however, is easily resolved by transposing יחדו from the first to the end of the second stichos. לאמים is indeed a natural and effective parallel to הגוים; but something is plainly out of order in the v.; for the antecedent of the pronominal suffix of בהם in the second distich and of עדיהם in the third distich can certainly not be the nations or peoples of the first distich, but can be only their gods. Obviously also the answer to the question in the second distich, "Who among them might foretell this?", can not be the nations, but must be their gods. Furthermore, just as

later in this address the prophet has Yahweh proclaim that Israel is His witness, who testifies to His reality and divinity, so here those who are challenged to produce their witnesses can be, not the nations at all, but only their gods. Accordingly for לאטים read אלהיהם, certainly a relatively simple and modest emendation. In the first distich for נקבצו read, with Torrey, as the context requires and in agreement with יָקבצו, ויאספו. In the second distich, with Cheyne, vocalize as a sing. יַשׁמִיעֵנוּ, to agree with יניד. Both verbs, it should be noted, are impfs., and so describe an action in either the present or the immediate future. In the first stichos of this second distich זאת, a monosyllabic word, must be linked with its governing verb, יניד, and the two words read as a single beat. Thus closely linked to the verb, זאת has the force of a pronominal suffix. Its antecedent must be some momentous event very soon to happen. This can be only, as the prophet, speaking in the name of Yahweh, develops in detail later in the address, Israel's deliverance from exile in Babylonia and its restoration to its ancestral land. Obviously the prophet is here once again resorting to his favorite, hortatory device, a supposititious court trial between the rival contestants, Yahweh and the foreign gods, to determine who is the one, true, universal God. And the test is once again, who of the gods, or of the supposed gods, can foretell future events. And of course, just as in every court trial, each side must have its witnesses to substantiate its case. The ו of both וראשנות and וישמעו connotes contrast, "or," rather than the customary "and." For צדק in the qal, "to show oneself to be in the right (through court-of-law processes)" cf. 43.26; 45.25, Ps. 143.2; Job 40.8, and passim.

At this point in the address 44.10, would be fittingly followed by 40.20, 19; 41.6–7; 44.9, 11 ff. These verses will be commented on in this order.

44.10. ופסל is here, just as again in 40.19, the object of נסך; therefore the two words can not be separated and assigned to different stichoi. Accordingly the v. at first glance seems to be a 3/2/2, certainly, as has already been stated, an awkward, uneuphonious meter and not convincingly attested. In all likelihood a word has been lost in the second stichos; and inasmuch as the natural object of נסך is מסכה, and since also the combined term, ומסכה פסל, occurs frequently as the designation of a single idol (cf. Deut. 27.15; Jud. 17.3, 4), particularly when just as, as seems to be the case here, the idol is made of wood overlaid with metal plating, we may very well supply ומסכה here following פסל. The v. thus becomes a 3/3/2 tristich, quite a common meter. Certainly 40.19–20 do not fit in where they stand now in MT, for quite plainly they interrupt the continuity of thought between vv. 18 and 21, while they themselves have little or no connection with the thought of the address in 40.9–21. On the other hand, they fit in perfectly, both as to thought and metrical form, here, where we have inserted them in this address. However, the order of the two vv. should be inverted, since v. 19 clearly continues the thought effectively begun in v. 20, viz. the manner of making the idol. The two introductory words of 40.20, המסכן תרומה, are disturbing in many ways. They are absolutely untranslatable and likewise can not by any possible means be fitted into the meter. Both G and S omit the two words; and that must be our procedure likewise. With these two words omitted, the text acquires perfect order and the v. becomes a normal 3/3/3 tristich. The v. describes quite graphically the first step in the making of this idol, viz. the selection of a suitable tree to form its body or base. The subj. of יבחר and of יבקש is of course the man who is having the idol made for his use. ימוט must of course be interpreted as reflexive in meaning.

40.19. Vocalize וּרָתוּקות; cf. I Kings 6.21; Ezek. 7.23; coming from the stem, רתק, "to bind," the word can mean only "links, joints." The second צורף should of course be emended to יצרף, to accord with ירקענו. The subj. of both verbs is צורף in the second stichos of the tristich. The v. clearly implies that at least two skilled artisans participate in the fashioning of the idol, the wood-worker, the חרש (cf. v. 13), and the metal-worker, the צורף. The realization of this fact paves the way to the linking of 41.6–7 with 40.19–20, a procedure proposed already by Duhm and Cheyne.

41.6–7. These two vv., describing a single procedure, and all manifestly in the same meter, actually constitute a 3/3 triple-distich. In v. 6 for יעזרו read the sing., יעזר, to agree with יאמר. The subj. of both verbs is of course איש. In the second stichos of the first distich of v. 7 there is plainly one word too many for the meter; likewise there is confusion in the thought. Certainly not פעם but פטיש must be the object of הולם; apparently פטיש was displaced from its original to its present position in the distich, and then the corruption, פעם, crept into its place. פעם is traditionally translated "anvil" (so V, S, Rashi and Kimchi), but inasmuch as the word would have this connotation in only this one place in the entire Bible, this interpretation may well be rejected. The v. seems to imply that not merely two, but rather four different artisans participate in the fabrication of this particular idol. It is noteworthy that in the first distich of v. 7 את is used with two nouns which seem undetermined, since neither has the article. But one stylistic characteristic of this address is that it dispenses with the use of the article constantly, where in ordinary prose the article would be indispensable, and yet the noun is determined, quite as if the article were there (in addition to these two vv. cf. 44.12–13).

44.9. This v. is plainly a double-distich. The first distich is a 4/3, and we would expect the second distich to be a 4/3 likewise; but it is anything but this; in fact in its present form it has no recognizable meter whatever. The vss. too seem to have had trouble with this half-verse, and to have in consequence paraphrased the entire v. rather than translating it literally. It should be noted that both G and S link the last two words of this v. with v. 10, quite as if they were not integral in v. 9. Moreover in v. 11, which in our rearrangement of the text follows immediately upon v. 9, יבשו occurs in its proper place; accordingly we may regard the word here at the end of v. 9 as a dittograph, and we may also see in this fact further evidence that in the original text v. 11 did indeed follow immediately upon v. 9, just as we have rearranged them. Accordingly these last two words of v. 9 may be elided as not a part of the original text. But the elision of these two words by no means solves all the difficulties of this second distich. The presence of המה after ועדיהם leads us to expect a nominal sentence here; but if so, the predicate, stating just who the witnesses to the vanity and impotence of these idols may be, is missing altogether. Furthermore, those who neither see nor know aught are certainly not these idol-makers, as the text in its present form seems to imply, but are rather the idols themselves. Unquestionably the clause, בל־יראו ובל־ידעו, should be transferred to follow immediately after בל־יועילו; moreover, since the negative quality of these idols is strongly stressed here, each of these בל's is emphatic and so must receive a full beat. Accordingly this transferred clause consists of four emphatic words, and in its new position constitutes the four-beat first stichos of the second distich for which we are seeking. The חמודים of the idol-makers are of course the idols themselves, the products of their hands. And plainly this word is the antecedent of the pronominal suffix of ועדיהם. Who then are the witnesses of the impotence and vanity of the gods whom these idols represent, and whom these gods are challenged in v. 9 to produce? The answer to this question will provide the missing predicate of the nominal sentence to which we have referred. It can be only one possible word.

Both *G* and *S* mention "their makers" in their versions of the v.; accordingly supply עשיהם to complete the nominal sentence. The very artisans who, with such pride, fashioned the idols of these gods are the very ones who must testify of them that they can neither see nor know aught, that they are utterly impotent and worthless. And this reconstruction furnishes for us the second 3-beat stichos of this 4/3 distich. As thus reconstructed the thought of the double-distich is compelling indeed, and is certainly essential to the effective presentation of the theme of this address.

11. For חבריו read חֲבֵרָיו (cf. Hos. 4.17). The antecedent of the suffix must be פסל in v. 9. The word must connote here "its associates," those who are linked to it in any way, its priests and its worshipers. The context requires that for וחרשים we read וחרשיו, with the suffix, and also that for the completely meaningless מאדם we read מאדמים, "are made to blush."

12. This v. too abounds in difficulties. For מעצד read, with Torrey, יעצב; for עצב, "to shape or make with the hands," cf. Job 10.8; moreover, עצבים were frequently, if not normally, made of metal; cf. Hos. 8.4; Ps. 115.4; 135.15. The v. is obviously in the 3-beat meter. Accordingly in the second distich of the initial tristich of the v. there is one word too many; therefore omit ופעל, a verb which occurs again in the very next stichos, and is here not only quite unnecessary, but is even disturbing. בפחם, "with glowing coal-fire," can hardly be the proper word here; in its stead, with only a rearrangement of the consonants, read בְּמַפֻּחַ, "with bellows" (cf. Jer. 6.29), and thus recover a proper and natural parallel to במקבות. Certainly we should, with *G*, insert לו after כח; the word was probably lost through haplography, of either sound or form, with the next word. For ויעף read of course וייעף, from יעף, "to be weary." The *'athnaḥ* should be set at כחו instead of in its present position. This would make the v. a 3/3/3, 3/3. The tristich would then describe the various procedures of the goldsmith in the making of the idol, while the distich would record the physical distress which he experiences as the result of his eagerness to complete his supposedly consecrated task, and from which, impliedly, the idol, or the god whom it is meant to represent, is unable to relieve him.

13. The v. is manifestly a 4/4 double-distich. But in the second distich there are two words too many; plainly the first יתארהו anticipates the second, at the end of the stichos and in its proper place, while similarly יעשהו anticipates the same word at the beginning of the second distich; the omission of these two superfluous words makes the picture here presented clear and vivid and likewise recovers the meter of the distich. Correspondingly the first stichos of the second distich lacks one beat; also the mention of the name of a tool of some kind would be appropriate immediately after ויעשהו and would add something to the vividness of the picture here; accordingly supply בחרט, "with graving-tool" (cf. Ex. 32.4). Finally it seems proper for כתפארת to read כתאר, certainly an emendation of minor degree. For ישב בית instead of ישב בבית cf. Gen. 4.20; 25.27; Jer. 36.22; Ps. 22.4.

14. Numerous difficulties are present in this v. also. For לכרת read, with *V*, יכרת, as the context suggests. Vocalize וְיִקַּח, as the context requires. Certainly the v. contemplates the selection and cutting down of only one tree; therefore for ארזים read ארז, to agree with the mention of the single tree, which follows. This is the only instance of the word, תרזה; accordingly, with Grätz, Cheyne and Marti, emend to תדהר (cf. Isa. 41.19; 60.13). The latter seems to have been, like the ארז and the אלון (cf. Gen. 35.8; II Kings 14.9; Hos. 4.13; Amos 2.9) a tree of large size and also suitable for sacred uses. Emend ויאמץ to ויֹמצא, with merely a simple rearrangement of the consonants. As the text now reads, this verb has no object; accordingly for בעצי־יער read, as indeed the context suggests, עץ מיער (cf. Jer. 10.3).

For the meaningless ארן, following a suggestion of *G*, read אל; for the ארזי אל cf. Ps. 80.11. The thought of the v. seems to be that only a tree of outstanding size and appearance, one which, so it seems, a god must have planted, and had planted for the express purpose that, when it reached its full growth, it might be made into an idol, an image of him, would be suitable for this purpose. This implies, in turn, that in the minds of the wood-carver and all concerned the tree possesses from the very first some quality of divinity. The v. is obviously a 3/3, 4/4.

15. This v. is a 3/3/3, 3/3, as are also vv. 12, 18–19a, 19bc. In all these passages the tristich comes first and expresses one idea, while the distich which follows expresses the contrasting idea. Here and again in v. 19bc the tristich describes the profane acts which the idol-maker performs, all for his own physical comfort, while the distich records his procedure in fulfilling his religious purpose. By describing the acts for physical comfort with three verbs and also by stating this first, while he describes the religious procedure with only two verbs and likewise puts it in second place, the prophet suggests, with biting satire, that considerations of physical comfort come first in the mind of the idol-maker. This is the implication again in v. 19bc. And a further implication of both passages is that in the life and thought of both idol-makers and idol-worshipers the shade of difference in the making of an idol between the sacred and the profane is infinitesimal and almost meaningless, and that the transition from the one to the other is easy, quick and of no import, further evidence that in the idol itself there is no real divinity or sanctity. מהם here is certainly misleading and not original; for it clearly implies by its plu. suffix that the idol-maker has in his possession quite a number of trees, whereas the context implies clearly that he possesses and works with only a single tree, a part of which he uses for the satisfaction of his physical needs and comfort and out of the remainder of which he makes the idol. מהם may well have sprung up here as a corrupt dittograph of ויחם. Instead of ויקח read, with Klostermann, ויקדח; and inasmuch as קדח always has אש as its object, supply this word here in place of מהם; this completes the second stichos of the tristich. Following a hint from DSIa, which reads או for the second אף, read here או for the first אף. The second אף is practically indispensable since it, in its customary usage, introduces the contrasting thought. Vocalize וְיָחֻם, וְיִקְדַּח, וְיִסֹד וְיִשְׁתָּחוּ, since all these verbs indicate action in the present or the immediate future. For עשהו read with *V*, יְעָשֵׂה. Inasmuch as it must be read with ויסגד as a single beat, it is probably well to read for למו the shorter and normal form, לו.

16. Vv. 16–17 together constitute a single thought-unit after the now established pattern. V. 16, another 3/3/3, 3/3, describes the physical, profane procedure of the idol-maker, while v. 17, a 3/3 double-distich, describes, again in briefer form, his religious procedure. In v. 16 the second and third stichoi of the tristich are badly confused. For this second חצין, following a hint from DSIa and *G*, with Klostermann and other scholars, read נחליו. Furthermore, following another hint from *G* and also as the sense requires, it is necessary to invert the order of the two verbs, יאכל יצלה, and also, as the sense again requires and as DSIa and *G* again suggest, for יאכל to read וְיֹאכַל. The final clause in the sentence may well be interpreted, with Dillmann, "I see a fire," and the very sight brings assurance, relaxation and comfort.

17. This v. is manifestly a 3/3 double-distich. The first stichos has one word too many for the meter; and since לאל is superfluous and even a bit disturbing, it may well be removed from the text. Also עשה should be emended to יְעָשֵׂה, to agree in tense and meaning with the verbs both preceding and following. Likewise the suffix, ו, should be detached from לפסלו and prefixed, as a ו connective, to the

following word, ויסגד. With these relatively simple emendations what was undoubtedly the original of the v. is recovered.

18. As has been already indicated, vv. 18–19a constitute a 3/3/3, 3/3 metrical unit, while v. 19bc constitutes a similar unit, in each of which the tristich presents a primary thought, which the distich supplements, frequently, as in v. 19bc, by presenting the contrasting thought. In v. 18 vocalize יֵדְעוּ again, so that this verb may agree in tense and meaning with the other verbs with which it is so closely linked. It is not altogether certain whether the subj. of the two plu. verbs in this sentence is the idols or the various idol-makers. But inasmuch as v. 19 speaks of the single idol-maker, it seems better to regard the idol-makers collectively as the subj. of the two verbs in v. 18. Moreover, while we might well speak of the idol's eyes, we could hardly speak of its heart or mind. For טח it is of course necessary to read טחו, since the subj. is plu. Also it is plain that a word is missing at the end of the third stichos of the tristich, clearly a verb in chiastic parallelism with טחו at the beginning of the preceding stichos; accordingly supply either כבדו or חזקו, preferably the former (cf. Morgenstern, "The Loss of Words, etc.," HUCA XXV [1954], 68 f.).

19. The text of v. 19a is in order, but it is necessary of course to read ולא־דעת and ולא־תבונה, each as a single beat. The prefixing of לא to a noun in this manner has much the same practical effect as the English negative prefix, "un-." In v. 19bβ it seems wise to omit ואף as a dittograph of the first letters of ואפיתי. It seems best to interpret לבול in v. 19c in the same sense as the corresponding term of Talmudic Hebrew, probably vocalized בּוֹל, meaning "a clod; a waste, useless piece." The designation here by the idol-maker of his idol as a תועבה, "an abomination," is especially meaningful at this point in the prophet's development of his theme, for it is the idol-maker's acknowledgement that this idol is false and worthless, and it paves the way readily for the next ensuing thought. Attention was called in the seminar to the fact that in vv. 19c–20 we have in part the same succession of verbs, used to describe the procedure of the idol-maker in dealing with his idol, as in v. 17, viz. עשה, סגד, אמר and הציל. Two verbs, however, in v. 15b, are missing here, viz. שחה and פלל. The same sequence occurs also in part in v. 15b. Moreover, the verb, סגד, occurs in the entire Bible only four times, all in Deutero-Isaiah, three times in this one address (44.15, 17, 19) and again in 46.6. Furthermore, in all these four passages, with the single exception of 44.19, it is regularly followed by שחה. It was therefore suggested that the same complete sequence should be expected here, and that accordingly we should supply a third stichos to the v., reading אשתחוה ואליו אתפלל. This would make v. 19c a 3/3/3 tristich. Furthermore, it does seem that the addition of these three words would complete the thought here expressed in most effective manner and likewise would strengthen considerably the import of the truth which the idol-maker must acknowledge, that this idol, to which he had not only bowed down in formal worship, but to which he had also prayed for actual deliverance from the evils which beset him personally, is only a תועבה, a vain and useless thing, totally unable to do aught for its devotees. Moreover, with this stichos added, this testimony of the idol-maker with regard to his god, would end in three 3/3/3 tristichs, certainly a most effective climax to the statement, which, as the witness for his god, he finds himself compelled to offer. Moreover, v. 20 commences with two words which are utterly meaningless and are also metrically disturbing where they stand. However, they might well represent a textual corruption of this missing, final stichos of v. 19c, misplaced to the beginning of the following v. And indeed, even though רטה in no way suggests an original reading אשתחוה ואליו אפר,

may very well have resulted from a corruption of אתפלל. All in all the emendation has very much to commend it and may accordingly be accepted, though with some reservation.

20. With the initial two words thus disposed of, the remainder of this v. is in perfect textual order. In the final stichos of the tristich ולא must be linked to יאמר as a single beat; but inasmuch as the first לא, in the preceding stichos, has been stressed by receiving a full beat, this procedure with ולא is natural and customary.

42.17. This v. is definitely out of place in its present position in *MT*, since it seriously interrupts the close unity of vv. 16 and 18. On the other hand it fits perfectly here and, in effective, climactic manner, provides the definitive judgment upon all idol-worshipers. The v. is obviously a distich; and inasmuch as v. 17b consists of four words and so forms a 4-beat stichos, we would expect v. 17a to constitute a similar stichos, and the distich to thus be in the 4/4 meter, a proper and dignified meter for the formulation of a court judgment. But in this first stichos, as it stands, there are plainly two words too many; accordingly omit the altogether superfluous יבשו בשת. Also vocalize בְּפֶסל, to agree with לְמסכה and to accord with the generalizing import of the judgment here pronounced. Likewise, as the sing. antecedent of the pronoun, מסכה, and also the sing. pred., אלהינו, indicate, אתם should be emended to the sing., אתה.

44.21. Having now demonstrated the complete unreality and utter futility of idols and of the gods whom they represent, the prophet, speaking of course in the name of Yahweh, now definitively proved to be the only true God, the one world-God, turns directly to Israel and brings home to it the full import of this now established truth. The v. is a 3/3 double-distich. But in the second stichos of the second distich there is obviously one word too many. Accordingly omit the altogether superfluous and weakening ישראל. תנשני, a *nif'al* with an object, is of course impossible; accordingly read, with Klostermann, Cheyne and Marti, תשני (cf. Deut. 32.15).

22. The thought of this v. might seem to fit in well at this point; but it seems to fit in better after 43.25, near the end of this address; accordingly we have transposed it thither.

23. This v. is certainly not integral in this address. It has all the characteristics of a psalmodic interpolation, probably linked in some way with the reading of this section of this address in the Synagogue as a part of the liturgy.

24. Inasmuch as here מבטן can modify only ויצרך, it is necessary to read, with *S* and in accordance with the obvious import of the clause, בבטן. And for מי אתי it is necessary for the same reason to read, with *V*, אתי מי, ואין, and likewise to read these two words together as one beat for the sake of the meter. Likewise אנכי יהוה must be interpreted as a variant form of the name of the Deity (cf. Morgenstern, "Deutero-Isaiah's Terminology for 'Universal God,'" *JBL* LXII [1943], 269–280), and so be read as a single beat.

25. *G*, *V* and *S* all interpret בדים as "diviners, soothsayers"; unquestionably they read here בָּרים, a Hebraization of the Babylonian *bârû*, "divining-priest"; this is certainly the correct reading here. Also, with *G* and *S*, for וקסמים read וְקסָמֶיהָ, "their divinations; their magical acts." Both וקסמיהם and ודעתם, being nouns, each with a prefix and a pronominal suffix, should be read as two beats, and thus make this v. a 3/3 double-distich.

26. As has already been indicated (above, p. 51), v. 26b, which has no thought-unity whatever with v. 26a, and also vv. 27–28 have been assigned to different positions in Deutero-Isaiah. V. 26a alone is integral in this position. The text is in perfect order.

43.10. The trial scene continues, and whereas the witnesses of the false gods, who had to testify to their unreality and utter impotence, were the very makers of these gods, Yahweh now declares that Israel, the people, are His witnesses, whose duty it is, as His chosen servant, to testify of Him and of His true, eternal and universal character and power to all the world, that He is the Existent One, the one and only true world-God. But before Israel can perform this task adequately and convincingly, they must themselves first learn to know Him, to understand Him and to have complete faith in Him. This is the theme of v. 10ab, a 3/3 double distich. Actually v. 10c is a unit in thought with v. 11, and with it forms a second 3/3 double-distich, the theme of which is the absolute unity and eternity of Yahweh as the sole world-God. The full import of the declaration in v. 10c, that prior to Yahweh no god had ever been formed, nor will there be any god to succeed or replace Him, becomes clear when we remember that both the Eastern and the Western Semites cherished the myth that the world had in the course of time passed through three stages or eras, during each of which a different god was supreme over gods and men. Babylonian mythology, with which these Jewish exiles were undoubtedly familiar, told of the successive eras of Anu, Bel and Ea, while the Western Semites told of the eras of 'Elyon or 'Eloah, Ba'al Shamem or Shaddai and 'El (cf. Morgenstern, "The Divine Triad in Biblical Mythology," *JBL* LXIV [1945], 15–38). V. 10c affirms, in significant contrast to this tradition or belief, that Yahweh, and He alone, had been God, the only God, from the very beginning of time, and would continue so until its very end. Here in this v. and again in 44.21, in our reconstruction of this address preceding this utterance by only a few sentences, the prophet speaks of Israel as Yahweh's servant. Furthermore, he affirms that Israel's service is to be Yahweh's witness, to bear testimony of Him, not only in the court procedure which the prophet envisions in this address, but at all times and to all the peoples of the entire world. Plainly the character of Israel's "service" is beginning to take shape in the prophet's mind, although it still seems to be somewhat undefined. And before Israel can testify of Yahweh truly and effectively, it must itself first learn to know Him as He really is and must also come to believe in Him with constant and un-shakable conviction. Only with such faith on its part can Israel testify of Yahweh unto the nations that He is the one and only God, and that besides Him there is, for the nations as well as for Israel, no other god and no other possible savior. Such is the thought set forth in the two 3/3 double-distichs in vv. 10–11.

11. יהוה here must be rendered "God" rather than as the name of the Deity (cf. Blank, "Studies in Deutero-Isaiah," *HUCA* XV [1940], 14–18). To translate it here merely "Yahweh" would make the passage utterly meaningless. The likelihood is that the prophet here and elsewhere interprets the name as a *qal* formation of היה, "to be," precisely as does the relatively late interpolation in Ex. 3.14, manifestly dependent upon Deutero-Isaiah (cf. Morgenstern, "The Elohist Narrative in Exodus 3.1–15," *AJSL* XXXVII [1921], 242–262). Thus interpreted, יָהְוֶה would mean "He Who Is" or "The One Who Is," and would be practically synonymous with the prophet's other, very frequent designation of the Deity by the pronoun, הוא, "He," i. e. "The One Who is; the Ever-Existent One."

12. V. 12 is manifestly a 4/4/4 tristich; but in each stichos there is some textual disarrangement. In the first stichos the thought sequence implicit in the present order of the three verbs is surprising and even disturbing. Repeatedly in the various addresses of the prophet הגיד is followed immediately by השמיע (41.22, 26; 42.9; 43.9; 48.3, 20) or the reverse (44.8; 45.21), without any other verb intervening. We expect the same sequence here. Undoubtedly והושעתי should be transposed to follow

והשמעתי; the displacement of the two verbs was due undoubtedly to their close similarity in their written form. As it stands now, the second stichos has only three beats; plainly a word is missing here. Moreover, the thought here expressed by the present wording, "And among you there is no stranger," is surprising and meaningless indeed. Accordingly before זר supply אל (cf. Ps. 81.10; also Ps. 44.21). This recovers the required fourth beat for the stichos. The third stichos has in its present form two words too many; accordingly, with G, omit the altogether super-fluous and even somewhat disturbing נאם יהוה and thus recover the original 4-beat text of the stichos. It is altogether possible that the prophet pronounced והושעתי with the accent upon the final syllable of the word. In such case the ו would be the ו consecutive, and we would have to translate the first stichos, "I have foretold, and I have proclaimed, and I shall work salvation." Either interpretation of the clause is possible, but of the two that which we here propose seems to us to be more probably the thought which the prophet intended to express.

13. For מיום with the connotation, "from today on," cf. 48.7 and its note. The implication of this v. seems to be that from this day of this court scene, in which Yahweh has definitely proved that the gods of the nations are non-existent, impotent unrealities and that He alone is God, the one God throughout the entire universe, it should be clear to all that there can be no opposition to His will and purpose from any source whatever, either human or divine.

14. This v. in its entirety is utterly meaningless and even untranslatable with any degree of certainty. Under no condition does it fit in either here or elsewhere in the address. It should accordingly be omitted as an altogether inexplicable intrusion.

15. Further and decisive evidence that v. 14 is an intrusion here is to be found in the fact that v. 15 continues directly the thought of v. 13. Actually the two vv. together constitute a single sentence, in which אני in the first stichos of v. 13 is the only subj. Metrically the sentence falls into two parts, in the first of which, the 3/3/3 tristich of v. 13, the universal character of Yahweh's divinity is stressed, while in the second part, the 3/3 distich of v. 15, His peculiar relationship to Israel, despite His universal character, is emphasized. From today on not only is He the one, sole God of the entire world and of all nations and all mankind therein, but He is also at the same time Israel's "peculiar possession," the primary connotation of קדוש, its Holy One and its King. אני־יהוה in v. 15 must be interpreted as another instance of the prophet's characteristic use of this compound term as the name of the Deity. His designation of Yahweh by the title, Israel's King, undoubtedly indicates that he conceives of restored Israel, no longer as a political entity, a kingdom ruled over by a king of Davidic descent, but rather as a religious unit or community, whose true head and sole ruler and king is Yahweh. There is also the implication, as we have already pointed out, of his applying to Cyrus the title, משיח יהוה, "Yahweh's Anointed One," hitherto borne, with the single exceptions of Saul and Jehu, only by kings of Judah of Davidic descent. The complete sentence implies further that in its relationship to Yahweh as contrasted with that of the other nations and peoples to Him as the sole world-God, Israel, as Yahweh's chosen people, created by Him for an especial mission, as His servant, is closest to Him, closer by far than any other people.

42.23. Here we would insert 42.23, for we feel that it fits in here better than in its present position in MT. With 43.16 a new section of the address begins, which announces Yahweh's impending deliverance of Israel from exile in Babylonia and its return, through the intervening desert, with all its natural dangers and hardships overcome by Yahweh's loving solicitude for His people, to its ancestral homeland.

To this section, rich in promise, 42.23 is indeed a fitting introduction. לאחור, literally, "to what is behind," i. e. "behind the present moment (as it draws near)," to events of the future (cf. 41.23), just as its antithetical phrase, לפנים, means "events of the past." The events of the future here referred to are of course Israel's impending deliverance in all its details.

43.16. For מים עזים as a synonym for ים cf. Neh. 9.11. Vv. 16–17 refer quite plainly to the tradition of the crossing of the Red Sea with divine help and deliverance at the time of the exodus from Egypt. This is confirmed by the charge in vv. 18–19 not to recall the events of the past but rather to think of the new deliverance which Yahweh will effect for Israel, this time, however, not through the sea but rather through the desert.

17. עזוז occurs elsewhere only in Ps. 24.8, where it has adjectival meaning, "strong; a strong being or person." This meaning hardly fits here; rather we expect a word which would parallel חיל, "might; army." Accordingly vocalize ועזוז, "strength (cf. 42.5; Ps. 78.4; 145.6), and give it a connotation which parallels חיל, "army"; accordingly render it "troop." As both thought and meter demand, יחדו must be incorporated into the first distich, as the final word of the second stichos thereof. This makes v. 17 a 3/3 double distich.

18. The "former things" are of course the traditional deliverance from Egypt; the "new things" are then the promised and now narrowly impending deliverance from Babylonian exile and restoration to ancestral land. For a similar contrasting of the "former things" with the "new things," about to be announced by Yahweh through the medium of the prophet, cf. 42.9. The v. practically says that there is no need longer for Israel to look back to its distant past for instances and evidence of Yahweh's solicitude for it and power to protect and deliver it, for He is now about to do a new thing in its behalf, to work a new deliverance for it, besides which that from Egypt in ancient times will pale into insignificance.

19. It must be admitted that הלוא, preceding תדעוה, is a surprising and rather awkward particle. Quite significantly G omits it. Similarly אף at the beginning of the second distich, preceding אשים, is equally surprising and awkward; and, significantly again, V omits it. Apparently only one particle stood here, and that too in its proper position before תדעוה, and this could have been, as in fact all the vss. seem to have read, only אף. Apparently אף became displaced in some way from its original position, and then some editor, sensing the necessity of a particle in this position to introduce the new thought, supplied הלוא. The manifest implication of עתה here is "now; in the immediate future." For נהרות read, following the suggestion of DSIa, נתיבות (actually the manuscript is blurred at this point, but it seems to read נתיבות rather than נתיבים, as transcribed by Burrows, in his edition of the text with photographs of the manuscript). This emendation recovers the close parallelism between this v. and v. 16. Finally a word essential to the 3-beat meter of the v. is missing at the end of the second distich; accordingly supply אתן and thus recover a close, chiastic parallelism between the two stichoi of this second distich of the v.

20. Inasmuch as the prophet is here announcing the actions which Yahweh is about to take in the immediate future in order to effect this new deliverance of His people, for נתתי read, with DSIa, אתן. Also after בישימון supply אשים, to provide the verb obviously missing at the end of the second stichos of the second distich and essential to completing the 3/3 meter and also to providing the expected chiastic parallelism between the two stichoi of the distich. As it stands now the v. is a 3/3, 3/3/3. But it seems better to prefix the final stichos of this v. to the next v., since the thought-linkage is closer with this arrangement. That would make v. 21 a 3/3/2,

which is certainly in this setting a more effective meter than a mere 3/2, as v. 21 would be otherwise without this rearrangement. Also this makes v. 20 a double 3/3 distich. Moreover, with this rearrangement we can account for the loss of אשים at the end of the second distich of the v., for it would then be another instance of the loss of a word at the end of a line of Biblical poetry.

21. Vv. 20–21 together voice a significant thought and pave the way to the section of the address which follows. They say that if the beasts of the desert honor Yahweh for providing water for them amply in their normally water-poor habitat, then how much the more should Israel praise and worship Yahweh for the marvelous deliverances and manifold other bounties which He has wrought for it throughout its long history, and this all the more so since He had actually brought Israel into being as His chosen people that it might recite His praise, and this too in the hearing of all the world, so that all nations and peoples might come to comprehend and believe in His oneness, His universal power and His saviorship, and might turn to Him in reverence. But, as the vv. immediately following relate in graphic manner, just this throughout its entire history, beginning with its very first progenitor, Israel had failed to do.

22. Note the unusual position and therefore the emphatic effect of אותי. כי here can be understood best as the כי of certainty, "verily." For יגע ב', "to grow weary of something," cf. Isa. 47.12; 63.8; Jer. 45.3; Ps. 6.7; 69.4.

23. This v., like vv. 22 and 24, all of which have a common theme, viz. Israel's disloyalty to Yahweh, is a 4/3 double distich. However, in the first stichos of the first distich there is manifestly one word too many for the meter. Accordingly omit the altogether unnecessary and even awkward and somewhat disturbing שה; with this elision the parallelism between the two stichoi of the distich becomes much more manifest and effective. It should be noted that not only is אותי in v. 22 emphatic, but this is true of all 1st pers. pronominal suffixes throughout the three vv. of this strophe. For וזבחיך read, with DSIa, ובזבחיך, as indeed the context requires. In the first stichos of the second distich of the v. העבדתיך must receive two beats; here this verb can mean only "I did not cause thee to worship" or "demand that thou worship."

24. Again in the first stichos of the first distich there is one word too many for the meter; accordingly omit the altogether superfluous and rather banal בכסף. With this omission the word-play of קנית קנה becomes more vivid and effective. הרויתני very properly takes a double-object; literally translated therefore, "and the fat of thy sacrifices thou didst not make me drink to satiety." אך here, with the connotation, "instead," has a significant meaning and so must receive a full beat; with this and also by giving בחטאותיך two beats, the expected 4-beat measure of the first stichos of the second distich is achieved. In the second stichos of this same distich בעונתיך must likewise be given two beats. In vv. 22–24 the prophet does not represent Yahweh as charging Israel with not offering sacrifices. On the contrary, the vv. imply clearly that Israel, and of course the Israel in exile, did offer sacrifices, and this even in abundance; but they were not offered to Yahweh. Accordingly they must have been offered consciously and directly to other gods; and these other gods could have been only the Babylonian deities. This is the crowning instance and proof of Israel's faithlessness to Yahweh.

25. This v. is certainly out of place at this point in this address, midway in Yahweh's denunciation of Israel for its faithlessness to Him. It fits far better after 44.8, whither we have transposed it.

26. הזכירני, literally "cause Me to remember," is tantamount to "challenge

Me." Yahweh magnanimously offers Israel the privilege of presenting its case first in the debate between them, in which Israel would presumably have the opportunity to vindicate itself of the charge of faithlessness to Him. But impliedly it can say nothing at all in defense of itself, and so, in the very next two vv., Yahweh resumes His denunciation of Israel and utters His final condemnation of it.

27. By "thy first father" the prophet certainly has in mind, as practically all scholars are agreed, Jacob, and not Abraham; note the frequency with which he speaks of Israel as the posterity of Jacob (44.5; 45.19; 48.1). No sin of Abraham is recorded in the Bible; but the sin of Jacob may well have been his supplanting of Esau (cf. Hos. 12.3–5). For ומליציך both *G* and *S* read either ומלכיך or ומשליך. Inasmuch as the former of these two words represents the lesser textual corruption, we prefer to regard it as original here.

28. For syntactical reasons it is necessary to read שרי הקדש. For ואתנה read, with DSIa, ואתן; there is no reason whatever for the enclitic ה' here; it may well, however, be the result of the misplacement of the article of הקדש. Just who these "holy princes" might be is not clear, but the most probable hypothesis would be that they were the priests of the Temple, who, in pre-exilic Judah, may well have stood second in rank and authority only to the king. לחרם in parallelism with לגדופים is somewhat surprising; and inasmuch as the regular parallel to גדופים is חרפה (cf. Isa. 51.7; Ezek. 5.15; Zeph. 2.8), we should undoubtedly emend לחרם here to לחרפה.

44.6. Insert, with DSIa and *S*, שמו after צבאות (cf. 47.4; 48.2); the addition of this word restores the original 3-beat stichos. Here once again (cf. 41.21; 43.15) the prophet applies to Yahweh the title, "King of Israel." Outside of these three Deutero-Isaianic passages this designation of Yahweh occurs, in all the prophetic writings, only in Zeph. 3.15. The import of this title for Yahweh we have considered in our discussion of 43.15. By יהוה צבאות, "Yahweh of Hosts," originally the formal designation of the god of the ark at Shiloh and then, after the transfer of the ark to Jerusalem and its eventual setting up in the Temple, the regular designation of the Yahweh of the Temple (cf. Eissfeldt, *Yahweh Zebaoth* [1950]), Deutero-Isaiah can mean, both here and in 48.2, only "Yahweh of the Hosts (of men)," i. e. Yahweh, the universal God. When, in the second half of this v., the prophet affirms that Yahweh is both the first and the last and that besides Him there is no other god, he not only gives vigorous expression to the principle of the absolute eternity and universality of Yahweh but he also reverts to the idea implicit in 43.10, which we have already discussed. Inasmuch as in the first stichos of the distich the first אני has a full beat, ואני, which follows, can be slurred over and read as one beat with אחרון.

7. This v. abounds in textual difficulties, all of which, however, in practical agreement with Torrey, can be resolved quite readily. The v. undoubtedly continues the enumeration of the attributes of Yahweh. Accordingly for יגידו read the sing., יגיד, in agreement with the other verbs in the sentence and the general context. לי is certainly a corruption; for it DSIa reads לוא, which is equivalent to the customary לו. However, it seems well to transpose למו from the end of the v., where it is both meaningless and metrically disturbing, to this spot in place of לי of *MT*. Inasmuch as in Deutero-Isaiah, as we have already noted, הגיד is regularly followed by השמיע, we miss the latter word here, and this really doubly so since יגיד occurs twice in the v.; accordingly for the altogether meaningless and confusing משומי עם־עולם read, with simple rearrangement of the letters, משמיע מעולם. With these relatively minor emendations the textual order of the v. is completely restored, and it becomes a 3/3 double-distich.

8. This is the only instance in Biblical Hebrew of a verb, רהה; accordingly

read, with DSIa, supported by *V* and *S*, תיראו. The pronominal suffix appended to השמעתיך is unnecessary and even somewhat surprising; and since the parallel verb, והגדתי, has no suffix at all, and also since the following 2nd pers. pronoun, and likewise the predicate noun are both plu., it seems wise to omit this suffix and read, with Duhm and others, merely השמעתי. The final stichos of the v. is textually completely disorganized. For ואין read, with Gordis (cited by G. R. Driver in "Notes on Isaiah," in *Von Ugarit nach Qumran: Festschrift für Otto Eissfeldt* [1958], 47), the interrogative particle, ואין (cf. I Sam. 21.9; Ps. 139.4). Emend צור to, in form closely similar, עוד. בלי־דעתי, absolutely meaningless in its present form, resembles closely מבלעדי just preceding; moreover, the obvious parallelism between the two stichoi of the final distich of the v. requires a word here of similar meaning. In all likelihood that original parallel word was זולתי, for which some careless copyist wrote בלעדי, which, in turn, was eventually corrupted to בלי־דעתי of *MT*. Here for the first time the prophet announces that Israel's task, as His servant, is to bear testimony of Him, to be His witnesses unto the peoples of the world. But he raises this thought here rather incidentally, quite as if it were only just beginning to take shape in his mind, and as if the wisdom or even the necessity of his defining just wherein Israel's service would lie had only now suggested itself to him.

43.25. הוא, "the Ever Existent One," is in apposition with אנכי, which is, in turn, the subject of the sentence, as the pronominal suffix of למעני indicates. The third stichos could easily be read with the required three beats by giving לא a full beat; however, it seems more in consonance with Hebrew linguistic procedure and also with DSIa to supply עוד at the end of the stichos and of the tristich, and so to read לא־אזכר as one beat.

44.22. At this point, and following immediately upon 43.25, this v. fits in perfectly, and the two vv. combined, and in this connection it may be noted that together they constitute a 3/3/3 double-tristich, voice a significant thought, viz. the form which Ezekiel's doctrine of "for His name's sake," with which, as we have established, Deutero-Isaiah inaugurated his prophetic ministry, had come to assume after he had functioned as a prophet of Yahweh for a number of years, and after his message had assumed its own distinctive shape. Just as Ezekiel had predicted, Yahweh will restore Israel to its ancestral land; in fact, according to Deutero-Isaiah, the moment for this is narrowly impending. And in connection with this restoration, so Ezekiel proclaimed, Yahweh will give Israel a new heart, or, as Deutero-Isaiah now puts it, Yahweh will blot out all Israel's transgressions and its sins He will remember no more, all this, in the thought of both prophets, so that henceforth Israel might be a sinless people, maintaining ever pure and faithful relations with Yahweh, its Holy One. According to Ezekiel, all this Yahweh will do למען שמו, "for His name's sake," for the sake of His reputation, for the evaluation which the various nations will put upon Him in comparison with their own gods. But according to Deutero-Isaiah, at the present stage of the evolution of his message, Yahweh does this not at all for the sake of His reputation, for, as has just been demonstrated conclusively, there are no other gods who might be compared with Him. Instead Yahweh does all this למעני, "for Mine own sake," i. e. for the fulfillment of His universal purpose, and that purpose is the salvation of all mankind. For the fulfillment of this purpose Yahweh needs Israel as His servant, as the agent of His universal salvation. And for this purpose He purges Israel of all its past iniquities and removes its transgressions from His memory, no doubt with the added implication that henceforth, in its role as His servant, Israel will sin no more, will, so the prophet probably meant, even be incapable of sinning further. This is almost certainly the implication of Yahweh's appeal to Israel, "return to Me, for I have redeemed thee," i. e. "return to Me and be My people and My faithful, unerring servant forever!" From the significant use of this one word, למעני, it becomes clearly apparent how far Deutero-Isaiah has now advanced over his predecessor and prophetic mentor, Ezekiel, and over his own starting-point in his prophetic ministry, and has evolved his own distinctive message and enlarged his stature as a prophet of Yahweh. In the second stichos of the tristich a word, indispensable for the required 3-beat measure, is missing; accordingly supply העברתי at the end of the stichos, thus creating once again an effective chiasm with the preceding stichos.

44.1–5. These five vv. constitute the closing and, in a sense, the climactic strophe of this poetic address. They are cast throughout in the dignified and impressive 4/3 meter. Their theme is Yahweh's future, happy relations with Israel, His servant, now, or at least in the very near future to be, redeemed by Him and purged of all transgression and inclination to sin. They serve as a very effective conclusion to this long, closely unified and very powerful address.

44.1. ועתה, "so now," introduces very forcefully the application to Israel's future, as Yahweh's servant and chosen one, of the principle of divine forgiveness of its sins and His taking it to Himself once again as a cleansed people, set forth in 43.25 and 44.22, as we have reorganized this passage.

2. In the light of the use of the same expression, of which the prophet was apparently fond, in 44.24, in the text as we have reconstructed it, we should probably construe מבטן with ויצרך and emend it to בבטן. For יעזרך it seems better, and in fact almost necessary, as the context requires, to read עזרך. The name here applied to Israel, ישרון, presents a problem. The name occurs in all Biblical writings only three other times, Deut. 32.15; 33.5, 26. In all of these passages the vss. interpret this word, not as a proper name, but rather as a descriptive term, an adjectival noun; nor is there agreement among them as to the meaning of the term. The thought is unavoidable, because of the similarity in form of the two words, that it is here a corruption of an original ישראל; but this same corruption would hardly have occurred in four different places. It is probably best then to retain the word as a secondary name or title of Israel. Plainly it is derived from the stem, ישר, "to be upright or straightforward," and designates Israel here as the "upright," or, as V renders it, "the most upright one." So interpreted, this title would be most appropriate for Israel at this point in this address, just after the prophet's pronouncement of Israel's purification by Yahweh from all its former sins and transgressions. In fact the use by the prophet of this new name for Israel at just this point suggests that by it he contemplates that new Israel, at which he had hinted previously, that new Israel, faithful and sinless, Yahweh's chosen servant. All this, because of lack of decisive evidence, must remain more or less hypothetical; but it certainly has much in its favor.

3. The v. is a double-distich, with plainly a close unity between the two distichs. And plainly too, even though MT does not bring this out adequately, a comparison is here set forth between the manner in which Yahweh provides abundant water for the thirsting soil and the manner in which He will now pour out His spirit upon Israel's offspring, His chosen servant. Accordingly insert, with DSIa, כן before the second אצק at the beginning of the second distich; moreover, this word is essential in order to complete the expected four beats of the first stichos of the second distich. And inasmuch as it must receive a full beat, it follows that the word voices an emphatic thought. But the appreciation of this vigorous comparison makes it imperative that the introductory word of the sentence, the word which must inau-

gurate this comparison, כי, at the beginning of the first distich, be emended to כאשר. Furthermore, since the figure is the same in both stichoi of the first distich, viz. the pouring of streams of water upon the dry and thirsty soil, and since יבשה here as well as all other nouns connoting the earth or the soil are always fem., it is necessary for צמא to read צמאה. In the respective distichs, על־יבשה and על־צאצאיך must each receive two beats.

4. As it stands now, v. 4 seems to be a 3/3; and even this would necessitate giving a full beat to the assuredly unemphatic בבין. Also for בבין, an altogether unparalleled union of two prepositions of like meaning, DSIa reads כבין, which certainly accords far better with the figurative thought here being unfolded. Moreover, in the midst of this series of 4/3's we expect this v. to be a 4/3 also. Furthermore, in conjunction with זרעך and צאצאיך in the preceding distich, we miss here very decidedly the most common word for "offspring," viz. בניך, "thy sons." And it is noteworthy that בניך and כבין have exactly the same letters; accordingly emend כבין to בניך and construe it as the subj. of וצמחו. This necessitates the supplying of the preposition, כ', before חציר, lost perhaps by haplography, coming, as it does, immediately after בניך. This necessitates our supplying some phrase to follow כחציר, which would parallel על־יבלי מים and would suggest the place where grass grows most abundantly; accordingly, in the light of Ps. 147.8, supply על־הרים, or perhaps על־ההרים. The parallelism between the two stichoi of the distich is thus made complete. And there can be no question that, with the v. thus reconstructed, the picture here set forth becomes far more vivid and both the literary and the hortatory effect are heightened greatly.

5. For יִקְרָא read, with a reflexive connotation, the nif'al, יִקָּרֵא (so Klostermann and others). Inasmuch as וזה at the beginning of the second stichos of the first distich is but the repetition of the זה at the beginning of the first distich, it may be readily slurred over and read with יקרא as a single beat. This recovers for the second stichos the expected three beats. For ידו read, as the context requires, בידו; the ב' was undoubtedly lost by haplography. For יְכַנֶּה read the pu'al, יְכֻנֶּה; and inasmuch as in Biblical Hebrew the word occurs only in the pi'el, it is justifiable to give to this passive form a reflexive connotation, "he shall entitle himself."

## Isa. 41

In the analysis and interpretation of the address contained in this chapter many problems of varying character present themselves, some of which can not be solved definitively for want of decisive evidence.

The theme of the address is the old one, so characteristic, it is now clear, of Deutero-Isaiah, a trial scene in court, or, perhaps better, a debate, between Yahweh and the gods of the nations, directed to the end of proving the total lack of reality and divinity of the latter and the sole, universal divinity and absolute power of Yahweh. The test is still the old one, which god is responsible for Cyrus' appearance upon the stage of history and for his conquest of the nations in such rapid succession, and who, as the primary author of Cyrus' world-plans and their successful execution, could and did predict all this in advance as the expression of his own divine world-plan and purpose. The witnesses of this trial scene or debate are the nations and peoples of the world, all of whom are summoned to be present in order to have demonstrated to them, so that they in turn might acknowledge, the total impotence and unreality of their gods and their complete discomfiture in their contest with Yahweh, Israel's god, the champion and advocate of His people.

This address has close affinities, both of thought and of manner of expression, with the addresses in both Isa. 45 and 42–44. But inasmuch as the concept of the role of Israel as the servant of Yahweh is developed here far beyond the point it attained in the address in Isa. 45 and even beyond that achieved in Isa. 42–44, it follows that this address must be later than that in 45 and probably also than that in 42–44. The tenses of the verbs in vv. 2–3 suggest that Cyrus' conquests are still vividly recent. And certainly the picture of the trial in 42–44 is more realistic and the satire which the picture there expresses is more biting than is the case here. And here, in vv. 11–13, we hear the entirely new note of enemies of Israel who rage against it, of which none of the earlier addresses, granting that 45.24b$\beta$ does not belong where it stands in *MT*, and so must be a misplaced fragment from some other address, probably now lost, has any intimation whatever. All in all then the weight of evidence, scanty and indecisive though it is, suggests that this address is the latest of all the addresses of the prophet which we have considered thus far.

Vv. 6–7 have long been recognized by scholars as not integral in this address; we have accordingly transposed them, together with 40.20 and 19, to the address in Isa. 42–44, inserting them after 44.10. But it is a question whether the remainder of Isa. 41 is a literary unit. Duhm, Marti and Cheyne omit v. 5 from the address; Duhm and Marti v. 24b also; and Marti vv. 11–16 likewise. Vv. 14–16 should under any condition be excluded from the address, for the picture which they offer of Israel's conquest and destruction of those hostile to it, whether nations, peoples or individuals, accords not at all with Deutero-Isaiah's dominant message of Yahweh's purposed salvation of all mankind, with Israel as His appointed agent thereof, nor yet with the prophet's picture of the world as a political unit, a single world-empire, under Cyrus, and presumably his dynasty after him, with Israel no longer a political entity, capable of waging a war of destruction. But it does accord closely with the hopes of the Nationalist party in Palestine in 520 B. C. and its program of world-conquest with Yahweh's aid and the establishment of a Jewish world-empire.[1]

---

[1] Cf. "Jerusalem — 485 B. C.," *HUCA* XXVII (1956), 155 ff.

Certainly this program and the passage which sets it forth, 41.14–16, can not possibly be from Deutero-Isaiah.

Vv. 11–13 speak of enemies, whom Israel is bidden not to fear and against whom Yahweh promises His protection. Israel in Babylon could have had as enemies no nation or people whatsoever; and indeed vv. 11–13 speak of these enemies as individuals rather than as nations. So far as we know, Israel in Palestine in 520 B. C. had no national enemies of whom it had to fear. But in 486 B. C. the situation was altogether different. Then Israel in Palestine was immediately threatened by the nations adjacent to it and was eventually, and that too very quickly, completely crushed by them. Accordingly the possibility must not be excluded that vv. 11–13 may be a literary unit with vv. 14–16, even as Marti holds them to be, and the entire passage may represent an editorial gloss interpolated into this address by some editor in or soon after 486 B. C. But all in all vv. 11–16 do not seem to be a literary unit. The enemy destined to be overcome and crushed by Israel in vv. 14–16 does not seem to be the same as the enemies in vv. 11–13, whom Israel is bidden not to fear. Moreover, vv. 11–13 are, quite properly, in the 3/2 elegiac meter, but, even though v. 14 is in this same meter, vv. 15–16 are in the customary 3/3 meter. Furthermore, the language of vv. 11–13 smacks very strongly of Deutero-Isaiah, whereas the language of at least vv. 15–16, with the exception of the title of Yahweh, קדוש ישראל, "the Holy One of Israel," at the end of v. 16, is in no way reminiscent of our prophet. This evidence is of course far from decisive; but it is the sole evidence available. Accordingly I prefer to regard merely vv. 14–16 as the gloss and to retain vv. 11–13 for Deutero-Isaiah, as an integral part of this address. And the Israel of these vv. I regard, as has already been adumbrated,[1] as the faithful minority in the Jewish community of Babylon, who accepted the message of the prophet and reaffirmed their loyalty to Yahweh by their response to the prophet's message, the new Israel, as I have called it, and in the prophet's sight the true Israel, while the enemies of Israel in these vv., whom it is bidden not to fear, are the faithless members of the Jewish community of Babylon, those who have forsaken Yahweh and have gone over more or less completely to the worship of the Babylonian gods, and who are resenting more and more bitterly and aggressively, as time passes, the prophet's denunciation of them for their disloyalty to the god of their fathers, and who openly manifest their hostility to the prophet and his followers.

Also vv. 17–20, with their picture of Yahweh's loving solicitude

[1] Cf. above, pp. 54–56, 62–67.

for His people in distress, apparently while on its difficult journey
from Babylon through the desert back to its ancestral land, is distinctly reminiscent of Deutero-Isaiah. However, inasmuch as this
address does not deal in any way with this journey through the
desert, and there is no place for any reference to this experience in
its theme and argument, it follows necessarily that these vv. must
be a misplaced fragment of some other address by the prophet, the
remainder of which has apparently been lost.

Largely, no doubt as the result of this quite considerable editorial
expansion of the original address here recorded, the present *MT* text
reflects a correspondingly extensive disarrangement of the words and
sentences of the address as these were first uttered by the prophet.
This condition we have endeavored to rectify as best we can by
rearrangement of the text in such manner as to bring out a logical,
effective and progressive development of the thought here set forth.
However, at the very best such procedure is always conjectural and
uncertain, and the possibility of some other textual rearrangement
must always be borne in mind.

Finally, we have interpolated 44.26b into this address, and have
thus salvaged this v. for Deutero-Isaiah.

| | | |
|---|---|---|
| 3/3 | יחדשו חיל איים / ולאמים יחליפו כח | I |
| 3/3 | ינשו אז ידברו / יחדו למשפט נקרבה | |
| 3/3 | מי־העיר ממזרח ‹כורש› / בצדק יקראהו לרגליו | 2 |
| 3/3 | יתן לפניו גוים / ומלכים יָרד ‹תחתיו› | |
| 3/3 | יתן כעפרת חרבותם / כקש נדף קשתותם | |
| 3/3 | ירדפם יעבר שלום / ארח ברגליו לא־יבוֹס | 3 |
| 3/3/3 | ראו איים וייראו / קצות הארץ נחרדו / קרבו ויאתיון ‹יחדו› | 5 |
| 3/3 | ראשון לציון הנני / ולירושלם מבסר אתנדב | 27 |
| 4/4 | קרבו ריבכם יאמר יהוה / הגישו מועצותיכם יאמר מלך־יעקב | 21 |
| | הגישו ‹ › לנו את־הקדמניות / הראשנות מה־הנה הגידו / ונשימה | 22 |
| 3/3/3 | ‹ › ונדעה אחריתן | |
| | או הבאות השמיענו / הגידו האתיות לאחור / ונדעה כי־אלהים | 23 |
| 3/3/3 | אתם | |
| 3/3 | אף תיטיבו ותרעו / ונשתעה ונראה יחדו | |
| 4/3 | הן־אתם אין ופעלכם אפס / תועה הבחר בכם | 24 |
| 4/3 | מי הגיד מראש ונדעָה / ומלפנים ונאמר צדק | 26 |
| 4/3 | אף־אין מגיד אף־אין משמיע / אף־אין שמע אמריכם | |
| 3/3/3 | ואראה ואין איש / ומאלה אין יועץ / ואשאלם וישיבו דבר | 28 |

| Meter | Hebrew | Verse |
|---|---|---|
| 4/3 | הן־כלם אין אפס מעשיהם / רוח ותהו נסכיהם | 29 |
| 3/3 | מי פעל ועשה / קרא הדרות מראש | 4 |
| 3/3 | אני יהוה ראשון / ואת־אחרנים אני הוא | |
| 3/3 | העירותיו מצפון ויאת / ממזרח־שמש קראתיו בשמו | 25 |
| 3/3 | ויבס סגנים כמו־חמר / וכמו־יוצר ירמס טיט | |
| 3/3/3 | ואתה ישראל עבדי / יעקב אשר־בחרתׂיך / זרע אברהם אהבי | 8 |
| 3/3 | אשר־החזקתיך מקצות הארץ / ומאציליה קראתיך | 9 |
| 3/3 | ואמר־לך עבדי אתה / בחרתיך ולא מאסתיך | |
| 3/3 | אל־תירא כי־עמך אני / אל־תשתע כי־אני אלהיך | 10 |
| 3/3 | אמצתיך אף־עזרתיך / אף־תמכתיך בימין צדקי | |
| 3/2 | הן יבשו ויכלמו / כל־הנחרים בך | 11 |
| 3/2 | יהיו כאין ויאבדו / אנשי ריבך | |
| 3/2 | תבקשם ולא תמצאם / אנשי מצתך | 12 |
| 3/2 | יהיו כאין וכאפס / אנשי־מלחמתך | |
| 3/2 | כי אני־יהוה אלהיך / מחזיק ימינך | 13 |
| 3/2 | האמר־לך אל תירא / אני עזרתיך | |
| 3/2 | האמר לירושלם תושב / וחרבותיה אקמם | 44.26b |

1. Let the Isles replenish (their) might
And peoples renew (their) strength.
Let them draw near, let them converse;
Together let us draw near for judgment.

2. Who stirred up Cyrus from the east,
With sure purpose summons him to attendance upon him;
Subdues nations before him
And kings reduces beneath him;
Makes their swords like lead,
Like driven chaff their bows?

3. He pursues them, he goes forward successfully
By a path which his feet do not tread down.

5. The Isles beheld and became afraid,
The ends of the earth, and they trembled;
They drew near and came (all) together.

27. First speaker for Zion, behold, I am,
And as advocate for Jerusalem I offer myself.

21. Present your case, sayeth Yahweh;
Marshal your arguments, sayeth Jacob's King.

22. Bring before us the earliest happenings,

The first things, what they were, declare;
>Yea, let us pay attention and let us know their out-
>come.

23. Or the events which are to come make us to hear;
>Tell (us) the things about to happen in the future,
>So that we may know that ye are gods.

Yea, ye may work good or work evil;
>Let us observe and behold it together.

24. Behold, ye are nothing and your work is naught.
>He goes astray who chooses you.

26. Who foretold aught from the very first so that we might
>know it,
>Or from former times, that we might say: (It is) truth?

Yea, there is not one who foretells, yea, not one who
>proclaims,
>Nor yet is there one who hears words of yours.

28. Yea, I looked, but there is not a single one,
>And from among these there is none who can give
>counsel;
>And when I ask them aught, do they give any answer?

29. Behold, all of them are nothing; naught are their works;
>Wind and vanity are their molten images.

4. Who has fashioned and produced,
>Who summoned the generations from the very first?

I, Yahweh am the very first,
>And with the very last ones will I be the Existent One.

25. I stirred him up from the north, so that he came,
>And from the place of sunrise I called him by his
>name,
>So that he tramples down rulers as mortar,
>Yea, even as the potter treads down the clay.

8. But thou, Israel, My servant,
>Jacob, whom I have chosen,
>Seed of Abraham, My friend,

9. Whom I have laid hold of from the ends of the earth,
>Yea, from its very edges have called thee
>And have said unto thee: My servant art thou;
>I have chosen thee and not rejected thee;

10. Fear not, for I am with thee;
>Be not dismayed, for I am thy God;
>I strengthen thee, yea, I help thee,
>Yea, I uphold thee with My trusty right hand.

11.    Behold they shall be put to shame and shall be humiliated,
           All those who inflame themselves against thee;
       They shall become as nothing, yea, they shall perish,
           The men who contend with thee.

12.    Thou mayest seek them out, but thou shalt not find them,
           The men who strive with thee;
       They shall be as naught and vanity,
           The men who war against thee.

13.    Verily, I, Yahweh am thy God,
           He who holds thee fast by thy right hand,
       Who says unto thee: Fear not;
           I am He who aideth thee;

44.26b  Who says of Jerusalem: She shall be repopulated.
           And her ruins will I restore.

1. For חחרישו אלי read, following a suggestion from G, יחדשו חיל; for חדש in a parallel usage cf. Ps. 103.5, and for חיל, "power," cf. I Sam. 2.4; II Sam. 22.40; Ps. 18.33, 40; 84.8. Thus emended, the parallelism between v. 1aα and β becomes perfect. נקרבה, the 1st plu. includes both Yahweh and Israel on the one hand and the various peoples and nations on the other. For a parallel sudden shift from the 3rd or 2nd plu. to the 1st plu. cf. v. 22. למשפט here may mean "for judgment" or "to the place of judgment."

2. העיר as a transitive verb must have an object; most commentators, with considerable violence to the text, regard צדק as that object. But metrical considerations establish clearly that צדק belongs in the second stichos. Clearly then the object of העיר is missing; and certainly the one who was stirred up was Cyrus. The thought of this distich parallels closely that of 45.13 and 46.11. For the missing object some figurative term, such as עיט in 46.11, might be supplied; but all in all it seems best to supply, just as is implicit in 46.11, the name itself, כורש. For צדק read, as in 45.13, בצדק; this is another instance of צדק having the connotation, "sure purpose." This interpretation of בצדק gives to the v. a very powerful, double implication. The essential question is not merely what god brought Cyrus from the east and sent him upon his mission of world-conquest, but also was this done by that god idly or with a sure and worthy purpose, and if the latter, what may that purpose have been? And the implicit answer to the question is that Yahweh, Israel's god, is the deity who stirred up Cyrus, and that in so doing, just as, by further implication, in everything that He does, Yahweh is acting with sure, wise and beneficent purpose, and that in this particular instance, as this is set forth more clearly in other addresses of the prophet, Yahweh's purpose is to effect the restoration of His people to its ancestral land, there to function as His servant, the agent of His world-wide salvation for nations, peoples and all mankind. So interpreted, and particularly with this connotation attributed to בצדק, the sentence becomes meaningful indeed, in fact the key-sentence of the entire address. For לרגלו, read, with G, לרגליו; for this term connoting personal attendance upon some one cf. I Sam. 25.42. ירד should certainly be vocalized יָרְד, from רדד, "to subdue." Metrical considerations suggest very forcibly that a word has been lost at the end of the distich, another graphic instance of the loss of a word at the end of a line in Biblical poetry; accordingly supply תחתיו; cf. Ps. 144.2. Certainly the comparison, in the third

distich of the v., of swords with dust is meaningless and ineffective; accordingly for כעפר read כעפרת; the figure of swords heavy as lead and therefore impossible of use, parallels effectively that of arrows flying aimlessly and uselessly through the air like chaff before the wind. For חרבו and קשתו read, with G, the plu., with plu. suffix, חרבותם and קשתותם. Actually v. 2ab constitutes one 3/3 double-distich, while vv. 2c–3 constitute a second 3/3 double-distich.

3. שלום is here an adverbial accusative; cf. I Sam. 16.4; 25.6; II Sam. 17.3; there is accordingly no need to emend to בשלום, as in Isa. 55.12; Job. 15.21. For יבוא read יָבוּס; cf. below, v. 25; Zech. 10.5.

5. This v. ends the first strophe of the address and tells that the various nations and peoples obeyed the summons, addressed to them in v. 1, and that they came together for the contest of their gods with Yahweh; but this they did in fear and trembling, in manifest anticipation that in this contest they and their gods would be worsted. As ראו and also the two verbs in the third stichos indicate, the action here set forth is all in past time; accordingly it is necessary to read וייראו and ניחרדו. As it stands in MT, the v. is a 3/3/2 distich; however 3/3/3 would certainly be a preferred meter; accordingly, with G and V, supply יחדו after ויאתיון; this is still another instance of the loss of a word at the end of a line of Biblical poetry.

27. This v. has always presented difficult problems, particularly in connection with the words ראשון and מבשר. G. R. Driver (in *Alttestamentliche Studien: Friederich Nötscher Festschrift*, [1950], 46 f.) has offered what seems to be the most plausible explanation of these terms. He holds that ראשון here connotes "the first speaker (in a trial by law or in a debate)." For מבשר he would read מבכר, on the basis of the Syriac בסב, "to refute; to rebuke," and would render it "refuter." Inasmuch as we are dealing in this address with a debate between the gods of the various nations on the one side, and Yahweh, Israel's god, on the other, with the various nations looking on and each eagerly yearning for the triumph of its own god, this interpretation of these two perplexing words, both apparently technical terms here, seems to be peculiarly appropriate. It is plain too that in this v. Yahweh is offering Himself as the spokesman for His people, Israel. Accordingly in the first stichos of the distich, where in MT there is manifestly one word too many for the obvious 3-beat meter, for the meaningless הנה הנם read הנני. In the second stichos אתן is meaningless and impossible; accordingly, and establishing a remarkably vigorous parallelism between the two stichoi, for אתן read אתנדב, an instance of the loss of the final two letters of a word at the end of a line of Biblical poetry. The thought of the v., as thus reconstructed, suggests strongly that it must have stood originally in the early part of the address; we have accordingly transposed it to follow v. 5.

21. In this v. Yahweh is quite obviously the speaker. He addresses the gods of the nations and challenges them individually to present each the evidence of his divinity, and particularly to show who among them, if anyone, it was, who summoned Cyrus to his career of world-conquest and made him so uniformly successful in all his undertakings. Plainly this v. records the initial words of Yahweh in His role of "first speaker" in the debate. We have accordingly transposed this v. and the entire passage which it introduces, vv. 21–24, 26, 28–29, to follow immediately upon v. 27. Certainly עצמותיכם is meaningless here; accordingly, following a hint from G and S, with a simple shift of two letters, read מועצותיכם, "your evil counsel or argument"; for מועצה with the connotation, "evil, stubborn counsel (which leads only to destruction)" cf. Jer. 7.24; Micah 6.16; Ps. 81.13; Prov. 1.31. מלך־יעקב must be read as a compound term with a single beat, both because the meter demands this and also because it is in parallelism with יהוה in the corresponding position in the first stichos. Very significantly the word, מלך, occurs only three times in Isa.

40–48 (41.21; 43.15; 44.6) and is always a designation of Yahweh. As we have already intimated, Deutero-Isaiah plainly conceived of Israel as no longer a political entity, ruled by its own king of flesh and blood, but as merely a province of the vast Persian Empire, and therefore subject to Cyrus, Yahweh's chosen "Anointed One." On the other hand, the prophet conceived of Israel as a religious community, a people whose supreme ruler and king was Yahweh, its god. Appreciation of this fact enables us to comprehend more clearly and precisely the role of Israel as Yahweh's עבד. Often the term עבד המלך designates a high official of the court, even the one second in authority to the king, the king's lieutenant or agent (cf. II Sam. 15.34; I Kings 11.26; II Kings 22.12; Neh. 2.10, 19 *et passim*). It is actually with this connotation that we should interpret the designation of Israel as the עבד יהוה, so characteristic of Deutero-Isaiah, actually not merely "the servant of Yahweh" but rather "the agent of Yahweh," of Yahweh, its King, the agent charged with a specific and highly responsible task, the salvation of all mankind in the name of Yahweh, the one, universal God, the divine Sovereign of all nations. So understood, it becomes apparent that the title, עבד יהוה, as coined by Deutero-Isaiah, implies for Israel, not a position of abject humility, but rather one of high responsibility, dignity and authority in relation to Yahweh, its King, on the one hand and to all the other nations on the other hand.

22. As it stands in *MT* this v. is plainly overloaded. The verse-division between vv. 22 and 23 should be immediately after אחריתן, and the final three words of v. 22 should, as in *G*, constitute the opening portion of v. 23. Thus rearranged, vv. 22 and 23a constitute a 3/3/3 double-tristich, with remarkably effective parallelism between the two tristichs and also between the stichoi of each tristich. In the first stichos of v. 22 in place of the present 3rd plu. impf., יגישו ויגידו, read, in conformity with all the other verbs immediately preceding and following, the impv. 2nd plu. Furthermore, there is here quite plainly one word too many for the meter; accordingly, since it occurs twice again, in the second stichos of this v. and also at the beginning of v. 23, omit והגידו here. Likewise, since the second stichos here speaks of events of the past, while the whole of v. 23 speaks of events of the future, we would certainly expect that the first tristich in its entirety should deal with the past. Viewed from this angle, את־אשר־תקרינה is certainly disturbing; accordingly, by a relatively simple emendation, for אשר תקרינה read הקדמניות "the former things"; cf. 43.18, where קדמניות is used in parallelism with ראשנות. The reference here is not necessarily, and probably not at all, to the events of creation, but rather to more recent events in history, which these gods of the nations, any one of them, might claim to have planned and carried through. In the final stichos there is obviously one word too many for the meter; accordingly omit לב; for שים, "to pay attention," with לב omitted but clearly understood, cf. Judg. 19.30.

23. As we have arranged the text, the three final words of v. 22 of *MT* should be linked to this v. V. 23a then is a 3/3/3 tristich, while v. 23b is a 3/3 distich. The text of the entire v. seems to be in perfect order. Both the tristich and the distich are introduced by conjunctions, או and אף, both of which, however, are emphatic and must therefore receive each a full beat. For אחור with the connotation, "the future," cf. 42.23 and the note to that v. V. 23b says, "Yea, ye may work either good or evil," but so long as it has divine character we will consider it evidence that ye are gods. Marti has very properly called attention to the biting sarcasm of this statement. Actually the sentence may well be directed at Persian Zoroastrianism; "ye may work good," i. e. like Ormuzd, or "work evil," i. e. like Ahriman.

24. For מאפע read אפס and for מאין read אין; in both cases the 'מ is the result of

dittography; for אפס ⸻אין as used here cf. vv. 12, 29 and also 40.17. The second
stichos emend, with Torrey, to read תועה הבחר בכם. It would seem that the prophet
represents Yahweh as, after His challenge in vv. 21–23, waiting dramatically for
the gods of the nations, or at least some one of them, to speak up and claim divinity
and divine power. But the total silence of these so-called gods in response to this
challenge leads necessarily to the conclusion, stated in this forceful manner, that
these supposititious gods are, all of them without exception, absolute nothings,
with the consequence that whoever accords worship to any of them certainly goes
astray.

26. V. 25 plainly interrupts the manifest thought-unity between vv. 24 and 26
and is an intrusion here. We have accordingly transposed it to follow immediately
after v. 4, with which it, in turn, comprises a perfect thought-unit. For וְנֵדְעָה it
seems better to vocalize וְנֵדְעָה. For צדיק read, with DSIa and G, צדק, "truth." The
threefold repetition of אף here seems characteristic of Deutero-Isaiah's style; cf.
40.24; 44.15–16; 46.11.

28. V. 28 continues directly the thought of v. 26 and paves the way for the
ultimate, general conclusion stated in v. 29. V. 27 is plainly a disturbing intrusion
here and fits better in the position to which we have transposed it. For וארא read,
with DSIa, וְאראה. The ו of the second ואין must be omitted. The v. climaxes the
debate and formulates the conclusion of the utter unreality and impotence of the
gods of the other nations. They stand mute and impassive. Among them there is
not a single individual who can act, nor any one who can serve as counsellor or
pleader in this debate. In fact when questions are put to them no answer is forthcoming. They are unreal, non-existent, imaginary things, with neither being, life
nor power. This this debate has demonstrated conclusively. For the expression,
אין איש, "there is no one," cf. 63.3. When יעץ is used with a god as the subject it
connotes "to make a decision; to decree," cf. 19.17; Jer. 49.20; 50.45.

29. For און it is necessary to read, with DSIa and S and also as the parallelism
with אפס indicates, אין. For נסכיהם with the connotation, "their idols," cf. 48.5;
Jer. 10.14; 51.17.

4. V. 4, followed by v. 25, presents rather succinctly, it must be admitted, the
positive side of Yahweh's argument, the affirmation that He has been, is and will
be the one, sole God from the beginning to the end of the world, and that accordingly He it was, and none other, who stirred up Cyrus from the very first and prospered him upon all of his campaigns. The text seems to be in perfect shape.

25. העירותי, a transitive verb, must have an object; accordingly, as in 45.13,
read העירותיו. The v. represents Cyrus as coming, at Yahweh's summons, from the
far east and also from the north, i. e. from the distant north-east, an effective descrip-
tion of the location of Persia with reference to Babylonia. Inasmuch as 45.4 states
that Cyrus did not, or perhaps even does not, know Yahweh, the statement here
that Cyrus calls upon Yahweh by name, i. e. accords Him homage and worship,
certainly can not be correct; accordingly emend יקרא בשמי to קראתיו בשמו בשמי. Thus
v. 25a repeats the thought already expressed by the prophet in 45.4b and 13a. For
ויבא again, as in v. 3, read, with Kittel, ויבס. Vocalize ירמס, giving both this word
and טיט a full beat; the subj. of this verb is not Cyrus, but is יוצר, immediately
preceding.

8. The text of vv. 8–11 seems to be in perfect order. The אשר preceding בחרתיך
must receive a full beat for the sake of the meter, whereas that preceding חזקתיך
in v. 9 must, for the same reason, be read with the verb as a single beat. For אהב
meaning "close friend" cf. I Kings 5.15. This title is applied to Abraham again in

II Chron. 20.7. Outside of this passage the name, Abraham, occurs in only six other passages in all the prophetic writings. Of these Isa. 51.2; 63.16 are Trito-Isaiah and so are certainly later than this. The mention of Abraham in Isa. 29.22 is clearly an interpolation into a passage itself probably late. Ezek. 33.24 comes at the very earliest from near the end of the Exile, has a definitely Palestinian setting and seems to voice the hopes of the Nationalist Party of regaining political independence and control of the land. The thought underlying both Jer. 33.26 and Micah 7.20 is that of Yahweh's covenant with David and His promise to the patriarchs as this latter is set forth in the J2 stratum of the Pentateuch. Manifestly all these passages must be linked with the program of the Nationalist Party in 520 B. C. or in 486 B. C. (cf. Morgenstern, "Jerusalem—485 B. C.," *HUCA* XXVII [1956], 155 ff.). Certainly then the reference to Abraham here is the earliest in all prophetic writings. Actually Deutero-Isaiah seems to have been the one who first conceived the idea that Yahweh chose Israel for the first time, not at Sinai, but rather when He called Abraham and with him made His initial covenant.

9. In this v. the prophet makes his most positive statement of the role of Israel as Yahweh's chosen servant. Moreover, this choice of Israel for this responsible role was not of recent occurrence, but was from the very time of Abraham, of Israel's origin as a people. This v. indicates plainly that by the time when this address was uttered the prophet had completely outgrown Ezekiel's doctrine of "for His name's sake," with which, as we have learned, he had inaugurated his prophetic ministry. ולא מאסתיך certainly refers to the interpretation put by other nations and peoples, and not impossibly even by some sections of the Jewish people also, upon the conquest of Judah by the Babylonians, loss of Judaic national existence and subsequent exile in Babylonia. Yahweh's choice of Israel at the very beginning of its existence as a people implied an eternal choice, with no possibility of these relations ever being terminated. For metrical reasons ומאצׁיליה must be read as two beats.

10. In the second stichos the first אף must receive a beat for the sake of the meter. The thought of vv. 8–9 is continued and reaches its climax in this v. The three verbs in the second stichos plainly imply the continuity of Yahweh's support of Israel in its service in His behalf from the moment when this service began in the distant past until the present moment, and with this the assurance of the continuance of this support on into the remote future.

Vv. 11–13 constitute a closely knit strophe announcing the certain and utter doom of the enemies of this new and faithful Israel and assuring it that it need not fear before them; accordingly it is very appropriately cast throughout in the elegiac 3/2 meter.

11. כל־הנחרים must be read as a single beat for the sake of the meter.

12. This is the only instance of מֵצָת in the entire Bible; מַצָּה, however, occurs three times, and so is well attested; it is probably wise therefore to, with Kittel, vocalize מַצָּתֶךָ.

13. כי here is the כי of certainty and so receives a full beat.

44.26b. This half-v., for which we can find no other suitable place in all of Deutero-Isaiah's addresses, fits in very well here both as to metrical form and as to thought. It gives to the new Israel the assurance, not merely of divine help in a general sense, but also in the specific direction of return to ancestral land and the rebuilding and restoration of Jerusalem to all its ancient glory.

## Isa. 40. 6–8, 12–31

Isa. 40. 1–5, 9–10a we have already shown to be a unit with 52.1–12[1] and have treated these vv. in detail. 40.10b–11 seem to be a gloss amplifying vv. 9–10a, or they may perhaps be a fragment of some other unidentifiable Trito-Isaianic utterance. Under no condition can they be integrated with the address contained in the major portion of this chapter.

This address presents numerous problems. There is no cogent reason to question its Deutero-Isaianic authorship. Various factors, such as the language and literary technique, the dominant universalism, the role of Yahweh as Creator of the world, the insignificance and transitoriness of foreign monarchs, all these and other considerations, as well as the position of this address with relation to the other addresses of the prophet, speak strongly for its Deutero-Isaianic authorship.

On the other hand, we miss in this address many of the dominant thoughts and motifs which we have found repeated again and again in all the other addresses of the prophet which we have already considered. Thus there is in this address not a word of denunciation of Israel in exile for its faithlessness to Yahweh and its coquetting with the Babylonian gods; there is in fact not the slightest suggestion of such faithlessness. Neither is there any trace of the Ezekelian doctrine of "for His name's sake," nor yet any suggestion whatsoever of the divinely appointed role of Israel as the servant or agent of Yahweh in the mission of bringing salvation to all mankind. There is likewise no mention of Cyrus, no contest or debate with the gods of other nations, no suggestion of Israel's divinely destined return to its ancestral land. The complete silence of the address with regard to these various motifs, all so integral in Deutero-Isaiah's total message, is significant indeed.

Furthermore, the address seems to envisage as its audience, not at all the entire Jewish community exiled in Babylonia, but only a section thereof, and that too seemingly not an overly large section. This group of Jews has apparently become disheartened and their faith in Yahweh, their god, seems to be shaken. It is not at all that they are turning from Him in order to attach themselves more or less closely to the cult of other, foreign gods. It is merely that their faith in Yahweh's ability to help them and protect them from some seemingly impending danger or calamity and to fulfill all His promise to them

---

[1] Cf. above, Part I note 22, pp. 10 ff.

seems to be wavering. Perhaps some grave disappointment or misfortune has recently befallen them or seems about to befall them, and they are beset with grave doubts with regard to Yahweh's ability to care for them and save them. From this distrust of Yahweh's power and of His purpose with them the prophet seeks to free the audience he is here addressing and to restore their shaken confidence in Yahweh and to enhearten them with faith in their divinely assured future.

All this permits only one conclusion, viz. that this is our prophet's very latest address, and that quite some time, several years perhaps, had elapsed between the delivery of his most recent address and this address. These had been, so it seems, momentous years for the prophet. Apparently the line of demarcation between his faithful followers, those who reverently accepted his message, and the great mass of, at least so it impressed the prophet, disbelieving and even faithless Israel in exile, had grown acute. The prophet's message is now directed to only the small group of his own hesitant followers. Them he need no longer convince that Yahweh is the one, sole God of the universe and that the so-called foreign gods are all vain and empty nothings. This basic principle of the prophet's message is devoutly accepted by his present audience and he need dwell upon it no further. Apparently too, as has been said, some grave misfortune has recently befallen them or now threatens them. Accordingly this is not the time for the prophet to dwell upon the theme of Israel as the servant of Yahweh charged with the responsible task of mediating to the nations and peoples of the world that universal salvation which Yahweh has destined for them. In its present mood the prophet's audience is not responsive to this message. His task at the moment is not at all to denounce them for loss of faith, but is rather to enhearten them, to restore their faith in Yahweh and their confidence in themselves and in their way of life, to make them believe once again that Yahweh is with them, keeps faith with them, and that therefore their future is assured. And this he does with such power and conviction that he could hardly have failed to achieve his purpose.

What the calamity or what the threatening danger which had thus affected this particular group's attitude towards Yahweh and their trust in Him may have been we have of course no way of knowing. We can only conjecture. As has been said already, Israel, now exiled in Babylonia for over fifty years, had no reason to fear foreign enemies, nor yet, so it would seem, antagonism from the Babylonians among whom they were settled. Most probably therefore the hostility and attendant threat to the group whom the prophet is here addressing came from within the ranks of Israel, from the mass of fellow-Israelites who in the process of integration with the culture of their Babylonian environment were repudiating Yahweh in greater or less degree and adjusting themselves with more or less conviction to the worship of the Babylonian deities. We have already suggested that in the course of time this section of the Jewish exiles in Babylonia came to resent the prophet's oft-repeated denunciation of them. And this resentment may well have extended itself in time to the little body of the prophet's immediate followers. And this may well have expressed itself in the open persecution of this latter little group, persecution all the more bitter and depressing because it was at the hands of their own fellow-Jews. The existence of such a hostile group we have already suggested in our discussion of 41.11; and it is not at all improbable that with the passing years the animosity of this group had increased in intensity and had extended itself to include not only the prophet himself but also his immediate, faithful followers. We can readily picture to ourselves what the humiliation and fear of this little group must have been when confronted by the distrust of their own Jewish brethren and persecution at their hands, and how, in consequence thereof, their faith in Yahweh and in His purpose with them may well have been shaken.

The theme of the address is clear and is closely unified. It is that Yahweh's faithfulness is absolute and assured, whereas that of man is at the very best uncertain and more or less evanescent. This theme is set forth clearly in the opening words of the address. It begins most effectively and dramatically by the prophet's declaration to his audience that he hears a voice calling, calling of course directly to him. This voice can be only either that of Yahweh Himself or of one of His heavenly messengers, speaking, however, in Yahweh's name. More probably it is the latter, as the use of אלהינו, "our God," in v. 8b would seem to indicate. The voice charges the prophet to call out, to speak, to proclaim a divinely communicated message. And in answer to the prophet's question, "What shall I proclaim,"? the answer comes back, contained in vv. 6b–8, that in the message which he is bidden to deliver he should contrast the absolute faithfulness of Yahweh in fulfilling His covenant obligations with the instability of mankind in so doing. There can be no question that the whole of v. 7 is a gloss which seriously interrupts and misdirects the course of thought. The entire v. is missing in the most reliable texts of G. Largely upon the basis of these considerations Gesenius, Hitzig and Oort regarded v. 7 as a gloss. This conclusion finds striking confirmation in the fact that the original manuscript of DSIa did not contain this v., but that it was inserted, written partly between the lines and partly down the left-hand margin of the column, by some later scribe. That he was certainly a later scribe is convincingly attested by the fact that he no longer wrote out the name of the Deity, יהוה, but instead indicated it by four dots, thus · · · · With v. 7, with its vague and disturbing thought, omitted, v. 8 follows smoothly and clearly and with perfectly unified thought upon v. 6.

The key-word of the sentence, and with this of the entire address, is חסדו in v. 6. The precise import of the word in this passage seems not to have been grasped by translators and commentators alike. G, V and S rendered the word as if it either read or were a synonym of הודו, "its glory." Influenced no doubt by the vss. the King James Bible and with it the Jewish Publication Society Bible have rendered the word "its goodliness." Torrey, in turn, renders it, with no textual emendation, "its beauty." Duhm would emend the word to הדרו, "its splendor." Kittel too would emend it to either הדרו or else to חמדו, "its splendor." Cheyne, Perles and Marti would emend it to חסנו, "its strength." To comprehend the true meaning of the word in this place we must understand something of the evolution of the covenant concept in ancient Israel.

Originally a ברית, a "covenant," was a mutual agreement between two parties by which each obligated himself to perform faithfully for the other some eagerly needed or desired function or service. By the terms of the covenant between Yahweh and Israel Yahweh undertook to be Israel's god and its alone, to favor, protect and prosper it in every way conceivable and at all odds. And Israel, in turn, undertook to worship and serve Him, and Him alone, to have naught to do with other gods, to do His will and carry out all His commands faithfully and eagerly. Failure of either contracting party to fulfill his assumed obligations warranted the repudiation of the covenant by the other party. According to the pre-exilic prophets Israel had been faithless to its covenant obligations with Yahweh. Therefore Yahweh was about to repudiate His covenant with it, to cast it off, leave it thus a people without a god to protect it; and of course a people so situated could do naught but perish. However, Jeremiah in his later years, as the final utterance of his rich, prophetic message, proclaimed that Yahweh would not cast Israel off despite its undeniable violation of its most essential obligations to Him. Instead He would discipline it through the bitter experiences of exile in Babylonia and would thus purge it of its inclination to go astray from Him. And when at last, after seventy years, this work of purgation and regeneration would have been completed, then Yahweh would terminate Israel's exile, restore it to its native land, make a new covenant with it, take it again as His people and function anew, as He had actually never ceased to function, as its god.

Not at all surprisingly this message of the new covenant formed by Yahweh with Israel captivated the imagination of the Jewish people, both those who had remained in Palestine and those who had been carried to Babylonia. Quietly the belief became firmly rooted in the heart and mind of Israel that it was still bound to Yahweh, its god, but by a new covenant, one which Yahweh had Himself imposed upon it, a new and eternal covenant, one which would never be broken.

However, despite the trials and sufferings of the exile, Israel did not become regenerate in the true and full sense of the term, as Jeremiah had anticipated. Its covenant relations with Yahweh continued to be much as those of its ancestors had been, loose and irresponsible. But the belief was now firmly implanted that the covenant relationship between Yahweh and Israel was eternal, unbreakable. Ezekiel's message of "for His name's sake" enhanced this concept of the eternal covenant immeasurably by its implication that for the sake of His reputation as a true god, a world-god, among the nations Yahweh needed Israel quite as much as Israel needed Him. The concept of the new, eternal covenant between Yahweh and Israel was now firmly established in the thought and life of the Jewish people. Regardless of how Israel might live and act henceforth, this covenant never would, and actually could not, be repudiated by either contracting party.

But it is readily clear that such a covenant was not a true covenant in the old and proper sense of the word, that it was not a ברית, a two-sided, mutual obligation. Of course there could be no question whatever that Yahweh would always fulfill His every obligation to Israel, His people. But there was no assurance that Israel would always fulfill its every obligation to Yahweh. In fact history quickly demonstrated that Israel was remiss in many particulars. Israel in Babylonia, for example, as we have seen, forsook Yahweh in very considerable measure and went over more or less completely to recognition and even to positive worship of the Babylonian gods. And yet, viewed from Yahweh's standpoint, Israel was still His people and He needed it, whether, according to Ezekiel's doctrine, for the sake of His reputation as a god, or, according to Deutero-Isaiah's doctrine, as His servant, the agent of His universal purpose for the peoples of the world. Whatever Israel's conduct in relation to Yahweh, He could not cast it off, could not repudiate His eternal covenant with it.

But, as has been said, call it what one will, such a relationship between god and people is not a true covenant in the old meaning of the term. All the obligation was now on one side. Yahweh, as god, could not of course but fulfill His every obligation to His people; but there was no assurance that Israel would fulfill its every obligation to its god. In fact it was reasonably assured that it would fail to do so. Small wonder then that in the prophetic utterances and also in the general literature of the post-exilic period the word, ברית, came to be used with less and less frequency and another word supplanted it to describe this new covenant relationship. This new word was חסד. In fact the primary and basic meaning of חסד was "a two-sided, mutually binding obligation."[1] As the passive implication of the form of the noun indicates, a חסיד was one who had been admitted into חסד, "covenant relationship," with Yahweh, with full awareness of the obligation which this relationship imposed upon him (cf. Deut. 33.8; Ps. 50.5; 89.20). This חסד relationship described the covenant between Yahweh and Israel (cf. Isa. 54.10; 55.3). חסד thus became almost synonymous, on the one hand, with ברית, and, on the other hand, with אמונה, "faithfulness," and אמת, "truth" (cf. Ps. 89.2–4, 15). The חסדי יהוה were the "faithful acts of Yahweh," which He performed in fulfillment of His covenant obligations (cf. Ps. 89.50). Accordingly חסד in this period acquired the fundamental meaning, "faithfulness," faithfulness in fulfillment of covenant obligations; loyalty; integrity; responsibility."

Just this is the meaning which the word has in Isa. 40.6. The address affirms that man's חסד, "faithfulness," is ephemeral like the flowers of the field, whereas Yahweh's faithfulness is eternal and sure for all those who wait for Him and put their trust in Him. This is the dominant theme of this stirring address, with its very effective climax, the assurance to those "who wait for Yahweh" that they will in due time find their faith and their hopes fulfilled in overflowing measure.

| | | |
|---|---|---|
| 3/3 | קוֹל אָמַר קרא / וְאוֹמַר מה אקרא | 6 |
| 3/3 | כל הבשר חציר / וכל־חסדו כציץ השדה | |
| 4/4 | יבש חציר נבל ציץ / ודבר אלהינו יקום לעולם | 8 |
| 4/3 | מי מדד בשעלו ימים / ושמים בזרתו תכן | 12 |

---

[1] Cf. Glueck, *Das Wort ḥesed im alttestamentlichen Sprachgebrauch als menschliche und göttliche gemeinschaftsgemässe Verhaltungsweise*, BZAW 47 (1927).

וכל בשלש < > ארץ / ושקל בפלס הרים / ונבעות במאזנים
<נטל>
3/3/3

מי תכן את־רוח יהוה / ו<מי> איש־עצתו ויודיענו
4/3    13

את־מי נועץ ויבינהו / וילמדהו ארח משפט / < > ודרך תבונות
הודיענו
3/3/3    14

הן גוים כמר מדלי / וכשחק מאזנים נחשבו
4/3    15a

והן־איים כריק יוטל / ולבנון אין־די בער / וחיתו אין־די עולה
3/3/3    15b–16

וכל הגוים כאין נגדו / כאפס ותהו נחשבו לו
4/4    17

ואל־מי תדמיון יהוה / ומה דמות תערכו־לו
3/3    18

הלוא תדעו הלוא תשמעו / הלוא הגד לכם מראש / הלוא הבינותם
מיסודת הארץ
4/4/4    21

הישב על־חוג הארץ / וישביה כחגבים <לפניו>
3/3    22

הנוטה כדק שמים / וימתחם כאהל לשבתו
3/3

הנותן רוזנים לאין / שפטי־ארץ כתהו עשה
3/3    23

אף־בל נטעו אף־בל זרעו / אף־בל שרש בארץ גזעם
4/4    24

וגם־נשף בהם וייבשו / וסערה כקש תשאם
3/3

ואל־מי תדמיוני ואשוה / יאמר קָדוש <ישראל>
3/3    25

שאו מרום עיניכם וראו / מי ברא <כל> אלה
4/4    26

המוציא במספר צבאם / לכלם בשם יקרא
3/3

מרב אונים ואמֶץ־כחו / איש לא נעדר
3/3

למה תאמר יעקב / ותדבר ישראל <עמי>
3/3    27

נסתרה דרכי מיהוה / ומאלהי משפטי עבר
3/3

הלוא ידעת אם־לא־שמעת / אלהי עולם יהוה / בורא קצות הארץ
3/3/3    28

לא ייעף ולא־ייגע / אין חקר לתבונתו
3/3

נתן לִיעֵף כח / ולאין־אונים עצמה ירבה
3/3    29

וייעפו נערים וייגעו / ובחורים כשול יכשלו
3/3    30

וקוי יהוה יחליפו כח / יעלו אבר כנשרים
4/3    31

ירוצו ולא ייגעו / ילכו ולא ייעפו
3/3

6.  A voice said: Proclaim!
        And I said: What shall I proclaim?
    All flesh is grass
        And all its faithfulness is as the flower of the field.
8.  The grass withers, the flower fades,
        But the word of our God stands forever.
12. Who has measured the ocean in the hollow of his hand,
        Or has marked off the heavens with his span,
    Or contained the earth in a measure,

Or has weighed the mountains in scales
Or the hills has suspended in a balance?

13. Who has compassed the spirit of Yahweh,
Or who was His adviser, who imparted knowledge to Him?

14. With whom did He take counsel, so that he made Him to comprehend,
And taught Him the course of justice,
And the way of discernment he caused Him to know?

15a. Behold, nations are as a drop from a bucket,
Even as a speck of dust on a scales are they reckoned.

15b–16 Behold the Isles are as something worthless cast away,
And Lebanon would not suffice for fuel,
Nor its animals for a burnt-offering.

17. Yea, all the nations are as nothing before Him;
As naught and vanity are they reckoned in comparison with Him.

18. Then to whom would ye liken Yahweh,
Or what appearance would ye ascribe to Him?

21. Do ye not know; will ye not hear;
Hath it not been told to you from the very first;
Have ye not comprehended it from the founding of the earth?

22. It is He who sitteth upon the circle of the earth,
And its inhabitants are as grasshoppers before Him,
Who stretcheth out the heavens as a spread,
And sets them up as a tent for His habitation;

23. Who bringeth princes to nothingness;
Who maketh the rulers of the earth (to be) as naught;

24. Yea, they are not planted, nor yet are they sown,
Nor yet does their stalk take root in the soil;
Moreover, when He breathes upon them they wither away,
And the tempest carries them off as chaff.

25. Then to whom would ye liken Me that I should be similar,
Sayeth the Holy One of Israel.

26. Raise your eyes aloft and see!
Who hath called all these into being,
Who bringeth forth the host of them in order,
Who summons each of them by name,
(So that) because of His abundant strength and mighty power
Not a single one is missing?

27.   Why sayest thou, O Jacob,
          And declarest, O Israel, My people,
      My way is hid from Yahweh,
          And my cause hath passed away from my God?

28.   Dost thou not know, or hast thou not heard?
          God everlasting is Yahweh,
              The Creator of the ends of the earth.
      He groweth not weary nor doth He become exhausted;
          There is no fathoming of His wisdom.

29.   He giveth strength to the weary
          And for him who is without power he multiplieth might.

30.   Even youths may grow weary and become exhausted,
          And young men may stumble completely.

31.   But they who hope in Yahweh shall renew (their) strength;
          They shall sprout forth wings as eagles,
      They shall run but not grow weary,
          They shall move onward but not grow faint.

---

6. For וָאֹמַר it is well, as indeed the context requires, to read, with *G* and possibly also with DSIa, וָאֹמַר, "and I said." But with this reading it seems wise instead of אֹמֵר to read אָמַר, and thus set both verbs in the past tense. Vv. 6b–8 are the answer given by the Voice to the prophet's question; as already said, they state the dominant theme of the address which the prophet is bidden to deliver. Read כל for the sake of the meter and to bring out the full emphasis of the word.

12–17. These vv. constitute a closely knit strophe with a unique metrical form. The theme of the strophe is the absolute incomparability of Yahweh. The strophe consists of seven metrical units, three 4/3—3/3/3's plus a 4/4, in which last the theme is summed up in climactic form. The effect is impressive indeed.

12. For מים read, with Kittel, ימים, "the Ocean" (cf. Gen. 1.10; 49.13; Deut. 33.19 *et passim*). For בזרת read, with DSIa, the Syriac translation of *G*, and *S*, בזרתו. With the pronominal suffix thus appended the word balances completely בשעלו in the first stichos of v. 12a. As comparison with vv. 14 and 15b–16 indicates, v. 12b must be read as a 3/3/3; accordingly in the first stichos there is one word too many; omit therefore, with Kittel, the altogether superfluous עפר; in fact with this word omitted, the parallelism between ocean, heaven and earth, the three integral parts of the world as then conceived, becomes complete. Also with Kittel, for הארץ read ארץ to conform to ימים and שמים, both nouns used here without the article. In the third stichos a word is missing, requisite for the expected three beats of the stichos; by inserting it at the end of the third stichos, a perfect, chiastic parallelism between the two stichoi is achieved; this is of course one more instance of the loss of a word at the end of a line of Biblical poetry. שעל is manifestly a unit of liquid measure, manifestly of small size (cf. I Kings 20.10). The זרת was a unit of longitudinal measure, "the span of a hand," also a relatively small measure. The שלש was obviously a unit of dry measure; the stem, שלש, suggests compellingly that it was one third of some larger, standard unit, presumably an ephah. The question here is obviously not merely who has measured ocean, heaven and earth, but rather who has measured

them so minutely and precisely by measurements each the smallest in its particular category.

13.  Since vv. 13 and 14 constitute the second of the series of three successive 4/3—3/3/3's it is obvious that the second stichos of v. 13 contains one word too few, while the third stichos of v. 14 contains two words too many. In v. 13b אִישׁ עֲצָתוֹ, since it is a somewhat conventional term expressing a single idea (cf. 46.11), should be read as a single beat. Accordingly, following G, V and S, insert מִי at the beginning of the stichos and shift the וֹ connective from וְאִישׁ to it and read וּמִי. Also, following G and V, prefix a וֹ and read וְיוֹדִעֶנּוּ; this would give to this verb the force of a relative clause, "who has imparted knowledge to him"; this וֹ was undoubtedly lost by haplography. Very interestingly and significantly this seems to be the only passage in the entire Bible where the רוּחַ יהוה is present in the Deity Himself; in every other passage it is an emanation from the Deity, which goes forth from Him and rests upon some distinguished person, a king (I Sam. 10.6, 10; 16.13), a prophet (I Kings 22.24; Ezek. 11.5) or some other leader of the people (Judg. 3.10; 11.29; 13.25) or one charged with an especial task (Ex. 31.3; 35.31). It always implies that the particular individual is filled with divine knowledge and power; and here too the concept of divine knowledge is implicit in the use of the term; the realization of this fact makes plain the thought-parallelism between the two stichoi of the v.

14.  It seems wise to, with G, V, and S, omit the בְ of בָּאֹרַח and make the noun the second object of וַיְלַמְּדֵהוּ. Likewise in the third stichos of the tristich there are plainly two beats too many. Moreover, the repetition of וַיְלַמְּדֵהוּ in this stichos immediately after its use in the preceding stichos is stylistically inelegant and awkward; accordingly, with G, omit וַיְלַמְּדֵהוּ דַעַת as a gloss; this restores the expected three beats within the stichos. Also for יוֹדִיעֶנּוּ in this third stichos it seems well to read הוֹדִיעֶנּוּ, to accord with the past tense expressed by the two verbs immediately preceding. Possibly מִשְׁפָּט in the second stichos, instead of being translated "justice," its conventional connotation, might here be translated better "government," i. e. the administration of the world by Yahweh, its שׁוֹפֵט or "ruler"; just this is the major theme of the remainder of this address.

Vv. 15-17 continue the picture of measuring and weighing, and, following immediately upon v. 14, say that whereas the spirit of God defies, is superior to, all weighing and measuring, nations, even entire nations, not only can be weighed and measured, but also, when so weighed and measured, in comparison with God are altogether insignificant, are but as a tiny drop from a full bucket or as a speck of dust upon a scale, utterly nothing, hardly meriting notice. This leads, in turn, very effectively to the question of v. 18, all this being so, how then can man liken God to anything, how can he seek to measure or depict or represent Him in human terms? How, above all, so the implication clearly is, can man continue to believe that an idol can resemble or portray God in any way? Vv. 21-24 then go on to describe God in the only manner comprehensible to man, by His creation and government of the universe and by His absolute, incomparable, irresistible power in comparison with which human beings are as grasshoppers, and even kings are as nothing; in fact He Himself has made them so, and His power, compared with theirs, is such that He carries them away as a breath. This leads properly and effectively to the repetition of the question in v. 25, "To what then would ye, insignicant human beings, liken God, Israel's own, peculiar, Holy One?" The emphatic affirmation here that He, the one, universal God, is in first degree Israel's own god, paves the way most effectively to the final assurance to anxious and troubled Israel that He has not forgotten it or His covenant (חֶסֶד, implicit here from v. 6) with it, and that He will care for it and deliver it from its present unhappy situation. But first, the primary, logical answer to the question of v. 25, to whom may man properly liken God? How shall they comprehend Him, the first, indispensable task in making any such comparison? Only by observing the wonder of His creation, its magnitude and precision, as evidenced by all the heavenly bodies and the punctuality of their movement. Therefore, knowing His solicitude for it, His people, Israel should realize that there is no ground for its fear that He no longer concerns Himself with it. Let them but have faith in Him and in His faithfulness and incomparable power, and they can feel reassured and can gather new hope and strength. Such is the theme of this address and the course of its development.

15. The final stichos in v. 15b must be dissociated from the distich in v. 15a and linked with v. 16 to form the 3/3/3 tristich here expected; note that with this rearrangment both the distich and the tristich begin with הן, and also that thus גוים is the theme of both parts of the distich, whereas in the tristich each stichos has a different subject. In order to achieve the expected four beats in the first stichos of the 4/3 distich הן here must be read with a full beat. The rather meaningless כדק ימול I would, following a suggestion of the Syriac translation of G and of 'A, emend to כריק יוטל.

17. Inasmuch as v. 17 continues directly the thought of vv. 15–16, it is well, with G, to prefix a connective ו to כל at the beginning of the v. and read וכל. For מאפס, a term which occurs nowhere else in the Bible, read, following G, with Kittel, כאפס. It seems well to read v. 17 as a 4/4, giving a full beat to וְכֹל in the first stichos and again to לו in the second stichos and thus bringing out the emphatic import of both words.

18. For אל read, with G, יהוה; certainly we expect here the proper name of the Deity rather than the title, אל, "the Supreme God," and this despite the fact that Deutero-Isaiah frequently employs אל as a designation of Yahweh.

21. Each הלוא must receive a full beat in order that its emphatic import may be appreciated; this makes the v. a 4/4/4 tristich. In the second stichos it seems well to transpose מראש to follow לכם and thus to link the latter word more closely with הגד. For מוסדות read, with Kittel, מיסודת (cf. Ps. 87.1).

22. The חוג הארץ is of course the encircling horizon of the earth. Inasmuch as the meter is plainly 3/3, a word is obviously missing in the second stichos of the first distich; accordingly supply לפניו, a word which is essential to the complete thought of the stichos; another instance of the loss of a word at the end of a line of Biblical poetry. For כדק, which is meaningless here and is plainly a corruption, V seems to have read כריק; following the hint which V thus offers, for כדק read, with many commentators, כרקיע; for נטה and רקע used in close association cf. Isa. 42.5; 44.24. For Yahweh's dwelling-place likened to a tent cf. Ps. 27.5.

23. For שפטי־ארץ cf. Ps. 2.10; 148.11; here the two words are closely linked and must, as the meter requires, be read as a single beat. תהו is used with the article (I Sam. 12.21; Isa. 29.21; Job 6.18) as well as without it (cf. v. 17 above); accordingly retain the article here, with MT.

24. The v. consists of two distichs, one a 4/4 and the other a 3/3. Each of the אף־בל's is emphatic and so must receive a full beat. שֹׁרֵשׁ must be regarded as a po'el perf. ויבשו should be written וייבשו, since it is a form of יבש, "to dry up;" the ו should be construed as a ו connective, so that the tense may agree with תשאם.

25. The ו of ואל has the force of "then." Inasmuch as the v. is manifestly a 3/3, the second stichos plainly has lost a word; accordingly supply ישראל after קדוש. The title קדוש ישראל, for Yahweh occurs nine times in Isa. 40–48, and so was obviously a favorite designation of the Deity by our prophet. This is of course yet another instance of the loss of a word at the end of a line of Biblical poetry.

26. It seems wise to insert, with *G*, כל before אלה since both context and meter suggest this; the first distich of the v. thus becomes a 4/4; since the reference here is obviously to the heavenly bodies, particularly the stars, the insertion of כל adds considerably to the effect of the passage. These words were undoubtedly accompanied by a sweeping gesture by the hand towards the heaven. Moreover, the passage suggests strongly that the prophet delivered this address at night, when the heavens were aglow with stars. And this suggests still further that upon this occasion the prophet's audience was small and assembled more or less secretly somewhere in the great outdoors. We can readily imagine the circumstances which, towards the end of the prophet's ministry, made an assembly under these circumstances advisable. "Who bringeth forth their host by number," i. e. in their assigned order. The sing., בשם, instead of the plu. בשמות, implies that each star is summoned in turn by its own name when the moment for it to become visible above the horizon arrives; this picture is graphic indeed. For אמיץ read, with DSIa, all the vss. and most commentators, אָמֵץ and, likewise with DSIa and all the vss. for כח read כחו.

27. The v. is plainly a 3/3 double-distich; obviously then a word is missing in the second stichos of the first distich; accordingly supply עמי (cf. 43.20; 47.6) after ישראל; still another instance of the loss of a word at the end of a line of Biblical poetry; the insertion of this word adds very much to the effect of this passage. משפטי, "my case at law; my cause" (cf. Isa. 49.4; Micah 7.9; Ps. 35.23; Job 34.5, 6). The second distich here exhibits a very effective chiasm. With this v. the prophet shifts from the 2nd plu. to the 2nd sing. in addressing Israel; this tends to make the message of reassurance which follows more personal and enheartening. The prophet seeks now to inculcate his hearers with faith in God; and certainly in the final analysis faith is a personal, individual matter; accordingly this transition here to the 2nd sing. is particularly effective. For יעבור read עבר, in order to agree in tense with נסתרה; this textual corruption resulted from dittography of the י of משפטי.

28. עולם had better be interpreted here as "the world" (cf. Ps. 66.7; Eccl. 3.11) rather than as "eternity," i. e. "the universal God" rather than "the eternal God," the universal God in the light of the fact, stated in the very next stichos, that He is the Creator of the earth unto its very ends. The v. states that neither the creation of this world nor anything else can weary or exhaust God, nor yet can there be, in man's efforts to comprehend the divine import of everything which befalls him, any adequate fathoming of God's all-wise plan and purpose. This thought paves the way for the message of faith set forth in vv. 29–31. יעף and יגע are not absolute synonyms; יגע means "to become weary or exhausted from extreme physical exertion," while יעף means "to become weary or faint from lack of food"; probably for this reason *G* renders every occurrence of יעף in this address by "hunger." It is plain from vv. 27–28 that the audience which the prophet is here addressing has become greatly disheartened by some, probably protracted catastrophe which had befallen it and that its faith in Yahweh, in His intentions towards it and in His ability to protect it has been severely strained. Instead of denouncing it for this loss of faith the prophet seeks to comfort his audience and restore its faith. Plainly the prophet is here addressing, not the entire Jewish community in Babylonia, as in his earlier addresses, but only a very small group thereof, one assembled at night and probably in some out of the way place, where it would not be disturbed by others, presumably, as we have suggested, the large mass of Israel in exile, now bitterly hostile to both the prophet and his faithful followers. And plainly too, this is a late address of the prophet, perhaps his very latest, as we have also suggested.

29. It seems well for לַיעֵף of *MT* to read לְיעֵף.

30. For ויעפו and וינעו of *MT* read, as in v. 31, וייעפו and וינעו.

31. "They shall sprout forth wings as eagles"; for this rendering of יעלו, "to cause to grow," cf. Jer. 30.17; 33.6; Ezek. 19.3. The reference is unmistakably to the myth of the phoenix and its annual renewal of its youth. That this myth, with the phoenix regarded as an eagle, was well-known in ancient Israel is evidenced by Ps. 103.5. The stichos says that those who hope in Yahweh shall renew their youth, even as the phoenix-eagle does in the myth; thus interpreted this second stichos offers a very vivid and effective parallelism to the first stichos.